CALAMITY at FREDERICK

*Robert E. Lee, Special Orders No. 191, and
Confederate Misfortune on the Road to Antietam*

Alexander B. Rossino

Alexander B R
10/21/23

SB
Savas Beatie
California

©2023 Alexander B. Rossino

All rights reserved. No part of this publication may be reproduced, stored in a retrieval system, or transmitted, in any form or by any means, electronic, mechanical, photocopying, recording, or otherwise, without the prior written permission of the publisher.

Names: Rossino, Alexander B., 1966- author.
Title: Calamity at Frederick : Robert E. Lee, Special Orders No. 191, and Confederate misfortune on the road to Antietam / Alexander B. Rossino.
Description: El Dorado Hills, CA : Savas Beatie, [2023] | Includes bibliographical references and index. | Summary: "The loss of Robert E. Lee's Special Orders No. 191 is one of the Civil War's enduring mysteries. This meticulous study presents a bold new interpretation of the evidence surrounding the orders' creation, distribution, and loss outside Frederick, Maryland, in September 1862. Rossino provides new information pinpointing where the orders were lost and offers a provocative hypothesis about who may have lost them, and the impact on Confederate operations. This is the Confederate companion to The Tale Untwisted by Gene M. Thorp and Alexander Rossino, which told the story from the Union perspective"— Provided by publisher.
Identifiers: LCCN 2023033022 | ISBN 9781611216905 (paperback) | ISBN 9781954547629 (ebook)
Subjects: LCSH: Maryland Campaign, 1862. | Antietam, Battle of, Md., 1862. | Confederate States of America. Army of Northern Virginia. Special Orders No. 191. | Lee, Robert E. (Robert Edward), 1807-1870. | Military orders—Confederate States of America.
Classification: LCC E474.61 .R664 2023 | DDC 973.7/336—dc23/eng/20230801
LC record available at https://lccn.loc.gov/2023033022

First Edition, First Printing

SB
Savas Beatie
989 Governor Drive, Suite 102
El Dorado Hills, CA 95762
Phone: 916-941-6896 / sales@savasbeatie.com

Savas Beatie titles are available at special discounts for bulk purchases in the United States. Contact us for more details.

Proudly published, printed, and warehoused in the United States of America.

For Ted Savas, with thanks for always believing.

"At the time the order fell into Genl. McClellan's hands, I considered it a great calamity and subsequent reflection has not caused me to change my opinion."

— Robert E. Lee to Daniel Harvey Hill, Feb. 21, 1868

Table of Contents

Abbreviations Used in the Text and Notes   vii

Preface   viii

Introduction   x

Chapter 1: Saturday, September 6: Illusion vs. Reality   1

Chapter 2: Sunday, September 7: General Lee Bides His Time   12

Chapter 3: Monday, September 8: Unexpected Events Force Lee's Hand   20

Chapter 4: Tuesday, September 9: The Creation and Distribution of Special Orders No. 191   39

Chapter 5: Where Did Barton Mitchell Find the Lost Orders?   62

Chapter 6: Who Lost Lee's Orders?   78

Chapter 7: The Importance of the Lost Orders to Wrecking Confederate Operations in Maryland   103

Conclusion   117

Appendix A: Who Wrote the Lost Copy of Lee's Special Orders No. 191?   123

Appendix B: Comparing the Text of Special Orders No. 190 and No. 191   131

Bibliography   139

Index   152

Acknowledgments   154

About the Author   156

List of Maps

Map 1: Confederate Encampments Around Frederick, September 7-9, 1862   7

Map 2: Advance into Maryland   26

Map 3: Distribution of Special Orders No. 191   59

Map 4: Monocacy Battlefield Lost Orders Map   65

Map 5: The Delashmutt/Myers Farm   67

Map 6: Lost Orders Discovery Site   70

Map 7: Federal Advance on Frederick   74

Map 8: Jeb Stuart's Headquarters   90

Map 9: Confederate Cavalry Defends Approaches to Frederick   95

Map 10: Early Morning March   104-105

Photos and illustrations have been placed throughout this book
for the convenience of the reader.

Abbreviations Used in the Text and Notes

ANBL: Antietam National Battlefield Library, Keedysville, MD
B&L: Battles and Leaders of the Civil War
MNBP: Monocacy National Battlefield Park, Frederick, MD
MOLLUS: Military Order of the Loyal Legion of the United States
NA: National Archives and Records Administration, Washington, DC
NC DNCR: North Carolina Department of Natural and Cultural Resources, Raleigh, NC
OR: Official Records of the War of the Rebellion
SHC, UNC: Southern Historical Collection, Wilson Library, University of North Carolina at Chapel Hill
SHSP: Southern Historical Society Papers

Preface

When I first began researching the Maryland Campaign for my book *Six Days in September: A Novel of Lee's Army in Maryland, 1862*, I never imagined writing a study of General Robert E. Lee's Special Orders No. 191. Of all the campaign's fascinating subjects, I believed there was surely nothing new to say about the orders' creation, their loss, or their discovery around noon outside of Frederick, Maryland, on September 13, 1862.

After many years of collecting evidence, and especially after publishing *The Tale Untwisted: General George B. McClellan, the Maryland Campaign, and the Discovery of Lee's Lost Orders* with Gene Thorp, I found my impression of the subject was wrong. There was more work to be done. This became particularly clear during the Q&A sessions Gene and I participated in following our presentations. The questions "who lost the orders?" and "where were they found?" inevitably came up even though *The Tale Untwisted* did not explore these topics. This made it clear that I should complete a companion study focused on the Confederate side of the story to go along with our study of McClellan's handling of the orders after they had been discovered.

There are parts of the Confederate story which by their very nature require speculation to handle. I have done my best to ensure that speculation is not idle, but is based on evidence, and that readers know when what they are reading is informed conjecture. This is the gray area of history. I present it at my own risk and hope that readers find they benefit from my investigation.

My only regret is that I did not complete this study sooner instead of relying on the conclusions of others for some of my earlier work. Had I done so the final shape taken by certain parts of my book *Their Maryland: The Army of Northern Virginia from the Potomac Crossing to Sharpsburg in September 1862* (Savas Beatie, 2021) would have been different. An author often does not know how a work will turn out until it is finished. This is a paradox that readers of history may not grasp. After all, if the basic framework of the events is well-known, how can the finished manuscript be that different? I contend it can be different, and sometimes surprisingly so. Writing this book proved that to me.

Alexander B. Rossino
Boonsboro, Maryland
July 2023

Introduction

The four days that General Robert E. Lee's Army of Northern Virginia spent near Frederick, Maryland, played a pivotal role in shaping events from September 10 through September 18, 1862. Victorious after a summer of campaigning from the James River peninsula east of Richmond to the Confederacy's "northern frontier," Lee's army had driven Northern troops from much of Virginia. These successes provided the general with an opportunity to test the strength of secessionist sentiment in Maryland, a slave state in the border South under Federal military occupation. Lee therefore launched an expedition (his term) with the objectives of feeding his army, pulling Maryland out of the old Union, entering Pennsylvania, and, at some point, winning a war-ending victory north of the Potomac.[1]

After watching the enemy's forces stream back to Washington following their devastating rout at the Battle of Second Manassas, Lee assumed he had weeks, if not months, to achieve his goals. However, less than 48 hours after his arrival near Frederick City, the Confederate general learned that Major General George B. McClellan, once again in command of the Army of the Potomac, had begun moving to intercept him. At the same time, news arrived that a Federal garrison consisting of several thousand men remained in place at Harpers Ferry.

Situated close to the Army of Northern Virginia's supply line, which Lee had begun shifting over the Blue Ridge Mountains into the Shenandoah Valley, the force at Harpers Ferry posed a serious threat that Lee could not ignore, particularly with McClellan's army on the move. These converging circumstances compelled Lee to design a plan for capturing the enemy garrison before he turned his army to

---

1 See Chapter 1 of Alexander B. Rossino, *Their Maryland: The Army of Northern Virginia from the Potomac Crossings to Sharpsburg in September 1862* (El Dorado, CA, 2021) for a detailed discussion of Lee's secessionist objectives.

face the oncoming enemy. It is in this context that he conceived Special Orders No. 191.

There is probably no other document in the history of the American Civil War with which even casual readers are so familiar. Lost outside of Frederick City, and discovered by a soldier with the 27th Indiana, the "Lost Orders," as they have come to be called, provided McClellan with the one piece of information he had not yet gleaned as of September 13, 1862—insight into Robert E. Lee's objectives. McClellan knew by September 11, less than 24 hours after it had set off, that most of Lee's army had departed from Frederick. By September 13, McClellan had also learned from communications with the War Department in Washington and Governor Andrew Curtin in Harrisburg, Pennsylvania, that parts of the Confederate force could be found west of South Mountain, it being the extension of the Blue Ridge north of the Potomac River. Some of Lee's army had even been reported crossing the Potomac back into (West) Virginia as far away as Williamsport, Maryland.

What all these movements amounted to remained a mystery to McClellan. He also did not know that Lee had separated his forces so widely. Reading the Lost Orders provided these key details. The knowledge "Little Mac" gained from the orders proved so invaluable that it enabled him to organize a two-pronged, en echelon attack on the passes (called "gaps" in Maryland) over South Mountain. These attacks, unanticipated by Lee, threw the Confederate commander off balance, forcing him to defend the mountain passes when he had never planned to do so, and, eventually, to face McClellan in the far bloodier fight along Antietam Creek that expelled the Army of Northern Virginia from Maryland.

Questions about the Lost Orders continue to swirl despite more than 160 years of scholarship. Where Indiana troops found the orders remains an open issue, as does identifying the man who lost them. The importance of the orders' loss to the course of the Maryland Campaign is also debated. This study addresses each of these issues and more. Organized into three parts, the first four chapters examine the context surrounding the orders' conception, drafting, and distribution. The two chapters that follow investigate the orders' loss, and the final chapter evaluates the consequences of that event for Confederate operations in Maryland. Two appendices then offer a detailed examination of the handwriting in the Lost Orders and a comparison of the lost copy with an earlier draft that Lee dictated to Maj. Charles Marshall.

New information is presented on each of these topics, along with a new interpretation of the history of the Lost Orders. Readers steeped in the existing history may find this interpretation provocative. It suggests that an individual not previously associated with the orders could have been responsible for losing them. This man then covered it up for the remaining years of his life, either out of shame or self-preservation since mishandling the orders might have led to charges of negligence in the face of the enemy.

The interpretation presented in this study also suggests that changes are needed to our understanding of certain aspects of Lee's Maryland Campaign. These include what we think we know about Lee's assumptions at the time, the strategy he hoped to employ north of the Potomac, and the extent to which he was able to see it through. Finally, this work reinforces a recent trend in the historical literature that attributes greater success to the efforts of George McClellan than has been acknowledged. Little Mac performed better in Maryland than most scholars, and certainly many Civil War enthusiasts, are prepared to accept. This study explains why that is even though it focuses primarily on the Confederate side of the story.

Chapter 1

Saturday, September 6:
Illusion vs. Reality

Crossing the Potomac River early in the morning at White's Ford, several miles from Leesburg, Virginia, General Robert E. Lee embarked upon the campaign in Maryland with a sense of optimism so palpable that it echoes down through documents from the time. Less than two days earlier, he had issued General Orders No. 102 as the first troops with Maj. Gen. Daniel Harvey Hill's division were wading across the Potomac at Check's Ford. These orders called the army's new operation "most important" and exhorted the ranks to avoid committing "excesses" that might "exasperate the people, lead to disastrous results, and enlist the populace on the side of the Federal forces in hostility to our own." The army was on the threshold of a "momentous" occasion, Lee added, hoping that by stressing the campaign's importance he could reduce the level of straggling which had already left a significant number of his men scattered across northern Virginia.[1]

Lee's army had recently crushed the Federal Army of Virginia at the Battle of Second Manassas, and the finality of that defeat on August 30 compelled Union forces to abandon most of the northern and eastern parts of the state. Lee then

---

1 *The War of the Rebellion: A Compilation of the Official Records of the Union and Confederate Armies*, 128 vols. (Washington, DC, 1880-1901), Series 1, Vol. 19, Part 2, 592-593. Cited hereafter as OR. Concerning Rodes's crossing see "Letter from Maryland, Camp of Rhodes' Brigade in *Columbus (GA) Sun,* Oct. 1862. Copy in Alabama Vertical File at the Antietam National Battlefield Library (ANBL), Keedysville, MD; and Jonathan W. Williams, *His Life and Times with the 5th Alabama, C.S.A. Company "D" Greensboro Guards* (Greensboro, AL, 1903), entry of Dec. 17, ANBL.

decided on September 2 to undertake the expedition north, following which he wrote to Confederate President Jefferson Davis on September 3 and 5 that he had determined the time had come to give Marylanders the "opportunity of throwing off the oppression," meaning martial law and occupation of the state by Federal troops, to which they had been subjected for more than a year.[2]

His ambulance rolling out of the Potomac's glimmering water on that bright, sunny day, Lee left his mounted security detachment at White's Ford to bring up stragglers before continuing north up the Chesapeake and Ohio Canal towpath. He then crossed over the canal into Montgomery County, parts of which contained hotbeds of pro-Confederate sentiment. Here he paused to write President Davis about the progress of his operation. Sending the following message to Warrenton, Virginia, by courier so it could be wired to Richmond, Lee informed Davis, "Thirteen miles from Fredericktown Md., 6th. [of Sept.]. Two divisions of the army have crossed the Potomac. I hope all will cross today. Navigation of the canal has been interrupted and efforts will be made to break up the use of the Baltimore and Ohio railroad."[3]

Good news about Maj. Gen. Kirby Smith's recent victory at Richmond, Kentucky, reached Lee at around this point, prompting him to issue General Orders No. 103. Combining a matter-of-fact tone with what for Robert E. Lee amounted to unbridled enthusiasm, these orders declared to the army "Soldiers, press onward! Let each man feel the responsibility now resting on him to pursue vigorously the success vouchsafed to us by Heaven." Lee then challenged his men, returning once again to the theme of liberating Maryland from Federal military occupation: "Let the armies of the East and the West vie with each other in discipline, bravery, and activity, and our brethren of our sister States will soon be released from tyranny, and our independence be established upon a sure and abiding basis." Then, after entertaining a visit by several local ladies who were

---

2 The Sept. 2 decision date comes from Armistead L. Long, *Memoirs of Robert E. Lee* (New York, NY, 1886), 204. OR 19:2, 590-591.

3 Douglas Southall Freeman, ed., *Lee's Dispatches: Unpublished Letters of General Robert E. Lee, C.S.A. to Jefferson Davis and the War Department of the Confederate States of America, 1862-65* (London and New York, NY, 1915), 61. Concerning Lee's bodyguards see Luther W. Hopkins, *From Bull Run to Appomattox: A Boy's View* (Baltimore, MD, 1908), 49. Although this message says it was wired from Maryland, there is no evidence the Confederates strung a functioning telegraph line across the river. The date "Telegram rec'd at Richmond Sept. 8" suggests that Lee sent a courier back to Warrenton where the only functioning wire south remained intact. This would account for the two days it took the message to reach Richmond. An accident on August 30 involving Lee's horse, Traveller, left Lee unable to ride until Sept. 16. For most of the campaign he travelled through Maryland in an ordinary army ambulance.

General Lee in 1863. Injured in late August, Lee traveled through Maryland on foot or in an army ambulance until Sept. 16. *Virginia Museum of History and Culture*

excited to see him, Lee pushed ahead to the rented farm of John T. Best at Monocacy Junction, located four miles southeast of Frederick City.[4]

The choice of this location was probably not a coincidence. There is for one thing the fact that the farm sat beside the iron bridge that took the Baltimore and Ohio Railroad over the Monocacy River. Lee had made cutting the rail line an objective of his operation, so camping his army astride the B&O was probably intended to accomplish that goal. In addition, Maj. Gen. Thomas J. "Stonewall" Jackson, whose troops led the Confederate column, deliberately adjusted his route of march to approach Frederick from the direction of Best's Farm. Jackson then chose the farm as the place to establish his headquarters ahead of Lee's arrival, something he surely would not have done without previously consulting his commander.

Known historically as The Hermitage, Best's Farm also happened to be the birthplace of Maryland's former governor, Enoch L. Lowe, Jr., a prominent figure who had early in the war declared support for secession before being forced to flee his home state for Virginia. Lee would write Richmond on September 7 "for ex-Governor [Enoch L.] Lowe, or some prominent citizen of Maryland, to join me, with a view of expediting ... arrangements necessary to the success of our army in this State." It seems reasonable to conclude that Lee chose to encamp a large part of his army, including the three divisions under Maj. Gen. James Longstreet, the reserve artillery, and the unattached commands of Maj. Gen. Richard H. Anderson and Brig. Gen. Nathan "Shanks" Evans, on ground symbolically associated with a vocal proponent of the Confederate cause.[5]

Upon reaching Best's Farm, most likely in the early afternoon, given the 13 miles he had to travel that morning, Lee ordered his headquarters established in a one-acre wide grove of oaks located on the western side of the Georgetown Pike.

---

4 OR 19:2, 596. "On the 6th the army began early in the morning to ford the river into Maryland.... The young ladies are wild to see Gen. Lee, and we agree to find him for them; so in the afternoon a caravan is made up of all the old family carriages in the country, and filled with pretty girls, and we escort them to where 'Uncle Robert' is resting. He is immediately surrounded, and kissed, and hugged, until the old gentleman gets very red in the face, and cries for mercy." William M. Owen, *In Camp and Battle with the Washington Artillery of New Orleans* (Boston, MA, 1885), 130. Also see Napier Bartlett, *Military Record of Louisiana* (New Orleans, LA, 1875), 129.

5 OR 19:2, 596. For the sources establishing which units camped at Best's Farm see Rossino, *Their Maryland*, Chapter 3. Jackson's command contained a large number of men from Maryland. Jackson had also urged Richmond to authorize an incursion into Maryland since 1861. His familiarity with the western part of the state suggests that Jackson may have been the one who encouraged Lee to set up his headquarters at Best's Farm.

Enslaved persons accompanying the headquarters group quickly set about pitching half a dozen canvas tents for Lee and his staff under the shade of the trees. The grove stood opposite the tents of Jackson's headquarters, which occupied "a hillside in a grassy field" on the eastern side of the pike.[6]

Jackson's three divisions led the army to the vicinity of Frederick in concert with the infantry division of Maj. Gen. D. H. Hill. But, unlike Jackson's command, which crossed back east of the Monocacy River near Buckeystown to approach Frederick from the direction of Washington, Hill's division marched up the Monocacy's west bank, traveling as far as the farm of George Markell along Ballenger's Creek, located four miles south of Frederick, before stopping to camp. General Longstreet then joined Lee, situating his headquarters in Best's Grove near two batteries of the Washington Artillery of New Orleans.[7]

At some point during the mid-afternoon, as Lee and his staff were settling in, Maj. Gen. James Ewell Brown "Jeb" Stuart rode into the new encampment. This took place after Stuart had led his command to the village of Urbana, located roughly eight miles to the southeast. Leaving his chief of staff, Maj. Heros von Borcke, to set up his headquarters in the yard of a sympathetic family named Cockey, Stuart continued toward Frederick around noon. He told Von Borcke to seek him out at the headquarters of Stonewall Jackson and later spent the evening celebrating with Confederate sympathizers in Frederick.[8]

Upon arriving at Best's Grove, Stuart reported to Lee to update him on the status of his command, and to inform Lee about what he had learned of the enemy. After learning that the Federals were assembling around Washington, Lee directed Stuart to "divide his cavalry and threaten both Baltimore and Washington . . . giving out [information] on each flank that he (Lee) was behind with his whole

---

6 *Baltimore American*, Sept. 10, 1862. The location of Jackson's headquarters was likely where the visitor's center of the Monocacy National Battlefield Park sits today. Also see James Power Smith, "With Stonewall Jackson in the Army of Northern Virginia," in *Southern Historical Society Papers*, 44 vols. (Sept. 1920), 43:17. Cited hereafter as *SHSP*.

7 *Baltimore American*, Sept. 10, 1862. "We are encamped (the two reserve batteries of the Washington Artillery) in a beautiful grove of oaks. On one side of us the headquarters of Gen. Longstreet are established, and with him is Gen. Lee. On the other side 'Stonewall' has pitched his tents. The latter passes our camp and our tent several times a day." Owen, *In Camp and Battle*, 131-132. Concerning D. H. Hill's march see Archie P. McDonald, ed., *Make Me a Map of the Valley: The Civil War Diary of Stonewall Jackson's Topographer* (Dallas, TX, 1973), 79.

8 "As General Stuart, always uncertain in his movements, was not at Jackson's headquarters, and was supposed to have gone into the town, I determined to ride there myself in the hope of finding him." Heros von Borcke, *Memoirs of the Confederate War for Independence*, 2 vols. (Edinburgh and London, 1866), 1:187.

Lt. Col. Elijah Viers White. A captain in September 1862, White brought Lee critical information about the continued occupation of Harpers Ferry by Federal troops on Sept. 8.
Thomas Balch Library

force." Brigadier General Fitzhugh Lee carried out this order on the following morning by sending the 3rd Virginia Cavalry and a portion of the 9th Virginia Cavalry to New Market on the National Road, which ran east from Frederick to Baltimore.[9]

Feigning an advance on Baltimore prompted a cautionary response from Maj. Gen. George McClellan, whom President Lincoln had just appointed to command the reconstituted Army of the Potomac. Due in part to his understanding of Baltimore's importance to communications between the Northern states and Washington, and the menace posed by Lee's army, McClellan sent the right wing of his force, under the command of Maj. Gen. Ambrose Burnside, to cut the National Road and halt any potential Confederate advance on the city.[10]

At some point after leaving Lee's tent, Stuart ran into Capt. Elijah Viers White, the commander of the Loudon Border Cavalry. White's men had served as scouts for Jackson and D. H. Hill during the advance to Frederick, and afterward they continued to work as foragers collecting livestock for the army in Frederick County. Stuart either personally disliked White, or felt he had little use for mounted auxiliaries in Maryland, so he ordered the captain back to Virginia to "watch for a

---

9 R. E. Lee to William Allan, Feb. 15, 1868, in Douglas Southall Freeman, *Lee's Lieutenants: A Study in Command*, 3 Vols. (New York, NY, 1945), 2:720. Walbrook D. Swank, ed., *Sabres, Saddles, and Spurs: Lieutenant William R. Carter, CSA* (Shippensburg, PA 1998), 12; Richard L. T. Beale, *History of the Ninth Virginia Cavalry in the War Between the States* (Richmond, VA 1899), 37.

10 There is no evidence Lee intended to march on Baltimore. For details on the punishing marches north to the National Road endured by the men of Maj. Gen. Joseph Hooker's corps see Gene M. Thorp & Alexander B. Rossino, *The Tale Untwisted: General George B. McClellan, the Maryland Campaign, and the Discovery of Lee's Lost Orders* (El Dorado, CA, 2023), 46-47, 54; see Steven R. Stotelmyer, *Too Useful to Sacrifice: Reconsidering George B. McClellan's Generalship in the Maryland Campaign from South Mountain to Antietam* (El Dorado, CA, 2019), 165, for a discussion of the controversy surrounding Lincoln's reappointment of McClellan to field command.

flanking force of the enemy expected by way of Dranesville, or Fairfax Court House." White protested vigorously against this order, declaring that as a native-born Marylander he had every right to serve the army in his home state. When Stuart would not change his mind, White demanded the matter be brought to Lee. This turned out to be an astute move on White's part because after hearing his plea, Lee sent White and his men scouting toward Harpers Ferry to gather intelligence.[11]

Lee's interest in the status of the enemy garrison was piqued by cannon fire from the direction of the ferry while on his journey from the Potomac River to Best's Grove. Word received a day or so earlier from Col. John H. S. Funk of Jackson's command said that the Federals had evacuated Winchester and were falling back to Martinsburg. Now, Lee hoped to hear that the enemy force at Harpers Ferry had also vacated its position. This would leave the lower Shenandoah Valley clear for the general to safely shift his army's supply line west of

---

11 Frank M. Myers, *The Comanches: A History of White's Battalion, Virginia Cavalry* (Baltimore, MD, 1871), 106-109.

the Blue Ridge Mountains. Intending to make Winchester his supply depot, and a collection point for reinforcements and stragglers, Lee planned to use the valley as a conduit to his army, either if he decided to stay in Maryland or to turn north into Pennsylvania. As Lee had informed Davis in a letter from Leesburg on September 4, "Should the results of the expedition justify it, I propose to enter Pennsylvania."[12]

Campaign histories have over the years focused on Lee's mention of Pennsylvania to the exclusion of the conditional statement written by the general in relation to it. At this point early in the Maryland Campaign, Lee did plan on entering the Keystone State, a conclusion confirmed by his comments concerning the Winchester depot. But while the general may have entertained this option, it can be argued with merit that he did not consider Pennsylvania his primary objective. He hoped instead to achieve a political victory by enlisting secessionist Marylanders in his cause. Fomenting rebellion would bring the state into the Confederacy, cut off Washington from the North, and render any military triumph he achieved above the Potomac even more decisive.[13]

Evidence for this can be found in a statement attributed to Lee that appeared in the *Philadelphia Inquirer* on September 12 under the heading "Our Baltimore Letter, Special Correspondence of the *Inquirer*. Near Baltimore, Sept. 11, 1862." This brief entry stated

> At last it appears to be a fixed fact that the Rebels are intent upon carrying out the plan proposed to be adopted by General Lee, or at least what he told a gentleman of this city it was, in an earnest conversation with him one day last week. Each day's movements go to prove the earnestness of the Rebel General's intentions. Lee said: "We have now come to redeem our pledge to the people of this State. We extend the olive branch to them, and, should they accept it, we shall welcome and protect them, with the assurance that the next battle ground will be in Pennsylvania. But, should they not come forward, after having been amply assured that their property would be unmolested, and every guarantee given

---

12 James Longstreet, *From Manassas to Appomattox: Memoirs of the Civil War in America* (Philadelphia, PA, 1896), 201-202; Joe D. Haines, Jr., ed., *The Diary of Col. John Henry Stover Funk of the Stonewall Brigade, 1861-1862* (Columbia, SC, 2022), 134; OR 19:2, 592.

13 Upon visiting Lee at his tent on the afternoon of September 6, S. Bassett French of Jackson's staff stated, "We are on our way to Pennsylvania" while expressing his need for a new mount. Lee did not correct him, suggesting that because he had not yet met with local secessionists the general still entertained the notion of invading Keystone State; see Glenn C. Oldaker, ed., *Centennial Tales: Memoirs of Colonel "Chester" S. Bassett French, Extra Aide-de-Camp to Generals Lee and Jackson, The Army of Northern Virginia, 1861-1865* (New York, NY, 1962), 57.

that the Southern army should remain on Maryland soil, for the maintenance of their sacred rights, then the battle ground must hereafter be in Maryland."[14]

The day when Gen. Lee uttered these words is hinted at by the phrase "one day last week." September 11, 1862, fell on a Thursday, meaning the meeting between Lee and the unnamed gentleman from Baltimore took place on either the previous Saturday (September 6) or Sunday (September 7) since the following Monday (September 8) marked the start of a new week. Of the two possible dates, September 6 is the most likely, since on that day Lee and his staff attended a dinner in Frederick held by Confederate sympathizers. In an essay he wrote after the war, Henry K. Douglas of Jackson's staff confirmed how on the afternoon of September 6 visitors from Frederick descended on Best's Grove to greet the newly arrived Southern commanders. It is probably during this crush of well-wishers that a representative from the local secessionist community invited Lee to his home.[15]

This social call is the only invitation Lee accepted during the three-and-a-half days his army rested near Frederick, indicating its importance. The news that a prominent visitor from Baltimore had traveled to meet him may have been the reason. This man surely carried information about the city that Lee wanted to know, especially because the general had made stoking secessionist hotbeds into flaming rebellion one of his main purposes for being in the state. It is likely, then, that Lee intended his comment to be publicized in order to make his plans for the people of Maryland known to them.[16]

14 *Philadelphia Inquirer*, Sept. 12, 1862.

15 "Early that day the army went into camp near Frederick, and Generals Lee, Longstreet, Jackson, and for a time 'Jeb' Stuart, had their headquarters near one another in Best's grove. Hither in crowds came the good people of Frederick, especially the ladies." Henry Kyd Douglas, "Stonewall Jackson in Maryland," in Robert Underwood Johnson and Clarence Clough Buel, eds., *Battles and Leaders of the Civil War*, 4 vols. (New York, NY, 1885), 2:620. Cited hereafter as *B&L*. For further details on the dinner Lee attended see Rossino, *Their Maryland*, 24.

16 The local newspaper made it clear that the arrival of the Confederate army "was undoubtedly known beforehand to the Secession sympathizers in our midst, some of whom had admonished their particular Union friends to leave." *Frederick Examiner*, Sept. 24, 1862; also see Paul and Rita Gordon, *Frederick County, Maryland: Never the Like Again* (Frederick, MD, 1995), 41-42: "A number of rebel officers, among them the Adjutant General of General Lee's staff... took lodging with a very worthy Union farmer, by the name of J. H. Finney, residing some three miles below Frederick. While here, they conversed freely among themselves... they came to the conclusion that they had no friends in Maryland. This was a positive fact, as the very men who had invited them turned their backs to them. One of Gen. Lee's Aides took a paper from his pocket with over one hundred names thereon, at the same time stating, "these

There are three additional reasons why the comments published in the *Inquirer* should be considered authentic. The first is that the course of events described in them matches those which in fact transpired. Lee's army marched northwest from Frederick on September 10 in accordance with the operation outlined in Special Orders No. 191. As he explained in his August 1863 campaign report, Lee made this move to capture the enemy garrison at Harpers Ferry and open "communications with Richmond through the Valley of the Shenandoah . . . [which would] by threatening Pennsylvania, induce the enemy to follow, and thus draw him from his base of supplies."

Even after nearly a year of war had passed, Lee recalled desiring to lure the Federals into Washington County, Maryland, by threatening Pennsylvania. This makes clear the meaning of the conditional statement he had written to Davis on September 4. If Maryland's people rose in rebellion, Lee would push his army north past the Mason-Dixon Line. If they did not, the Army of Northern Virginia would fight in the Southern border state of Maryland "for the maintenance of their sacred rights."[17]

Second, Lee wrote to Davis on September 12 that in Frederick he found "the citizens embarrassed as to the intentions of the army." This led him "to delay no longer in making known our purpose." Lee's statement is an indirect reference to the dinner he attended on September 6, and to the proclamation that he ordered his Maryland-born aide-de-camp, Maj. Charles Marshall, to compose. That document, which will be discussed in more detail below, stated Lee's objective with no ambiguity: "[O]ur army has come among you, and is prepared to assist you with the power of its arms in regaining the rights of which you have been despoiled. This, citizens of Maryland, is our mission, so far as you are concerned."[18]

Third, Lee's statement in the *Inquirer* expressed his intent to defend the rights of Marylanders, which is a sentiment that also comes through clearly in the general's August 1863 report. Writing "it was hoped that military success might

---

men wrote to us, and it was by their assurances we came here, and now they are our worst enemies, they will do nothing for us. . . . Most named were residents of Baltimore, a few were from Hagerstown, and eleven from Frederick. A pin hole had been placed opposite each Fredericktonian. The officer was particularly severe about these men, whose names were as follows: Hon. Richard H. Marshall, ex-Judge G. M. Potts, Robert Y. Stokes, Frederick Markell, Bob Johnson, George Hanson, A. B. Hanson, Dr. W. T. Wootton, John Ritchie, Mr. Ross, John Need."

17 OR 19:1, 144.

18 Long, *Memoirs of Robert E. Lee*, 208.

afford us an opportunity to aid the citizens of Maryland in any efforts they might be disposed to make to recover their liberties," Lee added, "The difficulties that surrounded them were fully appreciated, and we expected to derive more assistance in the attainment of our object from the just fears of the Washington Government than from any active demonstration on the part of the people, unless success should enable us to give them assurance of continued protection."

In other words, Lee learned late on September 6 that contrary to his earlier assumption he should not expect a popular uprising by Maryland's people unless his army could prove its ability to protect them by winning a victory in the state. This, and the other considerations outlined above, formed the backdrop against which Robert E. Lee began devising Special Orders No. 191 on September 8.

Upon entering Maryland, Lee had labored under the illusion that the presence of his army north of the Potomac would cause Confederate sympathizers in the state to erupt in rebellion against the Lincoln administration. Information collected throughout the day, however, made Lee realize that the reality of the political situation in Maryland was more complicated than he had believed. His army's presence alone would not be sufficient to pry the state loose. Instead, he would need to fight to pull Maryland into the Confederacy.

Once this became clear, Lee decided to appeal directly to secessionist sentiment via a proclamation, and then await the popular response. Until the public rendered a verdict on his presence in the state, the general would work to shift his army's supply line west in preparation for whatever step he needed to take next, be it entering Pennsylvania if Marylanders rose up, or fighting in Maryland to encourage them if they did not. By taking this course, Lee effectively relinquished the initiative he had won during his summer campaign. Waiting for a political outcome that he *hoped* would occur forced him to remain in one location until developments determined the next step he should take. This would become much clearer in less than 48 hours.

Chapter 2

Sunday, September 7: General Lee Bides His Time

Despite it being the Sabbath, Robert E. Lee began Sunday, September 7, as he always did, with correspondence. The fact that he could not use his hands to write due to injuries sustained in a fall from his horse on August 31 complicated this mundane task. For most of the Maryland campaign, Lee would dictate his thoughts to staff members acting as official stenographers. Aides Charles Marshall and Maj. Walter H. Taylor usually served in this capacity, but at times Lee would call on others, such as his military secretary, Col. Armistead L. Long, or, occasionally, his chief of staff, Col. Robert H. Chilton. During this early phase of the campaign, Lee also added to his staff Walter Taylor's older brother, Maj. Richard C. "Dick" Taylor.[1]

The documents Lee generated on the morning of September 7 reveal both what he knew about the enemy's activities and what he had learned from his hosts in Frederick on the night before. Two of the letters he composed went to Jefferson Davis, while a third went to the Confederate Secretary of War, George W. Randolph. A fourth letter then went to Gen. Gustavus W. Smith, the commander of Confederate forces defending Richmond. Informing the Confederate president that

---

1 "Mornings were Lee's preferred time for staff matters." J. Boone Bartholomees, Jr., *Buff Facings and Gilt Buttons: Staff and Headquarters Operations in the Army of Northern Virginia, 1862-1865* (Columbia, SC, 1998), 227. Also see Douglas Southall Freeman, *R. E. Lee: A Biography*, 4 vols. (New York, NY, 1934), 2:234-236. Concerning the presence of Dick Taylor see R. Lockwood Tower, *Lee's Adjutant: The Wartime Letters of Colonel Walter Herron Taylor, 1862-1865* (Columbia, SC, 1995), 43.

"all the divisions of the army have crossed the Potomac, unless it may be General [John G.] Walker's, from whom I have had no report since his arrival at Leesburg, on the evening of the 5th instant," Lee reported to Davis that "They occupy the line of the Monocacy." Thus far Maryland had provided his men with "plenty of provisions and forage... and the community have received us with kindness," but, striking a disappointed note, Lee added that some of the locals had balked at receiving Confederate currency as payment "for necessaries for the army." Nevertheless, the general intended to acquire the goods his army needed using "certificates of indebtedness of the Confederate States for future adjustment" if Marylanders would not take Confederate scrip.[2]

The items Lee required for his army included "horses, clothing, shoes, and medical stores," very little of which had reached him even though, as recent research by Jeffrey Dugdale has shown, the Confederate Quartermaster-General's Department sent copious amounts of supplies north from Richmond. To ease the shortages facing his men, Lee hoped it might "be convenient for ex-Governor [Enoch L.] Lowe, or some prominent citizen of Maryland [to join him] with a view of expediting these and other arrangements necessary to the success of our army in this State."[3]

The general then commented on the political situation, stating succinctly, "Notwithstanding individual expressions of kindness that have been given, and the general sympathy in the success of the Confederate States, situated as Maryland is, I do not anticipate any general rising of the people in our behalf. Some additions to our ranks will no doubt be received and I hope to procure subsistence for our troops." This statement contains yet another of Lee's conditional phrases that histories of the campaign often overlook. Focusing only on the words "I do not anticipate any general rising of the people in our behalf," historians and others have cited this comment as evidence that Lee never expected an armed rebellion to erupt in Maryland. The words "situated as Maryland is" go unheeded despite arguably being the more important part of the message.

[2] OR 19:2, 596.

[3] Jeffrey Dugdale, *Confederate Uniforms During the Maryland Campaign, September 1862* (Thatcham, Berks, UK, 2021) provides extensive evidence of supplies being sent to the Confederate army in September 1862. It appears, however, that only a portion of these goods made it to Lee's troops. Most probably ended up at the depot in Winchester where they were distributed to the men after the campaign in Maryland had ended. For a different approach to the subject see Keith S. Bohannon, "Dirty, Ragged, and Ill-Provided For: Confederate Logistical Problems in the 1862 Maryland Campaign and Their Solutions," in Gary W. Gallagher, ed., *The Antietam Campaign* (Chapel Hill, NC, 1999), 101-142.

What Lee meant by this comment has been partially addressed in the previous chapter. Marylanders sympathizing with the Confederacy confronted significant obstacles when it came to expressing their preferred allegiance. In particular, Maryland shared a long line with much larger Pennsylvania, meaning Northern forces could enter it at any point they chose. The national government also maintained a large number of troops around Baltimore and Washington. These forces effectively cut Maryland in half, separating the pro-secession counties of the eastern shore from the counties containing more mixed sentiment west of Baltimore and Annapolis. "The condition of Maryland," explained Lee in his August 1863 campaign report, "encouraged the belief that the presence of our army . . . would induce the Washington Government to retain all its available force [in the state] to provide against contingencies, which its course toward the people of that State gave it reason to apprehend." This is why Lee "hoped that military success" would encourage Maryland's secessionists to rise up in revolt. If the Army of Northern Virginia could protect them by winning a victory in the state, Southern sympathizers might gain enough confidence to rebel.[4]

Lee closed his letter with a brief summation of the military situation as it stood at the time. "As yet we have had no encounter with the enemy on this side of the river," he reported, "except a detachment of cavalry at Poolesville, which resulted in slight loss on both sides, 31 of the enemy being captured. As far as I can learn, the enemy are in their intrenchments around Washington. General Banks, with his division, has advanced to Darnestown. The Shenandoah Valley has been evacuated, and their stores, &c., at Winchester are stated to have been destroyed."

The information Lee conveyed shows that he possessed only a partial understanding of the situation. Stuart's report about the cavalry engagement at Poolesville was accurate. The 5th and 3rd Virginia Cavalry had clashed with Federal troopers on September 6. This skirmish was less important, however, than the other facts Lee communicated. Enemy troops had advanced to Darnestown, Maryland, but they belonged to the Sixth Corps under the command of Maj. Gen. William B. Franklin and not to Maj. Gen. Nathaniel P. Banks.

That Lee would be unclear on this point is not surprising given the confusion which attended McClellan's rapid reorganization of disparate Federal forces into the new Army of the Potomac. More important still, the general's reference to

---

4 OR 19:1, 144. The "condition of Maryland" referred to by Lee meant its occupation by Federal troops. Lee hoped that the fear of a rebellion, prompted by the suspension of Habeas Corpus and the imposition of martial law, would compel Washington to keep a large portion of its army in the state.

Winchester conveyed information sent by Col. Funk, and which Lee had read in the September 4 edition of the *Baltimore Sun*, before he crossed the Potomac River. Neither of those sources reported the Shenandoah Valley clear of the enemy. Funk, for example, reported only that the enemy had fallen back to Martinsburg, some "22 miles distant," and the column in the *Sun* stated, "Winchester was yesterday evacuated by our troops."[5]

Lee believed that enemy forces had cleared out of the Shenandoah Valley because he had heard a rumor to that effect. We know this from a letter he dictated that morning to the Confederate Secretary of War, George W. Randolph. In it the general stated, "I learn from rumor" that troops with Brig. Gen. Julius White's Union command had "retreated to Pennsylvania." Shockingly, for a man engaged in a high-stakes military operation, General Lee appears to have taken this rumor to heart. This in turn reinforced the belief that he had sufficient time to shift his supply line, and eventually his entire army, west of the Blue Ridge without any interference from McClellan. His letter to Gustavus Smith on the same morning describes why. "[O]fficial reports from the valley state that Winchester was abandoned on the night of September 2," Lee explained, adding "General White, commanding at that place, is stated to have retired into Pennsylvania." Since he had heard nothing of a Federal advance from the capital, Lee concluded from his available information: "I think the enemy will concentrate about Washington."[6]

As for the morning's second letter to Davis, it concerned an issue that had long vexed the general—large numbers of men leaving the ranks without permission. Straggling, pronounced Lee, was "one of the greatest evils" besetting his army and the Southern cause. Lee blamed it on the army's rapid organization in the early days of the war and "its constant occupation and hard duty . . . [which] has not been improved by the forced marches and hard service it has lately undergone." Nevertheless, the general retained confidence in his force, stating, "the material of which it is composed is the best in the world, and, if properly disciplined and instructed, would be able successfully to resist any force that could be brought

---

5 OR 19:2, 597; OR 19:1, 25. McClellan converted Banks's II Corps, Army of Virginia, into the XII Corps, Army of the Potomac, and placed it temporarily under the command of Brig. Gen. Alpheus S. Williams. See M. Chris Bryan, *Cedar Mountain to Antietam: A Civil War Campaign History of the Union XII Corps, July-September 1862* (El Dorado, CA, 2022), 200-201. Concerning the Poolesville clash see Laurence H. Freiheit, *Boots and Saddles: Cavalry During the Maryland Campaign of September 1862* (Iowa City, IA, 2013), 152. Haines, Jr., ed., *The Diary of Col. John Henry Stover Funk*, 134.

6 OR 19:1, 139; OR 19:2, 599.

against it." Instilling the necessary discipline and good order required creating the position of "a proper inspector-general, with sufficient rank and standing, with assistants, [who] could be appointed to see to the execution of orders, and to fix the responsibility of acts."

Unfortunately for Lee, he did not possess the legal authority to introduce such a reform, and so he hoped Davis could be convinced to implement the change in his stead. "I assure you some remedy is necessary," Lee closed the letter, "especially now, when the army is in a State whose citizens it is our purpose to conciliate and bring with us. Every outrage upon their feelings and property should be checked." Here again Lee confirmed an important reason why his army had entered Maryland in the first place—to enlist the state's people and resources on the side of the South.[7]

With his daily correspondence completed, Lee turned his attention to other matters, including the draft proclamation to Maryland's people. That Charles Marshall likely composed this document on September 7 is deduced from the fact that it was printed and publicly distributed on September 8. It would have taken time for Marshall to write the text and for Lee to review, edit, and approve it before the finished copy was sent to a local press for typesetting. The time required for each of these steps makes it almost certain that Marshall wrote the document on the day before its publication.

Lee's proclamation summarizes the reasons why he led his army north of the Potomac, and what he hoped to accomplish in so doing. Addressed "To the People of Maryland," Lee affirmed that "It is right that you should know the purpose that brought the army under my command within the limits of your State . . . The people of the Confederate States have long watched with the deepest sympathy the wrongs and outrages that have been inflicted upon the citizens of a commonwealth allied to the States of the South by the strongest social, political, and commercial ties. They have seen with profound indignation their sister State deprived of every right and reduced to the condition of a conquered province." These sentences illustrate how in September 1862 Gen. Lee, in line with his government, most of his army, and many in the Confederacy, considered Maryland a lost Southern state kept in the Union by a tyrannical government in Washington.[8]

Emphasizing this aspect of Lee's thinking is important since most Civil War histories have referred to Maryland as in "the North" and to Lee's presence there as

---

7 OR 19:2, 597-598.

8 Long, *Memoirs of Robert E. Lee*, 208-209.

A native Marylander, Maj. Charles Marshall (shown here with the rank of Lt. Col.) composed the proclamation "To the People of Maryland" signed by Lee and distributed on Sept. 8. *Tulane University Library*

an invasion of "the North." In actuality, Lee had good reason to believe he might attract Marylanders' support. Located below the Mason-Dixon Line, which had long been considered the geographical boundary between the North and South, Maryland was a border state in the South. Furthermore, while a majority of the population supported the Union, this reality was neither clear at the time nor recognized by Confederates seeking to bring Maryland into their new nation. Indeed, had Lee considered Maryland "the North," he would not have carried out his operation in the manner he did. As Lee's aide Walter Taylor later recalled of that time, "now comes the 'tug of war.' The invasion policy is begun."[9]

What is more, Lee and others in his army were not the only ones who questioned Maryland's loyalty to the Union. No less a pro-administration newspaper than the *New York Herald* wrote at the end of August 1862, "The condition of affairs in Maryland is not satisfactory to loyal Union men. It is well known that the rebels there are openly organized in every county in the State, and there is reason to believe they are fully prepared with arms, and only wait an opportunity to raise the black flag of rebellion. The military authorities are strongly urged to require the disarming immediately of all who will not take the oath of allegiance."[10]

The *Herald's* reporting supported its editorializing. A story titled "Maryland Rebels 'Skedaddling' into Virginia," recounted recent rumors "that thousands of

---

[9] None of this is to say that Lee and others in the army ignored the evidence of divided sentiment in the state. Walter Taylor, for example, wrote on Sept. 7, "I think the population about equally divided in sentiment. I can judge only from what demonstrations as I see. Some appear rejoiced at our advent amongst them; others manifest either indifference or a silence which bespeaks enmity." See Tower, ed. *Lee's Adjutant*, 42-43.

[10] *New York Herald*, Aug. 27, 1862.

men have passed over into Virginia, principally from the eastern counties of Maryland. An entire company of cavalry left Montgomery County on the Upper Potomac last week, and squads are constantly moving into Virginia." So many Confederate supporters departed for the Confederacy that the *New York Daily Tribune* wryly commented, "Maryland will be a loyal State, if the migration of her Rebels into Virginia goes on a few weeks at the present rate."[11]

The *Philadelphia Ledger* echoed the sentiment, reporting that "private accounts from Maryland are not such as the loyal men of the nation would desire, for it is boldly stated that, should Jackson succeed in getting his army into the State, he will be joined at once by no less than 60,000 of its inhabitants. The aim is said to be to make Baltimore the Headquarters of the Confederate army, cut off the northern communication with Washington, and maintain a threatening attitude towards that city to result finally in its capture and destruction."[12]

Lastly, the *New York Times* declared in its September 14 edition: "That part of the State which it (Lee's army) occupied, though not entirely loyal, is its most loyal section," hinting at Maryland's pro-Confederate persuasion. And lest readers think only hyperbolic newspapermen held such a view of the situation, Lincoln's secretary of war, Edwin M. Stanton, is said to have commented in October 1862 that the government "wanted no more recruits from that state (Maryland), giving for a reason that they have enough rebels in the Northern army already." In short, the evidence suggests that describing Maryland as "the North" in September 1862 is a distortion which twists our understanding of what conditions in the state were at the time and obfuscates what Lee hoped to accomplish when issuing his proclamation.[13]

Returning to the proclamation itself, Lee recounted the violations of Marylanders' constitutional rights, such as arrest and imprisonment without charge, and he appealed directly to Baltimore's secessionists. "The government of your chief city has been usurped by armed strangers," he declared, "your legislature has been dissolved by the unlawful arrest of its members; freedom of the press and of speech has been suppressed; words have been declared offenses by an arbitrary

---

11 *New York Herald*, Aug. 27, 1862; *New York Daily Tribune*, Aug. 27, 1862. The cavalry referred to may be related to Capt. E. V. White's Loudoun Border Cavalry. White maintained close relationships with families along the river in Montgomery County.

12 *Philadelphia Ledger* quoted in the *Mobile Advertiser and Register*, Vol. XXX, No. 141, Friday, Sept. 12, 1862.

13 *New York Times*, Sept. 14, 1862; *Fayetteville (NC) Observer*, Oct. 2, 1862.

decree of the Federal Executive, and citizens ordered to be tried by a military commission for what they may dare to speak." These alleged misdeeds encouraged "the people of the South . . . to aid you in throwing off this foreign yoke, to enable you again to enjoy the inalienable rights of freemen, and restore independence and sovereignty to your State. In obedience to this wish, our army has come among you, and is prepared to assist you with the power of its arms in regaining the rights of which you have been despoiled. This, citizens of Maryland, is our mission, so far as you are concerned."

In these final sentences Lee repeated for the sixth time, if one includes the letters to Davis of September 3 and 4, General Orders No. 103, his comment recorded in the *Philadelphia Inquirer*, and his letter on September 7, that he led his army north of the Potomac to provide the armed support he and other Confederates believed Marylanders needed to rebel. "This army will respect your choice, whatever it may be," Lee concluded, "and while the Southern people will rejoice to welcome you to your natural position among them, they will only welcome you when you come of your own free will."[14]

Appearing in print on September 8, Lee's proclamation announced publicly for the first time the political motives that he had expressed only within the pages of letters and army orders up to that point. The proclamation thus represented a culmination of sorts. No longer convinced that Maryland's secessionists would rise up unless his army proved it could protect them, Lee would need to wait to see if his words produced the desired effect. Little did the general know, however, that the time he thought he had in abundance to accomplish this end had already run out. Around nightfall on September 7, McClellan arrived at Rockville, Maryland, to take command of the Army of the Potomac in the field. He would begin pushing it toward Frederick on the next day.

---

14 *OR* 19:2, 601-602.

Chapter 3

Monday, September 8:
Unexpected Events Force Lee's Hand

General Lee summoned the members of his staff to his tent "at the usual hour" ahead of what would turn out to be a critically important day. Dictating his first message to President Davis that morning, Lee wrote, "Since my letter to you of the 7th instant, nothing of interest, in a military point of view, has transpired." It may have appeared that way, but, unbeknownst to the general, George McClellan had placed the reconstituted Army of the Potomac in position to begin its advance toward Frederick. Cobbled together from portions of the old Army of the Potomac, as well as from John Pope's former Army of Virginia, Ambrose Burnside's expeditionary force from North Carolina, and the Kanawha Division of Brig. Gen. Jacob D. Cox from western Virginia, Little Mac had worked furiously to get his army into fighting trim. Lee knew none of this at the time, however, and his ongoing belief in the enemy's lethargy appears to have lulled him into a dangerous sense of complacency.[1]

Writing, "As far as I can learn, the enemy are not moving in this direction, but continue to concentrate about Washington," Lee either did not admit to Davis or did not know that the enemy already occupied positions running from Dawsonville and Rockville (25 and 30 miles from Frederick) to Brookeville, Maryland, approximately 33 miles from Frederick. If the latter is the case, then the blame for Lee's ignorance falls on the shoulders of Jeb Stuart, whose pickets should have kept

---

1 OR 19:2, 600-601. The News Leader, "Col. Walter H. Taylor, A. A. G," in *SHSP*, Vol. 41, No. 3 (Sept. 1916), 83. For a detailed treatment of McClellan's activity in the days leading to September 7 see Chapter 2 of Thorp and Rossino, *The Tale Untwisted*.

him apprised of Federal movements. Lee, in any event, remained content to shift his army's supply line west of the Blue Ridge as if he had no reason for deeper concern. Informing the Confederate president, "I am endeavoring to break up the line of communication as far back as Culpeper Court-House," the general intended to "turn everything into the Valley of Virginia, in accordance with the plan which I have heretofore made known to you."

Lee also informed Davis that weapons "captured on the plains of Manassas, of which some 10,000 or 12,000 were collected at Gainesville," remained unaccounted for. This caused Lee to fear these valuable arms might "all be lost, for want of transportation to remove them." He had made "the best arrangements" in his power to collect them, but "being compelled to move the army away . . . the wagons that had been ordered to go by Gainesville to take arms back were taken to transport sick and wounded back to Warrenton." The last Lee had heard of them "they were still at Gainesville," adding, "so far we have had no difficulty in procuring provisions in the country, though we have not relied exclusively upon them for our subsistence."[2]

The general then turned to a separate matter in a second letter to Davis—proposing peace to the Lincoln administration. Arguing that "[t]he present position of affairs, in my opinion, places it in the power of the Government of the Confederate States to propose with propriety to that of the United States the recognition of our independence," Lee claimed that "[s]uch a proposition . . . being made when it is in our power to inflict injury upon our adversary, would show conclusively to the world that our sole object is the establishment of our independence and the attainment of an honorable peace. The rejection of this offer would prove to the country that the responsibility of the continuance of the war does not rest upon us, but that the party in power in the United States elect to prosecute it for purposes of their own." In addition, he hoped, "The proposal of peace would enable the people of the United States to determine at their coming elections whether they will support those who favor a prolongation of the war, or those who wish to bring it to a termination, which can but be productive of good to both parties without affecting the honor of either."[3]

Histories of the Maryland Campaign often cite influencing the outcome of Northern elections as one of General Lee's primary goals. The emphasis on this

---

2 In his campaign report, Jeb Stuart notes that he detailed the 6th Virginia Cavalry to "collect arms" at Centreville. See OR 19:1, 816.

3 OR 19:2, 600.

subject appears to arise, however, from a distorted understanding of Lee's desire to incite a secessionist rebellion in Maryland which would help him defeat the Federals north of the Potomac River. Unwilling to acknowledge that Lee simultaneously pursued both political and military agendas in Maryland, historians and others have sought other rationales, such as influencing Northern elections, to explain the general's actions.

In truth, Lee wrote about Northern elections only after he had crossed the Potomac, and while he waited to make his next move. His mention of the subject appears to say more about the time he had to ruminate on broader political issues than it does about his belief that Richmond's actions could shape public opinion in the Northern states. If offering a peace proposal could help turn the Northern public against the war then so much the better, but there is little evidence beyond this single letter to suggest that Lee felt strongly about the issue one way or the other. He mentioned elections only this one time in 1862, and after writing about it to Davis, he never again returned to the subject. Even in his post-campaign report, Lee did not discuss influencing elections as a motivating factor for his operation. His suggestion concerning it on the morning of September 8 thus seems to have been an expression of something Lee considered a realistic possibility given the outward inaction of his much "weakened and demoralized" opponent rather than a potent motivating idea. Information that Lee received shortly after dictating his letter to Davis would in any case rapidly disabuse him of the presumption.[4]

His thoughts to the Confederate president duly recorded, Lee requested that Col. Robert Chilton write General Samuel Cooper, the army's Adjutant and Inspector General in Richmond, concerning the "Many convalescents, anxious to rejoin their commands, [who] are scattered between this and Culpeper Court House, subject to capture by passing scouts of Federal cavalry." Asking of Cooper "that all recruits, convalescents, &c., destined for this army, may be retained in Richmond, employed as guards or at the school of instruction, until in sufficient force to be sent forward as an organized detachment, under command of officers, to Culpeper Court-House, and thence, after drawing rations sufficient for the march, to Winchester, by the way of Luray and Front Royal," Lee confirmed once again his intention to march the army west-northwest into the lower Shenandoah Valley in preparation for a move against Pennsylvania.[5]

---

4 Ibid., 590.

5 Ibid., 601.

Monday, September 8: Unexpected Events Force Lee's Hand | 23

Commander of the ill-fated Harpers Ferry garrison, Col. Dixon S. Miles stayed put when ordered to by Maj. Gen. John E. Wool of the Eighth Corps/Middle Department. Miles's continued presence proved to be a thorn in the side of Robert E. Lee, forcing the Confederate commander to devise Special Orders No. 191.
Library of Congress

It was around this time, either after completing the morning's staff business, or perhaps even during it, that Lee received two pieces of intelligence. These proved to be so important that their receipt immediately altered the general's plans. One bit of news came from Capt. E. V. White, who had just returned from his scouting mission to Harpers Ferry. As the history of White's cavalry mentions, after "learning of the condition of affairs about Harper's Ferry, and gathering much valuable information; without, however, being required to engage the enemy," White told the general that contrary to rumor the enemy garrison had not evacuated to Pennsylvania. Instead, as many as several thousand men still occupied the position.[6]

The other information Lee received came from Jeb Stuart, who reported that contrary to what the commanding general had just written to President Davis, there was indeed a significant development on the military front—the Army of the Potomac had begun to move. Stuart, recalled Lee in a February 1868 letter to D. H. Hill, "reported that Genl. McClellan had reached Rockville and was marching very slowly with an extended front, covering the roads to Washington and to Baltimore." This news must have come as a shock to Lee because it immediately

---

6 Myers, *The Comanches*, 109. White could have reported to Lee on the evening on Sept. 7 but there is no evidence for this. We do know White had returned to Frederick by Sept. 8 thanks to Lewis H. Steiner, *Report of Lewis H. Steiner, Inspector of the Sanitary Commission Containing a Diary Kept During the Rebel Occupation of Frederick, MD, and an Account of the Operations of the U.S. Sanitary Commission During the Campaign in Maryland, September, 1862* (New York, NY, 1862), 13-14, 16. The following statement about Lee's learning of the enemy at Harpers Ferry is not verifiable, but is included to be thorough: "This officer was still maintaining his position. This to General Lee was a matter of great surprise, as being contrary to all military prudence and principle. He said, on receiving this report, 'Is it possible those people have not retired?' and at once made disposition to capture the force"; George W. Booth, *Personal Reminiscences of A Maryland Soldier In The War Between The States, 1861-1865* (Baltimore, MD, 1898), 71.

eliminated the assumption that he could "detain the enemy upon the northern frontier until the approach of winter." His army would now need to confront the Federals within a matter of days instead of weeks or months.[7]

Lee's statements concerning the situation at that time have created some confusion on this point. Although the general wrote in his August 1863 report that "[t]he advance of the Federal Army was so slow at the time we left Fredericktown as to justify the belief that the reduction of Harper's Ferry would be accomplished and our troops concentrated before they would be called upon to meet it," testimony from Richard H. Anderson and Lafayette McLaws suggests that Lee felt more urgency than he later recalled. Anderson stated in a letter to D. H. Hill after the war, for example, that upon calling him to headquarters to explain the Harpers Ferry operation in the late afternoon of September 8, Lee said repeatedly, "Harpers Ferry must be taken against Thursday evening (September 11)." McLaws commented similarly, noting, "It is evident from the whole tenor of the order (i.e., Special Orders No. 191) that little, if any delay, was contemplated at Harper's Ferry."[8]

These statements are reinforced by the fact that Lee voiced the need for urgency in notes to Jeb Stuart on September 12 and to Lafayette McLaws on September 13. Concerning the former missive, Lee dictated through Charles Marshall at 2:30 p.m. that he feared "the enemy will be in Fredericktown" before Stuart could evacuate the 430 sick and wounded men the Army of Northern Virginia had left behind. Lee assumed correctly that the enemy would "follow in your footsteps," and he urged Stuart to resist the Army of the Potomac's advance as best he could. Writing, "I do not wish you to retire too fast before the enemy, or to distribute your cavalry wide apart," Lee admonished his cavalry chief to "[k]eep me advised of the movements of the enemy, and do not let them discover if

---

[7] R. E. Lee to D. H. Hill, Feb. 21, 1868, D. H. Hill Papers #2035-z, Southern Historical Collection, The Wilson Library, University of North Carolina at Chapel Hill, cited hereafter as SHC, UNC. The possibility exists that Stuart reported this information in person; see R. Channing Price in Robert J. Trout, *With Pen and Saber: The Letters and Diaries of J. E. B. Stuart's Staff Officers* (Mechanicsburg, PA, 1995), 96: "Monday [Sept. 8]. I went up [to Frederick] again with Gen. Stuart." Frederick's civilian population had heard rumors of the Federal army's advance, too. See Entry for September 7, 1862 in Ann R. L. Schaeffer, *Records of the Past: Civil War Diary, September 4–23, 1862* (Frederick, MD, no date).

[8] OR 19:1, 144-145. R. H. Anderson to D. H. Hill, Nov. 14, 1867, Daniel Harvey Hill Manuscript (Mss.), Record ID PC.93.1, Daniel Harvey Hill (1821-1889) Papers, State Archives of North Carolina, Raleigh, NC. Anderson wrote that this conversation with Lee took place on the evening of September 8; Lafayette McLaws, "The Maryland Campaign" (Savannah, GA, 1896) in McLaws Papers, SHC, UNC.

Maj. Gen. George B. McClellan. Reinstituted as field commander of the Army of the Potomac, McClellan's advance toward Frederick, MD, on Sept. 8 took Robert E. Lee by surprise. *Library of Congress*

possible our movements." To McLaws, meanwhile, Lee wrote through Col. Long, "He is anxious that the object of your expedition [against Harpers Ferry] be speedily accomplished. The enemy have doubtless occupied Frederick since our troops have abandoned it, and are following our rear."[9]

It seems from these dispatches that the moment he decided to send Jackson to capture Col. Miles's garrison, Lee knew he was taking a significant risk by dividing his army in the face of an approaching enemy force. Assuming that McClellan would be methodical in his approach, Lee took his chance anyway. He then openly fretted about his decision when the operation began to fall behind schedule. In short, Lee gambled that Jackson and the others could make quick work of Harpers Ferry, after which they could then rejoin the other parts waiting for them west of South Mountain. The general also seems to have believed that Jeb Stuart could keep the Federals at bay long enough for Jackson to complete his operation. Choosing this course of action, however, committed Lee and his army to an operational timetable beyond the general's control and fateful consequences would attend the decision.

The return of George McClellan to field command clearly influenced Lee's thinking about what he thought his men could accomplish. Joseph Harsh has called into question Lee's knowledge of McClellan's return, arguing, "there is no contemporaneous evidence that Lee knew as early as the 9th [of September] it would be McClellan" in command. This is an unfortunate overstatement. There is sufficient evidence, both explicit and circumstantial, to show that Lee knew about McClellan's position at the head of the new army. Lee knew as of September 3, for example, "that some of Buell's cavalry have been joined to General Pope's army." He also had "reason to believe that the whole of McClellan's, the larger portion of Burnside's and Cox's, and a portion of Hunter's, are united to it." This told Lee that McClellan had arrived in northern Virginia and was no longer with what remained of his force near Richmond.[10]

One day later, the *Baltimore Sun* provided Lee with additional information. Writing, "Major General McClellan had, in accordance with the general order of yesterday, issued an order resuming the chief command of the aggregated army

---

9 R. E. Lee to J. E. B. Stuart, Sept. 11, 1862, J. E. B. Stuart Military Papers, mss SA, Box 2, Huntington Library, San Marino, CA; OR 19:2, 606; *Washington Evening Star*, Sep. 15, 1862. Lee's fears proved to be well-founded as all of the sick and wounded left behind fell into Federal hands.

10 Joseph L. Harsh, *Taken at the Flood: Robert E. Lee and Confederate Strategy in the Maryland Campaign of 1862* (Kent, OH, 1999), 84-85, 130, 141; OR 19:2, 591.

(Pope's and Burnsides's) thus assembled for the defense of the capital," the paper's editors added in a second column on the same page, "Major Gen. McClellan, we hear, has to-day reestablished his headquarters in the building on Pennsylvania avenue, opposite the State Department, occupied by him for the same purpose before the departure of his army of the Potomac from this vicinity." If this information did not provide confirmation enough, yet another column stated that "Gen. McClellan has assumed command of the entire Federal forces in and around Washington."[11]

These reports informed Lee, who mentioned this issue of the newspaper in his September 4 letter to Davis, that McClellan had been named chief of the combined forces (i.e., "the aggregated army") of the recently defeated John Pope (the Army of Virginia) and of Ambrose Burnside (troops from North Carolina), in addition to his own men from the Army of the Potomac. The *Baltimore Sun* article made it clear that the president had relieved Burnside and Pope, both of whom were senior field officers, of their respective commands. It seems a reach to conclude, therefore, that Lee would have assumed someone other than McClellan would take command of the new army in the field. This conclusion is also reinforced by the fact that men in the ranks of the Army of Northern Virginia, from lowly privates to Brig. Gen. Dorsey Pender, learned while in Frederick that Lincoln had put McClellan back in command. Lee surely heard this news as well given that he had spent time in the city on the evening of September 6.[12]

Learning that McClellan's army had begun moving toward him, and that a sizable enemy force still occupied Harpers Ferry, immediately changed the static situation in which Lee had planned his next move. With his army then in an unenviable position between the two enemy forces, Lee needed to move it before the situation became untenable. Nevertheless, Lee did not think in defensive terms. He chose instead to assume the offensive and summoned Stonewall Jackson to meet with him, thereby setting in motion the planning that culminated in Special Orders No. 191.

Why Lee called on Jackson and not Longstreet for this task is often attributed to the fact that two days earlier while on route to Frederick, Lee had heard cannon fire from the west and proposed that Old Pete "organize forces to surround and

---

11 *Baltimore Sun*, Sept. 4, 1862.

12 For details on the news in Frederick concerning McClellan's return to command see Rossino, *Their Maryland*, 33-34.

Maj. Gen. Thomas J. "Stonewall" Jackson. General Lee issued a verbal command on Sept. 8 placing Jackson in charge of the operation against Harpers Ferry despite Jackson's desire to engage Federal forces near Frederick. *Library of Congress*

capture the works and the garrison." Longstreet had for his part balked at this, expressing the opinion that he

> thought it a venture not worth the game, and suggested, as we were in the enemy's country and presence, that he would be advised of any move that we made in a few hours after it was set on foot; that the Union army, though beaten, was not disorganized; that we knew a number of their officers who could put it in order and march against us, if they found us exposed, and make serious trouble before the capture could be accomplished; that our men were worn by very severe and protracted service, and in need of repose; that as long as we had them in hand we were masters of the situation, but dispersed into many fragments, our strength must be greatly reduced.[13]

It may be that Lee recalled his conversation with Old Pete and turned instead to Jackson. Yet there were other compelling reasons to assign the operation to the hard-marching Virginian. For one thing, Jackson knew Harpers Ferry and the surrounding countryside intimately. He had begun the war in command of the place, which gave him knowledge of its strengths and, more importantly, its weaknesses. For another thing, a small portion of Jackson's command already occupied Winchester, so there existed the potential for Old Jack to cooperate with it instead of Longstreet, who did not know the terrain or the section of the valley wherein Harpers Ferry lay. Lastly, as has been discussed, Lee hoped to make quick work of the garrison by swiftly forcing its surrender. This meant employing Jackson's vaunted "foot cavalry" against Harpers Ferry instead of relying on the often slower-moving command of James Longstreet. In short, it made sense on multiple levels for Lee to send Jackson despite the doubts that Old Pete had voiced about the operation.

13 Longstreet, *From Manassas to Appomattox*, 201-202.

Lee and Jackson discussed a number of subjects during their conference. The first of these involved the plan to shift the army west of South Mountain. Lee had already planned to make this move before receiving word that the Federals still occupied Harpers Ferry. However, according to Maj. Robert Lewis Dabney, Jackson's wartime biographer and one-time Assistant Adjutant General, Stonewall preferred defending the line of the Monocacy. "Two ... plans remained [to Lee]: the one was to leave Harper's Ferry to itself for the present, and fight McClellan as he advanced," wrote Dabney. "The other was to withdraw the army west of the mountains, as at first designed ... and then to re-assemble the whole at some favorable position in that region for a decisive struggle with McClellan. The former was advocated by Jackson ... lest the other system of movements should prove too complex for realizing that punctual and complete concentration which sound policy required."[14]

Jackson's idea did not suit Lee because he wanted to engage the Federals as far from their base of operations as possible in order to avoid a repeat of the incomplete victory his army had won at Second Manassas. Despite having crushed Pope's Army of Virginia in that battle, Lee found he could not follow up the triumph because the fugitives from Pope's force had streamed into the safety of the entrenchments around Washington. Lee described his thinking about this subject in his Maryland campaign report, explaining that he

> decided to cross the Potomac east of the Blue Ridge, in order, by threatening Washington and Baltimore, to cause the enemy to withdraw from the south bank, where his presence endangered our communications and the safety of those engaged in the removal of our wounded and the captured property from the late battle-fields. Having accomplished this result, it was proposed to move the army into Western Maryland, establish our communications with Richmond through the Valley of the Shenandoah ... induce the enemy to follow, and thus draw him from his base of supplies.

---

14 Robert L. Dabney, *Life and Campaigns of Lieut.-Gen. Thomas J. Jackson* (Richmond, VA, 1866), 549. Dabney served as Jackson's A. A. G. until Aug. 15, 1862, when he resigned the position due to illness and returned to Richmond. His claim about Jackson wanting to defend the Monocacy near Frederick is unique and likely based on interviews of Jackson's staff after the campaign; see Henry K. Douglas, *I Rode with Stonewall* (Pennington, NJ, 1995), 118.

Then, as if to emphasize the point, he repeated three paragraphs later, "It had not been intended to oppose its [the Army of the Potomac's] passage through the South Mountains as it was desired to engage it as far as possible from its base."[15]

Jackson and Lee also must have considered sending the entire army to reduce Harpers Ferry instead of just a few parts of it. Evidence for this comes from a letter sent by D. H. Hill to Robert Dabney in 1864. Explaining how "[a]fter the Battle of Fredericksburg Genl. J[ackson] asked me if an officer had a right to divulge the opinions expressed by him at a Council of War," Hill wrote, "I gave him my opinion about it, naming the circumstances which would justify such a course. After a good deal of distraction, he said, 'at the Council held at Frederick I opposed the separation of our forces in order to capture Harper's Ferry. I urged that we should all be kept together.'"[16]

General Longstreet agreed. While visiting army headquarters that morning, Longstreet happened to stumble onto the meeting taking place between Jackson and Lee. "I found the front of the general's tent closed and tied," recalled Longstreet in his postwar memoir. "Upon inquiring of a member of the staff, I was told that he was inside with General Jackson. As I had not been called, I turned to go away, when General Lee, recognizing my voice, called me in." Old Pete found Lee and Jackson engaged at that moment in planning what would become Special Orders No. 191. "The plan had been arranged," wrote the general. "Jackson, with his three divisions, was to recross the Potomac by the fords above Harper's Ferry, march via Martinsburg to Bolivar Heights; [Lafayette] McLaws's division by Crampton's Gap [would march to] to Maryland Heights; J[ohn]. G. Walker's division to recross at Cheek's Ford and occupy Loudoun Heights, these heights overlooking the positions of the garrison of Harper's Ferry."[17]

---

15 OR 19:1, 145; William Allan, *The Army of Northern Virginia in 1862* (Boston, MA, 1892), 331, picked up on this as well: "Lee designed to give battle where, in case of success, the distance of the Federal army from Washington and Baltimore would be too great to admit of its reaching speedy shelter."

16 D. H. Hill to R. L. Dabney, July 21, 1864, in Robert L. Dabney Papers and Miscellaneous Papers, Microform VSY Reel 62, Union Presbyterian Seminary, William Smith Morton Library, Richmond, VA.

17 Longstreet, *From Manassas to Appomattox*, 202-203; also see James Longstreet, "The Invasion of Maryland," in Johnson and Buel, eds., *B&L*, 2:663. Longstreet's explanation of Walker's part in the operation is a clear example of hindsight because at the time Lee had not yet decided what Walker's role should be. He would not decide this until late on the following morning.

Maj. Gen. James Longstreet. Opposed to separating the army for the operation against Harpers Ferry, Longstreet sought to strengthen the portion of his command sent with Lafayette McLaws to capture Maryland Heights. *Library of Congress*

Learning that Lee intended to cannibalize his command to augment the force Jackson could bring against the Federals must have come as a surprise to Longstreet, but he did not complain when writing about it decades later. Lee desired to bring the operation to a swift conclusion by ensuring that Confederate forces encircled the garrison, giving the hapless Federals no hope of relief or escape. This comes through clearly in paragraphs III and V of Special Orders No. 191 demanding that Jackson's and McLaws's forces be in position by Friday morning, September 12.[18]

As for the rest of the army, Longstreet learned that "D. H. Hill's division [was] to march by the National road over South Mountain at Turner's Gap, and halt at the western base, to guard trains, intercept fugitives from Harper's Ferry, and support the cavalry, if needed; the cavalry [was] to face the enemy and embarrass his movements." Concerning his own command, Longstreet recorded it "was to march over the mountain by Turner's Gap to Hagerstown." With "their minds . . . settled firmly upon the enterprise," he continued, "I offered no opposition further than to ask that the order be so modified as to allow me to send R[ichard] H. Anderson's division with McLaws and to halt my own column near the point designated for bivouac of General D. H. Hill's command. These suggestions were accepted, and the order so framed was issued."

Here we see Longstreet, much like Jackson, endeavoring to keep together as large a portion of the army as possible. Yet this still would not settle his mind, and so "Not satisfied with the organization of McLaws's column, [Longstreet] . . . obtained permission on the 10th [of September] to strengthen it by three other brigades, [Cadmus] Wilcox's, under Colonel Alfred Cumming; [Winfield S.]

18 OR 19:2, 603.

Featherston's [under Carnot Posey], and [Roger A.] Pryor's, which were attached to R. H. Anderson's division." In the end, Lee would reconcile Longstreet's and Jackson's concerns about dispersing the army in the face of the enemy with his own plan to bring it back together west of South Mountain by adding paragraph IX of Special Orders No. 191. This stated, "The commands of Generals Jackson, McLaws, and Walker, after accomplishing the objects for which they have been detached, will join the main body of the army at Boonsborough or Hagerstown."[19]

Upon the meeting's conclusion, Lee issued "verbal instructions [placing Jackson] in command of the expedition" before later putting those orders in writing on September 9. Jackson then ordered D. H. Hill to select a brigade from his division to act as the army's rear guard during its march away from Frederick City. The evidence for this rests in the fact that Hill chose the brigade of George B. Anderson for this duty and ordered it to march from where it had been camped at White Oak Springs southwest of Frederick to a new position on the hills east of the Monocacy River, near the bulk of Jackson's command. Private James Shinn of the 4th North Carolina Infantry recorded this movement in his diary:

> Sept. 8. We lay in camp after being aroused very early, until nearly 10 a.m. expecting to march every minute. At the above ... hour the drums rolled and soon the shouts of mules sounded through the grove. The line of march was soon formed and we learned that we would only march about 3 miles to camp with the division, who had been resting there a day or two while our brigade was marching hard exploring the Va. side of the river. We crossed the railway and also the Big Monocrisy on the turn pike bridge about where the railway crossed. By 2 ½ o'clock we camped in a beautiful grove of chestnuts on a high ridge.[20]

His perspective limited to that of a man in the ranks, Shinn mistook this change of location as intended to bring together all the brigades of Hill's division. Three of the other four brigades under Hill were at that time, however, still camped four miles south of Frederick along Ballenger's Creek west of the Monocacy River. Roswell Ripley's brigade, meanwhile, remained as far away as Buckeystown, where it guarded a bridge over the Monocacy River. This minor error notwithstanding, Shinn added an important detail, writing how he and his comrades "expected to rest a few days," but received orders in the early evening "to draw '3 days rations'

---

19 Ibid; Longstreet, *From Manassas to Appomattox*, 205.

20 James W. Shinn Diary, Edwin Augustus Osborne Papers, #567, Folder 166, Vol. 76, SHC, UNC; Lee to Hill, Feb. 21, 1868, D. H. Hill Papers #2035-z, SHC, UNC.

and cook it." This they did, although cooking the rations did not take place until the following day.

Shinn's diary supports the conclusion that the headquarters meeting between Lee, Jackson, and Longstreet took place on the morning of September 8 and not on September 9. If the conference did not take place on September 8, there is no way to explain why D. H. Hill ordered one of his brigades to move east of the Monocacy River. Hill clearly received an order from Jackson to make this redeployment as part of his division's designation as the Army of Northern Virginia's rear guard. Soldiers in both armies also knew from experience that orders to cook rations signaled that either a movement or an engagement was imminent.

Hill communicated this instruction to Anderson on the evening of September 8, which suggests he did not know about a planned general movement of the army until later in the day. This implies that Hill did not receive orders concerning the upcoming march all at once. Rather, he got them in stages with Jackson transmitting the instruction to move a brigade east of the river before later informing Hill of the need to cook rations. The possibility also exists that Hill gave the order to cook rations on his own authority after Jackson had instructed him to position a brigade east of the Monocacy. Without corroborating evidence it is simply impossible to know.

All of this took place before D. H. Hill received a copy of Special Orders No. 191 from Jackson's headquarters on the following day. Why Old Jack would issue a written copy of the orders to Hill is explained by the command situation at the time. During this phase of the Confederate operation, encompassing Friday, September 5, when his three divisions crossed the Potomac River, to the morning of Wednesday, September 10, when his command moved out, Jackson exercised direct command over Hill's division. Hill recalled this fact after the war, writing that during the army's time in Frederick, "we drew all our supplies and received all our orders through General Jackson." Lee knew this as well, replying to a letter from D. H. Hill in February 1868: "[I]t was proper in my opinion that a copy of the order (i.e., Special Orders No. 191) should have been sent to you by the Adjt. Genl. . . . as you were by it withdrawn from Genl. Jackson's Command." In other words, Lee confirmed that Hill remained under Jackson's command until the operation against Harpers Ferry commenced on September 10. From that date onward, Hill's division operated under the command of Lee himself, not Stonewall Jackson.[21]

---

21 "My division was the first to cross the Potomac . . . I then learned that Gen. Jackson had crossed and wished to see me. After a rapid ride, I found him at the head of his division

The reversion of Hill's command to "unattached" status meant that on September 9 the army's headquarters staff would need to generate a copy of Special Orders No. 191 for Hill. It is worth noting that at this point in the war, Lee often sent orders to division commanders directly, so the arrangement was not unusual. Sir Frederick Maurice, the editor of Charles Marshall's papers, observed of Lee concerning this practice:

> He was, as regards the plans and operations of his army, in a great measure his own chief of staff. He but rarely issued elaborate written orders for operations; when he did, he usually drafted them himself and gave them to his personal staff to make the necessary copies. In the field preliminary orders were usually given direct to his divisional and corps commanders, subsequent orders being delivered verbally by his aides-de-camp.... There is no doubt that Lee's reliance upon verbal explanations and messages was sometimes carried to excess.[22]

Upon concluding his conference with Jackson and Longstreet, Lee then entertained a visit from Brig. Gen. William Nelson Pendleton, the commander of the army's Reserve Artillery, who had just arrived in the area. "After reporting to General Lee, Monday morning (September 8)," recalled the artillery commander in a letter home, "I spent the day in calling on my old friends in Frederick." Pendleton then revealed in this same letter, written on September 10: "To-day we go farther inward; I must not indicate where lest my letter fail and give some clue where I would not have information gotten. Suffice it that General Lee seems well to understand what he is about." Reading between the lines, it appears that Lee informed Pendleton verbally about the upcoming operation against Harpers Ferry.

---

examining a map held by Captain (afterwards Colonel) E. V. White, who still lives. He said, 'You have been placed under my orders, I wish your division to join me, to-night, near Frederick.' I returned and brought up my division that night. General J. was disabled the next morning by his horse falling back upon him, and I was put in charge of the corps.... For the next two or three days, we drew all our supplies and received all our orders through General Jackson"; Daniel Harvey Hill, "The Lost Dispatch," in *The Land We Love*, 6 vols. (Charlotte, NC, 1868), IV:274; Lee to Hill, Feb. 21, 1868, D. H. Hill Papers #2035-z, SHC, UNC.

22 Frederick Maurice, ed., *Lee's Aide-De-Camp: Being the Papers of Colonel Charles Marshall Sometime Aide-De-Camp, Military Secretary, and Assistant Adjutant General on the Staff of Robert E. Lee, 1862–1865* (Lincoln, NE, 2000), xxxviii-xxxix.

This may have then removed the need to send a written copy of Special Orders No. 191 to Pendleton once they were issued.[23]

For the rest of the day on September 8, Lee attended to further planning his operation and to handling other army business. In the meantime, engineers Col. Thomas H. Williamson and First Lt. Thomas T. L. Snead of Jackson's staff led a team placing explosive charges under the piers of the Baltimore and Ohio Railroad bridge. They then blew up the structure, dropping it into the Monocacy River. The destruction of the bridge on September 8, while seemingly unconnected to the other events discussed above, provides evidence that Jackson was preparing to move his command. If he was not getting ready to march then Lee could have assigned the task of destroying the bridge to Longstreet and have the demolition carried out on September 9. Jackson, however, got it done immediately to complete the task before he and his men moved out.[24]

Toward sunset on September 8, Lee received an unusual visitor. Federal General Columbus O'Donnell owned a farm in Weverton, Maryland, near Harpers Ferry, and pressing business required him to travel to Baltimore. Leaving his homestead at about 2:00 p.m., the general and his son, Oliver, reached the outskirts of Frederick several hours later. Pickets halted them outside of town before waving them through to the office of Col. Bradley T. Johnson. Johnson informed O'Donnell that he could not issue a pass to send him through the lines, but Lee could, and so O'Donnell rode to the Best Farm to secure the required pass. According to the *Baltimore American* newspaper, which reported on the story:

> On reaching the camp General O'Donnell approached the tent of General Lee, when he was met by Charles Marshall … with who[m] he was also personally acquainted. Marshall was acting as an aide of General Lee, and on General O'Donnell making known to him that his business was to secure a pass to Baltimore, he told him that General Lee was very busy and could not be seen, but that he would make known his request to him. Marshall entered the tent, and soon returned with the pass required, and informed General O'Donnell that General Lee requested him to say that it afforded him great pleasure to grant his request.[25]

---

23 Susan P. Lee, *Memoirs of William Nelson Pendleton* (Philadelphia, PA, 1883), 211; Rossino, *Their Maryland*, Appendix B outlines a speculative case for Pendleton to have been given a copy of Special Orders No. 191 on this date while at Lee's headquarters. This speculation is probably incorrect.

24 McDonald, ed., *Make Me a Map of the Valley*, 79-80; Government Printing Office, *List of Staff Officers of the Confederate States Army, 1861-1865* (Washington, DC, 1891), 155, 180.

25 *Baltimore American*, Sept. 10, 1862; also see *Baltimore Sun*, Sept. 10, 1862.

O'Donnell traveled onward and, upon reaching Baltimore the next day (September 9), he reported to Maj. Gen. John Ellis Wool, the commander of the Federal Middle Department/Eighth Corps. Wool promptly wired McClellan a message confirming that O'Donnell had observed "[t]he position of the rebel army [when he] passed through their camps" near Frederick. Wool did not mention another interesting bit of information that O'Donnell allegedly told the *Baltimore American*. Reporting O'Donnell's visit to Lee's headquarters, the newspaper stated on September 10 that the Confederates "were preparing to retire before McClellan's army." The general denied in writing that he had ever said such a thing and whether he did or not is irrelevant. The important point is that however they got the information, the editors of the *Baltimore American* knew by September 9 that Lee's army was readying itself to move out. If this information did indeed come from O'Donnell, then it means he noticed these preparations late in the day on September 8. This would reinforce the conclusion that the Lee-Jackson-Longstreet conference took place that morning and not on the following day.[26]

By the time darkness arrived on September 8, Robert E. Lee faced a very different strategic situation than he had at daybreak. Believing early in the morning that enemy forces remained inactive around Washington, Lee had been content to continue shifting his supply line into the Shenandoah Valley. Once this task had been completed, he could take whatever step he chose next, be it to march his army into Pennsylvania or, with luck, to support an uprising by Maryland's people against the old national government. All of this had changed by late morning after Lee learned about McClellan's advance toward Frederick. Suddenly, Longstreet's warning on September 6 that "[t]he Union army, though beaten, was not disorganized," seemed prophetic.[27]

---

26 OR 19:2, 231; O'Donnell's information confirmed to George McClellan that Lee's army remained in place along the Monocacy River. O'Donnell subsequently wrote an open letter to the *Baltimore American* that it had incorrectly reported on what occurred. Writing, "To the Editors of the American: Gentlemen: — We have seen a statement in your paper this morning giving an account of our visit to the Confederate army, which we regret to find entirely incorrect. We have no knowledge of the extent of the army or its intended movements. We were kindly received, and General Lee gave us a pass to return home, with the request that we would give no information about the extent or intentions of the army. Our property was not injured, nor from all the information we could procure, was the property of any of the inhabitants of the county taken, or any of them disturbed in any way. We found good order prevailing in the city, and everything quiet and orderly. Respectfully, yours, Columbus O'Donnell and C. Oliver O'Donnell." *Alexandria Gazette*, Sept. 11, 1862.

27 Longstreet, *From Manassas to Appomattox*, 202.

Lee also learned that the Federal garrison at Harpers Ferry remained in place. This information, when combined with the news about the Army of the Potomac, told Lee that the abundance of time he thought he had to move farther north no longer existed. Harpers Ferry needed to be taken as soon as possible to secure the army's rear, meaning that Lee also could not afford to wait for sympathetic Marylanders to respond to his proclamation. The need for haste quickly replaced the notion of operating at length in the enemy's territory until winter. Lee would instead need to test the resolve of the state's secessionists by fighting McClellan's army sooner rather than later. As the general wrote of this moment, he hoped "that military success might afford us an opportunity to aid the citizens of Maryland in any efforts they might be disposed to make to recover their liberties . . . Influenced by these considerations, the army was put in motion."[28]

McClellan's impressive ability to breathe life into the defeated Federal army, and put it back into the field only five days after he had assumed command of the Washington defenses on September 2, forced Lee's hand at a moment when the Confederate commander least expected it. As a result, Lee "proposed to move the army into Western Maryland, establish our communications with Richmond through the Valley of the Shenandoah, and, by threatening Pennsylvania, induce the enemy to follow, and thus draw him from his base of supplies." By the time he began dictating Special Orders No. 191 to an aide late the next morning, Lee had therefore abandoned the idea of marching his army into Pennsylvania. Moving in the direction of Hagerstown and the Pennsylvania state line would instead serve as bait. All that remained to be done, so Lee believed, was to await the outcome of Jackson's operation and identify the place where the battle he planned to win in Washington County would be fought.

---

28 OR 19:1 145.

Chapter 4

Tuesday, September 9: The Creation and Distribution of Special Orders No. 191

Several matters on the morning of September 9 occupied Gen. Lee's attention before he could turn to dictating the text of Special Orders No. 191. Foremost among these was the need to write his daily missive to Jefferson Davis. Curiously, Lee informed the president that "[n]othing of interest, in a military point of view, has transpired since my last communication." He then turned to the subject of provisions, spending more time telling Davis about this than he did about either the military or political situation. Thus far, the army had been "able to obtain forage for our animals and some provisions, but there is more difficulty about the latter," Lee wrote, although "[m]any of the farmers have not yet gotten out their wheat, and there is a reluctance on the part of millers and others to commit themselves in our favor." As he had intended from the campaign's beginning, Lee promised to "open our communication with the valley, so that we can obtain more supplies," following which he reported that "[s]ome cattle, but not in any great numbers, are obtained in this country. The inhabitants are said to have driven many off to Pennsylvania."[1]

Lee then proceeded to contradict himself by explaining to Davis how reports reaching him from the cavalry indicated "the enemy are pushing a strong column up the Potomac River by Rockville and Darnestown, and by Poolesville toward Seneca Mills. I hear that the commands of Sumner, Sigel, Burnside, and Hooker are

---

1 OR 19:2, 602.

advancing in the direction above mentioned." Describing the advance of McClellan's army as "nothing of interest," while at the same time failing to inform Davis that the enemy still held Harpers Ferry, is perplexing given that it is this combination of events which forced Lee to move his army. Rather than being of no interest, they could instead be considered illustrations of the Confederate commander's flawed assumptions to that point. He had learned one day earlier, for example, that contrary to the rumors he had heard (and believed), Federal troops remained in strength in the Shenandoah Valley. Similarly, Lee appears to have believed that the enemy's apparent inactivity around Washington indicated it would sit by idly as he marched the Army of Northern Virginia wherever he chose to take it.

Late night socializing with Confederate sympathizers by Jeb Stuart on the night of September 8 could be a reason why the information Lee conveyed to Davis seems confused and contradictory. Screening the army's eastern flank from New Market to Barnesville, Stuart appears to have done a credible job of keeping Lee informed up to September 8. He reported details of the clash at Poolesville that made it into Lee's missive on September 6 and, as is noted above, he informed Lee about the enemy columns approaching Frederick. Yet Stuart seems not to have made any specific mention of enemy activity on the Georgetown Pike or the National Road. This is curious because there were developments on that front. A rather serious engagement at Hyattstown between Wade Hampton's men and the 1st New York Cavalry took place on September 8, for example, but Stuart does not appear to have reported it to army headquarters.

The other possibility is that Lee simply neglected to mention it in his correspondence. This would have been strange, however, considering the tactical details he described to Davis on other occasions. It is probably no coincidence that the Hyattstown clash took place on the same night as the famous "Roses and Sabers" ball at Urbana. Stuart's staff prepared all day for the ball and, except for the time they took to respond to the fight at Hyattstown that evening, they danced with the ladies of Urbana until "the first glimmer of dawn." According to Heros von Borcke, "The sun was high in the heavens when we rose from our camp pallets the following day." Jeb Stuart then did not appear at army headquarters near Frederick until well after Lee had finished his correspondence for the day.[2]

---

2 Von Borcke, *Memoirs*, 1:197-198; Freiheit, *Boots and Saddles*, 166 is also critical of Stuart's actions on the evening of September 8: "Federal cavalry was beginning to come up near the eastern side of Parr's Ridge so Stuart would have begun to have difficulty in learning about

Returning to Lee, a courier bearing a message from Davis reached army headquarters at some point early in the morning. Written from Rapidan Station in central Virginia on September 7, Davis's letter informed Lee that he was traveling north to Leesburg, after which he intended to join the army in Maryland. According to James Longstreet, Davis did not make this journey on a whim. Rather, he and Lee had planned it beforehand. "It had been arranged that the Southern President should join the troops and from the head of his victorious army call for recognition," wrote Old Pete. "Maryland would have put out some of her resources, and her gallant youth would have helped to swell the Southern ranks— the 20,000 soldiers who had dropped from the Confederate ranks during the severe marches of the summer would have been with us. Volunteers from all parts of the South would come, swimming the Potomac to find their President and his field marshal."[3]

Longstreet's comments are of interest because if accurate they provide additional evidence that Lee undertook the expedition into Maryland based on more than his own initiative. Longstreet implies instead that Lee had discussed the subject with Davis while the army pushed back McClellan's force near Richmond. This suggests that Lee did not cross the Potomac because he had no other choice, as Lost Cause advocates such as Charles Marshall and Bradley T. Johnson claimed in the decades after the war. Histories of the campaign have long characterized the operation as a result of Lee casting about for what to do after the victory at Second Manassas. Unable to remain where he was due to a lack of food and fodder in northern Virginia, Lee could not retire south because it would surrender the initiative to the enemy and give up all of the ground his army had fought and bled for that summer. Lee also could not move west into the Shenandoah Valley, because doing so would open the path to Richmond. Neither could he attack the fortifications of Washington because his army was too weak. The general, therefore, had no option at the end of August but to embark on a so-called "defensive-offensive" operation north of the Potomac River.[4]

Union movements to the east starting as early as September 8, had he deigned to send scouts out that far. At the very least, the increased Federal cavalry pressure should have warned Stuart that it was likely Union infantry was not far behind, yet his attention on 8 September turned to more joyful pursuits."

3   Longstreet, *From Manassas to Appomattox*, 285.

4   For a longer discussion of this subject See Rossino, *Their Maryland*, 3-7.

The notion of Gen. Lee facing a dilemma after Second Manassas is a tall tale ginned up by former Confederates after the war. It has nevertheless become a part of most modern Maryland campaign histories. The truth about the matter is simple. Lee made it clear on September 5 that he faced no dilemma. Writing to Jefferson Davis on that day, "in the event of falling back it is my intention to take a position about Warrenton," Lee explained that once there "should the enemy attempt an advance on Richmond, I should be on his flank; or, should he attack me, I should have a favorable country to operate in, and, bridges being repaired, should be in full communication with Richmond."[5]

Lee found instead that after Second Manassas he did not need to fall back. He therefore chose to cross the Potomac to carry out Richmond's policy of bringing Southern border states into the Confederacy. Walter Taylor added an important detail about this initiative in a letter to his sister on September 12, 1862, explaining that Lee sent him "from Frederick City Maryland to meet his Ex. the President & Ex Govr Lowe." As is noted in Chapter One, Lee had camped a large part of his army at Lowe's ancestral home and called for the pro-secession governor to join him in Maryland as a political representative. Davis traveling with Lowe illustrates the political ambitions that both men entertained in support of Lee's effort to pry Maryland from the Union.[6]

Returning to Lee's second letter to Davis on the morning of September 9, he warned the president about the danger of crossing the Potomac. "You will not only encounter the hardships and fatigues of a very disagreeable journey, but also run the risk of capture by the enemy," cautioned the general, who added that he was sending his adjutant, Major Taylor, "to explain to you the difficulties and dangers of the journey, which I cannot recommend you to undertake." Lee then described the next phase of his operation using vague language that once again contradicted his earlier statement about nothing of military interest being afoot. Explaining that he was "endeavoring to break up the line through Leesburg, which is no longer safe, and turn everything off from Culpeper Court-House toward Winchester," Lee revealed his plan to "move in the direction I originally intended, toward Hagerstown and Chambersburg, for the purpose of opening our line of communication through the valley, [and] in order to procure sufficient supplies of

---

5 OR 19:2, 593.

6 Tower, ed., *Lee's Adjutant*, 43; also see Joseph L. Harsh, *Confederate Tide Rising: Robert E. Lee and the Making of Southern Strategy, 1861-1862* (Kent, OH, 1998), 9-10. Braxton Bragg would attempt to accomplish the same objective in Kentucky later that month.

flour. I shall not move until to-morrow, or, perhaps, [the] next day, but when I do move the line of communication in this direction will be entirely broken up. I must, therefore, advise that you do not make an attempt that I cannot but regard as hazardous."[7]

This letter hints at the operation Lee would outline just a short time later in Special Orders No. 191. Those orders also make it clear that Lee had decided to march the next day and not the day following, as he had communicated to Davis might be an option. This aspect of the missive is bizarre unless the possibility is taken into account that Lee feared his correspondence might be captured. If that occurred, his letter would cause the reader to think that Chambersburg was his objective (it was not by that time) and that he might not move his army until September 11.

Soon after he had finished writing Davis for the second time, Lee entertained a visit from Brig. Gen. John G. Walker, who had just arrived in the area with his small division of two brigades under the command of Brig. Gen. Robert Ransom and Col. Van H. Manning. John Sloan of the 27th North Carolina recalled this occurring at "[a]bout 10 o'clock, [when] we reached Frederick city." Walker's visit to Lee's headquarters probably took place at around this time. Upon speaking with Lee, Walker received orders to retrace his steps to the Potomac and "destroy the aqueduct of the Chesapeake and Ohio Canal" at the mouth of the Monocacy River. Lee had of course assigned this task to D. H. Hill when his division first crossed into Maryland on September 4, but Hill had failed to accomplish it due to a lack of equipment. Walker would achieve the same disappointing result for the same reason. As Capt. Vines E. Turner of the 23rd North Carolina recounted, "On the night of 9 September, 1862, our division was sent to the mouth of Monocacy river to destroy the aqueduct where the canal crosses. This we were unable to do for want of proper tools."[8]

General Walker later described his meeting with Lee in an article for *The Century Magazine* that appeared in the *Battles and Leaders* series. Written in the mid-1880s, this piece offered a lengthy and suspiciously precise account of what Lee had told him only a short time before dictating Special Orders No. 191. Walker

---

7 OR 19:2, 603; OR 51:2, 617; Walter H. Taylor, *Four Years with General Lee* (New York, NY, 1878), 66.

8 OR 19:1, 912. John A. Sloan, *Reminiscences of the Guilford Grays* (Washington, DC, 1883) 40-41; Vines E. Turner and H. C. Wall, "Twenty-Seventh Regiment," in *Histories of the Several Regiments and Battalions from North Carolina in the Great War, 1861-'65*, 5 vols., Walter Clark, ed. (Goldsboro, NC, 1901), 2:431.

claimed in the article that Lee described the Harpers Ferry operation in depth, stating "there are between 10,000 and 12,000 men at Harper's Ferry, and 3,000 at Martinsburg." Lee also allegedly identified Harrisburg, Pennsylvania, as his ultimate objective.[9]

Details this extensive render Walker's account highly suspect. The historian Joseph Harsh dismissed Walker's account on exactly this basis, writing with justification that "[i]t stretches credulity to believe the usually secretive Lee—who did not discuss grand strategy beyond the small circle of Davis, Longstreet, and Jackson—would have promptly unburdened himself to a nonintimate acquaintance such as Walker." D. Scott Hartwig concluded similarly in his history of the campaign, adding, "Walker's report clearly states that he did not learn about the Harpers Ferry operation until the early-morning hours of September 10. If this important fact, which conflicts with his alleged conversation with Lee, is true, then the credibility of the rest of the discussion, as Walker related in his article, must be regarded with skepticism."[10]

To these cogent critiques can be added the fact that by his own admission Lee had already abandoned the idea of invading the Keystone State before he left Frederick, preferring instead "by threatening Pennsylvania [to] induce the enemy to follow, and thus draw him from his base of supplies." An analysis of Lee's correspondence at the time also shows that he declined to describe his plans to Jefferson Davis. Furthermore, neither Jackson nor Longstreet mentioned the possibility of an incursion into Pennsylvania in their campaign reports. If anyone in the Army of Northern Virginia should have been privy to that information, it would have been those two officers. For John Walker to insist that Robert E. Lee shared such detailed plans with him when he did not share them with more senior commanders stretches credulity indeed.

Then there is the number of Federal troops allegedly described by Lee. Lafayette McLaws recalled after the war that contrary to the total of 13,000-15,000 men at Harpers Ferry and Martinsburg stated by Walker, Lee told him "there was a force of 7000 or 8000 men in garrison at Harper's Ferry; but he was inclined to think the number was exaggerated, and that there was not, perhaps, more than 3000 or 4000." Walker's estimate is at least double, if not triple, the enemy troop

---

9 John G. Walker, "Jackson's Capture of Harper's Ferry," in Johnson and Buel, eds., *B&L*, II:604-606.

10 Harsh, *Taken at the Flood*, 135. D. Scott Hartwig, *To Antietam Creek: The Maryland Campaign of September 1862* (Baltimore, MD, 2012), 120.

strength that McLaws remembered Lee telling him. The minimum total of the two garrisons mentioned by Walker is also suspiciously close to the 12,500 men that Jackson captured. It is entirely possible that John Walker could have learned about this number in the twenty-plus years between the events themselves and the publication of his article.[11]

The truth of the matter seems to be that Lee discussed only three subjects with Walker on September 9: he informed the brigadier that the army would be marching toward Hagerstown the next day (September 10), he ordered Walker to wreck the C&O Canal aqueduct, and he told Walker to rejoin the army by way of Jefferson and Middletown, Maryland, after he had finished the aqueduct's demolition. Walker would not find out about the rest of Lee's plans until he received a copy of Special Orders No. 191 overnight.[12]

Once Walker had left his tent, Lee finally found himself with the latitude he needed to dictate the text of his orders for the Harpers Ferry operation. The time was now between 10:30 and 11:00 a.m. based on the estimate of Walker's arrival around 10:00 and the "12 noon" notation on the lost copy of the orders addressed to D. H. Hill. Major Taylor did not take down Lee's words because Lee had already charged him with intercepting Jefferson Davis in Virginia. Taylor would have needed at least a brief period to collect his personal effects, to make sure that any outstanding duties he had would be handled by another member of the staff, to draw water and rations for the journey, and to have his horse readied.[13]

The evidence documenting when Taylor rode out of headquarters is provided by two sources. The first of these is a letter he sent to President Davis from Warrenton, Virginia, on September 10. Reporting that he had left "Frederick City at noon" on September 9, Taylor informed the president that "General Lee expected . . . I would meet you and Governor Lowe, and gave me dispatches in addition to verbal instructions." Once he reached Warrenton, however, Taylor found that Davis had already turned back to Richmond, so he rode on to Winchester and had the documents forwarded by courier. The second source is paragraph II of Special Orders No. 191 itself. This states "Major Taylor will

---

11 McLaws, "The Maryland Campaign."

12 The details concerning Lee comments come from Walker's campaign report; see OR 19:1, 912-913.

13 The noon notation on the Lost Orders is clear, but it also could have been a mistake by the writer. See the analysis of the document in Appendix B for further discussion.

proceed to Leesburg," proving that at the time it was written, Lee's adjutant had not yet left for Virginia.[14]

As for the orders' creation, the following description of that process is based on the premise that a draft copy held at the Library of Virginia in Richmond is the original dictated by Lee to Charles Marshall. This claim rests on five presuppositions, beginning with the fact that the copy is labeled Special Orders No. 190. All of the other existing copies of the order are labeled Special Orders No. 191. Second, the penmanship in this copy is indisputably Marshall's, whom Lee frequently called on to compose letters and other important documents. Lee would have leaned particularly hard on Marshall for support once he had instructed Walter Taylor to ride back to Virginia. Third, Special Orders No. 190 is the only copy to appear with Lee's personal papers, suggesting it is a draft that was never sent out. Fourth, the orders are not marked "Confidential" at the top of the document, as were the official copies sent out later that day. Fifth, and perhaps most importantly, the second page of Special Orders No. 190 does not include the endorsement of the staff writer in the lower left corner across from the signature of Lee's proxy, Col. Robert Chilton. All official documents emanating from Lee's headquarters, and even some informal ones dashed off in the field, contained this endorsement. The absence of the endorsement in Special Orders No. 190 indicates that the document is most likely a draft and not an official copy.[15]

Like the lost copy of Special Orders No. 191, Special Orders No. 190 contains only paragraphs III through X. The text is reproduced below, including all the punctuation, spelling, and abbreviations unique to the original:

---

14 OR 51:2, 617.

15 Robert E. Lee, Letters, 1862-1865, Accession No. 23458, Personal Papers Collection, Library of Virginia, Richmond, VA. Taylor provided evidence for not being involved in the creation and distribution of the orders, writing long after the war, "I was sent to meet Mr. Davis and so did not supervise the promulgation of this order"; Walter H. Taylor, *General Lee: His Campaigns in Virginia, 1861-1865, with Personal Reminiscences* (Norfolk, VA, 1906), 125; See Lee to Pendleton, Sept. 17, 1862, William Nelson Pendleton Papers, Collection #01466, Folder 27b: 15-23 September 1862: Scan 12, Filename: 01466_0027b_0012.tif, SHC, UNC, for an example of Charles Venable endorsing an informal note sent during the fight at Sharpsburg/Antietam. Available online at https://finding-aids.lib.unc.edu/01466/ #folder_27b#1. There may have been some confusion concerning the sequence of special orders at Lee's headquarters. A copy of Special Orders No. 188, issued on Sept. 5, 1862, appears in OR 19:2, 595, but the next printed order in the sequence is No. 191. It may be that much like No. 190, Special Orders No. 189 also never made it into the *Official Records*.

Tuesday, September 9: The Creation of Special Orders No. 191 | 47

III. The army will resume its march to-morrow taking the Hagerstown road. Genl Jackson's command will form the advance and after passing Middletown, with such portions as he may select take the route towards Sharpsburg cross the Potomac at the most convenient point, and by Friday morning take possession of the Balto. + Ohio R. R. capture such of the enemy as may be at Martinsburg and intercept such as may attempt to escape from Harpers Ferry.

IV. Genl. Longstreet's command will pursue the main road as far as Boonsboro, where it will halt, with reserve, supply and baggage trains of the army.

V. Gen'l McLaws, with his own division and that of Genl R. H. Anderson will follow Gen'l Longstreet, on reaching Middletown will take the route to Harpers Ferry and by Friday morning possess himself of the Maryland Heights and endeavor to capture the enemy at Harpers Ferry and vicinity.

VI. Gen'l Walker with his division after accomplishing the object in which he is now engaged, will cross the Potomac at Cheek's Ford ascend its right bank to Lovettsville take possession of Loudon Heights, if practicable by Friday morning, Keyes Ford on his left and the road between the end of the mountain and the Potomac on his right. He will, as far as practicable cooperate with Gen'l's McLaws + Jackson + intercept retreat of the enemy.

VII. Gen'l D. H. Hill's division will form the rear guard of the army pursuing the road taken by the main body. The reserve artillery, ordnance and supply trains +c., will precede Gen'l Hill.

VIII. Gen'l Stuart will detach a Squadron of Cavalry to accompany the commands of Genl's Longstreet, Jackson and McLaws, and with the main body of the Cavalry will cover the route of the army bring up all stragglers, that may have been left behind.

IX. The commands of Gen'l's Jackson, McLaw's + Walker after accomplishing the objects for which they have been detached will join the main body of the army at Boonesboro or Hagerstown.

X. Each Regiment on the march will habitually carry its axes in the Regimental ordnance wagons for use of the men at their encampments to procure wood +c.

By command of Genl. R. E. Lee
R. H. Chilton,
A. A. G.

Special Orders No. 190 contains numerous signs of being written in haste. Many of these errors then made it into later copies. The sloppy punctuation, abbreviations, and spelling are all hallmarks of rapid composition. In addition,

Head Quarters Army of No. Va.
September 9th 1862

Special Orders }
No. 190 }

III The Army will resume its march tomorrow taking the Hagerstown road. Genl Jackson's command will form the advance and after passing Middletown, with such portion as he may select take the route towards Sharpsburg cross the Potomac at the most convenient point and by Friday morning take possession of the Balt. & Ohio R.R. capture such of the enemy as may be at Martinsburg and intercept such as may attempt to escape from Harpers Ferry.

IV Genl. Longstreet's command will pursue the main road as far as Boonsboro, where it will halt, with reserve, supply and baggage trains of the Army.

V— Genl McLaws with his own division and that of Genl. R. H. Anderson will follow Genl. Longstreet, on reaching Middletown will take the route to Harpers Ferry and by Friday morning possess himself of the Maryland Heights and endeavor to capture the enemy at Harpers Ferry and vicinity.

VI Genl Walker with his division after accomplishing the object in which he is now engaged, will cross the Potomac at Cheek's Ford ascend its right bank to Lovettsville take possession of Loudon Heights if practicable by Friday morning, Keyes Ford on his left and the road between the end of the mountain and the Potomac on his right. He will as far as practicable cooperate with Genl's McLaw's & Jackson & intercept retreat of the

Front side of Special Orders No. 190, the draft copy that Lee dictated to Maj. Charles Marshall between 10:30 a.m. and noon on Sept. 9, 1862. *Library of Virginia*

enemy

VII Gen'l D. H. Hill's division will form the rear guard of the Army pursuing the road taken by the main body. The reserve Artillery, Ordnance and Supply trains &c. will precede Gen'l Hill.

VIII Gen'l Stuart will detach a squadron of Cavalry to accompany the commands of Gen'ls Longstreet, Jackson and McLaw's, and with the main body of the Cavalry will cover the route of the Army bring up all stragglers, that may have been left behind.

IX The commands of Gen'ls Jackson, McLaw's & Walker after accomplishing the objects for which they have been detached will join the main body of the army at Boonesboro or Hagerstown

X Each Regiment on the march will habitually carry its axes in the Regimental Ordnance wagons for use of the men at their encampments to procure wood &c.

By Command of Gen'l R. E. Lee
R H Chilton
A. A. General

Reverse side of the two paragraph copy of Special Orders No. 190. Note the signature of Col. Robert H. Chilton. *Library of Virginia*

multiple sentences are punctuated incorrectly, resulting in run-ons. The word "General" is also abbreviated inconsistently throughout the document and the word "and" is written out in some places while in others it is expressed as a "+" mark. Sentence two of paragraph V is even missing the word "and" between "Longstreet" and "on." There are as well other sentences where words appear to be missing, such as in paragraph IV, which lacks the word "the" between the words "with" and "reserve." The last sentence of paragraph VI contains this omission, too, between the words "intercept" and "retreat."

A thorough analysis of the document must also account for the absence of paragraphs I and II. The reason they are not included in Special Orders No. 190 is that General Lee instructed they be written out separately. This is clear from the structure of Special Orders No. 190, which contains no space at the top of the document for paragraphs I and II. Why General Lee created the documents apart from one another is not clear, but it could have to do with the difference between general orders and special orders.

J. Boone Bartholomees explains in his study of the Army of Northern Virginia's staff operations that regulations formally defined "two varieties [of orders] . . . General orders contained information of interest to the entire command, or at least multiple segments of it. Special orders pertained to individuals or single units. The distinguishing factor between the two types was whether the whole command needed to know the information." Lee's instructions appear to fall between the definition of general and special orders. Paragraph I's orders for troops not to enter Frederick unless on official business certainly applied to the entire army, but paragraph II addressed Walter Taylor's forthcoming ride to Virginia, and that information was not relevant to anyone but Lee himself.[16]

Whatever his reasoning, we know that Lee ordered paragraphs I and II to be written out as a distinct document because a copy of it is available at the U.S. National Archives and Records Administration (NA) in Washington. Contained in Record Group 109, the "War Department Collection of Confederate Records," this copy, labeled Special Orders No. 191, consists of only the first two paragraphs. They are written in the hand of Capt. Arthur P. Mason of Lee's staff, signed by Col. Robert H. Chilton, and addressed to Gen. Samuel Cooper in Richmond, the Confederate army's Inspector General and highest-ranking officer. This copy is almost certainly not the original since Charles Marshall did not write it. Presumably, Marshall took down Lee's dictation for the first draft before handing it off to

---

[16] Bartholomees, Jr., *Buff Facings and Gilt Buttons*, 238-239.

Tuesday, September 9: The Creation of Special Orders No. 191 | 51

Mason. The text of these two paragraphs reads as follows, including the punctuation, spelling, and abbreviations found in the original:

> I. The citizens of Fredericktown being unwilling while overrun by members of this Army to open their stores, in order to give them confidence, and to secure to officers and men purchasing supplies for benefit of this command, all officers and men of this army are strictly prohibited from visiting Fredericktown except on business in which case they will bear evidences of this in writing from Division Cmdrs. The Provost Marshall in Fredericktown will see that his guard rigidly enforces this order.
>
> II. Maj. Taylor will proceed to Leesburg Va, and arrange for transportation of the sick + those unable to walk to Winchester securing the transportation of the country for this purpose. The route between this + Culpepper C. H. east of the mountains, being unsafe will no longer be travelled. Those on the way to this army, already across the river will move up promptly, all others will proceed to Winchester collectively + under commands of officers at which point being the General Depot of this Army, its movements will be known and instructions given by Comdg Officer regulating further movements.
>
> By command of General R. E. Lee
R. H. Chilton
A. A. General

The document's numerical designation as Special Orders No. 191 is curious. There appear to be three possible explanations why the eight-paragraph document is labeled Special Orders No. 190 and the two-paragraph document is labeled Special Orders No. 191. The first of these is that Capt. Mason, either on his own or according to instructions, corrected an error made by Charles Marshall and standardized the numbers on the copies of each document to read 191 before he sent them to General Cooper. The second possibility is that General Lee intended the documents to be separate from the moment of their creation. The third possibility is that Lee dictated paragraphs III through X first and ordered these labeled Special Orders No. 190 before he turned to the text for paragraphs I and II and designated them Special Orders No. 191. Lee then clarified that both sets of orders should be combined and labeled Special Orders No. 191. Capt. Mason copied the combined document into the headquarters order book at some point after this, which created the only complete copy that remains in existence.[17]

---

17 The order book contained all official headquarters documents arranged by date and number (e.g., General Orders 102, 103, etc.).

Front side of the two paragraph copy of Special Orders No. 191, written by Capt. Arthur Mason of Lee's staff and addressed to General Samuel Cooper, Adjutant General and Inspector General, Confederate States Army. *National Archives*

Reverse side of the two paragraph copy of Special Orders No. 191. Note the signature of Col. Robert H. Chilton, making this an official copy. *National Archives*

Federal forces captured the headquarters order book when the Army of Northern Virginia surrendered at Appomattox in April 1865. The War Department then printed the complete ten paragraph copy in the *Official Records* three decades later. This printed complete copy has for more than a century led readers to think that the orders distributed on September 9 must have always contained all ten paragraphs when at the time there were two separate and distinct copies. One of these copies, which Lee did not order distributed, contained only paragraphs I and II. The other copy contained paragraphs III through X and it is this copy, originally designated Special Orders No. 190, that Lee had his staff send out. The lost copy of the orders found near Frederick and given to McClellan confirms this interpretation because it consisted of only paragraphs III through X.

When it came time for the draft special orders to be copied and distributed, either Col. Chilton, acting in his capacity as army chief of staff, or Robert E. Lee himself, assigned the responsibility to Maj. Richard C. "Dick" Taylor. The evidence for this comes from Lee's aide-de-camp, Lt. Col. Charles S. Venable, who wrote in his unpublished memoir of the war that "The order, a dictation by General Lee was copied carefully in the Adjutant's tent (by Colonel Taylor's aid and brother) in the camp at (Frederick) City." Dick Taylor then sent these copies "to [the] Commanders of Corps and Divisions who were concerned" with the copies marked "confidential" at the top of the document. This process took place at around noon, as is indicated by the underlined "12" next to the crossed-out date at the top of the copy made for D. H. Hill. In other words, if Venable is to be believed, Lee (or Chilton) entrusted the distribution of a critically important document to an utter novice on the staff.[18]

The orders went out throughout the day, with the first copies being sent to Jackson and Longstreet. These men were Lee's senior subordinates and their respective headquarters were physically closest to General Lee's. Upon receiving his copy, Longstreet read it carefully and "used [it] as some persons use a little cut of tobacco (i.e., he chewed it up), to be assured that others could not have the benefit of its contents." As for Jackson, it is not known when he received his copy, but it was early enough in the day for him to write out a copy and send it to D. H. Hill. In addition, Jackson's staff topographer, Lt. Jedediah Hotchkiss, mentioned in his diary that he spent September 9 drawing maps, including "one of Washington Co., Md." Hotchkiss completed this work based on instructions from Jackson, who had finally received a written copy of Lee's orders authorizing the Harpers Ferry operation. Receipt of this document confirmed in greater detail the verbal instructions that Lee had issued on the previous day, which led Jackson to have Hill move G. B. Anderson's brigade to a new position east of the Monocacy River.[19]

Lee then communicated his plan for the coming operation both verbally and in writing to the generals in command of detached operations. Major General Lafayette McLaws described this process in detail and his words are worth reproducing in full:

---

18 Charles S. Venable, "Personal Reminiscences of the Confederate War" (Sept. 28, 1889), 60, McDowell-Miller-Warner Papers, Accession #2969-a, Box 5, Special Collections Dept., University of Virginia Library, Charlottesville, VA. Walter Taylor held the rank of major at the time, not colonel.

19 Longstreet, *From Manassas to Appomattox*, 213. Jackson referred only to "instructions from the commanding general" in his official campaign report; see *OR* 19:1, 953; McDonald, ed., *Make Me a Map of the Valley*, 80.

Tuesday, September 9: The Creation of Special Orders No. 191

In the evening (i.e., afternoon) of Tuesday, September 9, 1862, while camped near Fredericktown, Md., on the left bank of the Monocacy, I received notice by an orderly that Gen. Lee wished to see me. I at once proceeded to his headquarters, and was then told by the General himself that 'the whole army would move the next morning (Wednesday), taking the Hagerstown road, and that Gen. R. H. Anderson of South Carolina would be directed to report to me, and that I would follow with Anderson's and my own division in the rear of the army, until, reaching Middletown, I would take the route to Harper's Ferry, and by Friday morning the 12th, possess myself of Maryland Heights, and endeavor to capture the enemy at Harper's Ferry and vicinity.'

I remarked to the General that I had never been to Harper's Ferry, nor in the vicinity. He replied, intimating that it did not matter. He then went on to inform me that it had been reported there was a force of 7000 or 8000 men in garrison at Harper's Ferry; but he was inclined to think the number was exaggerated, and that there was not, perhaps, more than 3000 or 4000, and asked if my division was not enough, or with the addition of one or two brigades of Anderson's, with which to undertake the expedition.

I replied that I would go, of course, with whatever force he ordered, and would do all I could with it, but as the force at Harper's Ferry was unknown, but reported to be larger than the strength of my division, my preference would be to have the whole of Anderson's division with me; that Gen. Anderson was a classmate and friend, and I would like to have him with me particularly. But little more passed between us, and I returned to my headquarters.

That evening I received a copy of special orders No. 191 . . . wherein the movements which were to be made were designated.[20]

Major General Richard H. Anderson, the commander of an unattached division during the campaign, recalled something similar in a letter he wrote to D. H. Hill after the war. Writing, "I received no written instructions from Genl. Lee when I was sent with McLaws to operate against Harpers Ferry from the north side of the Potomac," Anderson clarified his place in the army's command hierarchy:

> 20 McLaws, "The Maryland Campaign." In his campaign report, McLaws wrote simply, "On the 10th ultimo, in compliance with Special Orders, No. 101, of September 9, 1862, from your headquarters, I proceeded with my own and General Anderson's division, via Burkittsville, to Pleasant Valley, to take possession of Maryland Heights, and endeavor to capture the enemy at Harper's Ferry and vicinity." OR 19:1, 852. I have broken up McLaws's long paragraphs for readability. In 19th century parlance the term "evening" meant any time after noon. It is thus interchangeable with the modern term "afternoon" unless the event described is specifically designated as taking place after nightfall.

> From the time of my promotion to Major General shortly after the battles around Richmond until the formation of corps for Longstreet and A.P. Hill the division which I commanded constituted a separate body and was subject only to Genl. Lee's orders. On the evening before the detachment marched from our camp near Frederick my tent being quite near Genl. Lee's Head Quarters he sent for me and gave me instructions verbally. Since I was to be merely a subordinate (McLaws being in command) I thought it somewhat unusual that he should speak to me so particularly as to what were his objects, his expectations and his opinions as to the best steps to be taken etc. He repeatedly said 'Harpers Ferry must be taken against Thursday evening.' When I joined and reported to McLaws I went over to him all that Genl. Lee had said to me, thinking that perhaps Genl. Lee was under the impression that I was the superior officer. I am perfectly sure that no written instructions were ever given to me.[21]

As for Walker, Lee's courier found him at the confluence of the Monocacy and Potomac Rivers, where he was "accomplishing the object in which he is now engaged," the attempt to wreck the C&O Canal aqueduct. The fact that Special Orders No. 191 referred to this mission as in progress further documents the fact that Lee had sent Walker to destroy the aqueduct before the orders' creation. Describing the event in his campaign report, Walker wrote:

> On September 9 I was instructed by General Lee to proceed from Monocacy Junction, near Frederick, Md., to the mouth of the Monocacy, and destroy the aqueduct of the Chesapeake and Ohio Canal. We arrived at the aqueduct about 11 p. m., and found it occupied by the enemy's pickets . . . The movement of our main army from Frederick toward Hagerstown, which I had been officially informed would take place on the 10th, would leave my small division in the immediate presence of a very strong force of the enemy, and, while it would be engaged in destroying the aqueduct, in a most exposed and dangerous position. I therefore determined to rejoin General Lee by way of Jefferson and Middletown, as previously instructed by him.

Walker's report adds details about his interview with Lee that indicate the commanding general did not initially intend for Walker's division to participate in the operation against Harpers Ferry. Noting that Lee had mentioned the pending movement of the army toward Hagerstown, Walker revealed that the general did not tell him to cross the river back into Virginia. Walker was instead to complete his task and then rejoin the army at Middletown, Maryland. This suggests Lee changed

---

21 Anderson to Hill, Nov. 14, 1867.

Tuesday, September 9: The Creation of Special Orders No. 191 | 57

his mind after Walker had left headquarters and issued the modification of Walker's instructions in paragraph VI of Special Orders No. 191. Walker noted this change in his campaign report, writing that before he marched his two brigades away from the still intact aqueduct, he "received instructions to cross the Potomac at Cheek's Ford and proceed toward Harper's Ferry, and cooperate with Major-Generals Jackson and McLaws in the capture of the Federal forces at that point."[22]

As for D. H. Hill, Lee did not summon him to headquarters even though by his own admission Special Orders No. 191 released Hill from Jackson's command. Lee evidently considered Hill to be still subordinate to Jackson until the army marched out on September 10. He failed to make this clear to Hill, however, with the result that the staff wrote out a copy of Special Orders No. 191 for Hill that Hill was never told to expect. Hill was therefore not on the lookout for marching orders, which he would have been if Lee had briefed him at headquarters as he did Anderson and McLaws. This oversight on Lee's part meant that Hill never knew he should report having not received the orders, thus contributing to the confusion that attended their going astray.

The final participant to consider in this drama is Jeb Stuart. No evidence has been found of a courier being sent to Stuart with a copy of Special Orders No. 191, yet Stuart's campaign report mentions them. Writing that he abandoned his defensive line eight miles southeast of Frederick on September 11, Stuart noted that he had remained in place "longer than was contemplated by the instructions covering the investment of Harper's Ferry (found in the orders appended to this report)." Stuart's men then took up new positions just west of the Monocacy River defending the covered bridge over the Georgetown Pike at Monocacy Junction and at the Jug Bridge, where the National Road crossed over the river. There is, however, a problem. The copy of Special Orders No. 191 that Stuart claimed to have appended to his report is missing. This document could have been lost over the years, but it is strange that the general's report survived the war intact, while a supporting document he sent with it did not.[23]

It is clear in any case that Stuart possessed a copy of Special Orders No. 191. The means used to get him the orders is not known, but the strong possibility exists

---

22 *OR* 19:1, 912-913. It may be that Stuart's report of a Federal column advancing up the left bank of the Potomac River led Lee to attach Walker's division to the Harpers Ferry operation as a way of keeping his men safe.

23 *OR* 19:1, 815.

Maj. Gen. Jeb Stuart's cavalry crossing the Georgetown Turnpike bridge over the Monocacy River near the Best Farm. Artist Francis H. Schell (1834-1909). *The Becker Collection*

---

that Stuart picked them up in person. Catherine Markell, a member of a secessionist family in Frederick, confirmed in her diary that Stuart visited the town on September 9, writing, "General Pryor called, also General J. E. B. Stuart, the latter is a gay, rollicking cavalier and a great favorite with the girls." Stuart most likely stopped at headquarters before he left the area and received a copy of the orders at that time. The sources show that he then returned to Urbana where he and Maj. Heros von Borcke "were invited to dine with the doctor of the place, at whose pleasant dwelling we passed a few hours most delightfully. The universal verandah looked out upon the same beautiful landscape that we had admired from other points, and afforded us a cool retreat for cigars and conversation."[24]

The morning's work completed, army headquarters then endured a flood of well-wishers from Frederick City who had come out to bid Lee and the other Confederate luminaries farewell. The presence of these people indicates that word

---

24 Catherine Susannah Thomas Markell, "Frederick Maryland in Peace and War, 1856-1864" (Frederick, MD, n. d.), 107. Stuart may have also reported in person on the advance of the enemy's columns that Lee mentioned in his missive to Jefferson Davis that morning; see OR 19:2, 602; Von Borcke, *Memoirs*, 1:198-199.

Tuesday, September 9: The Creation of Special Orders No. 191

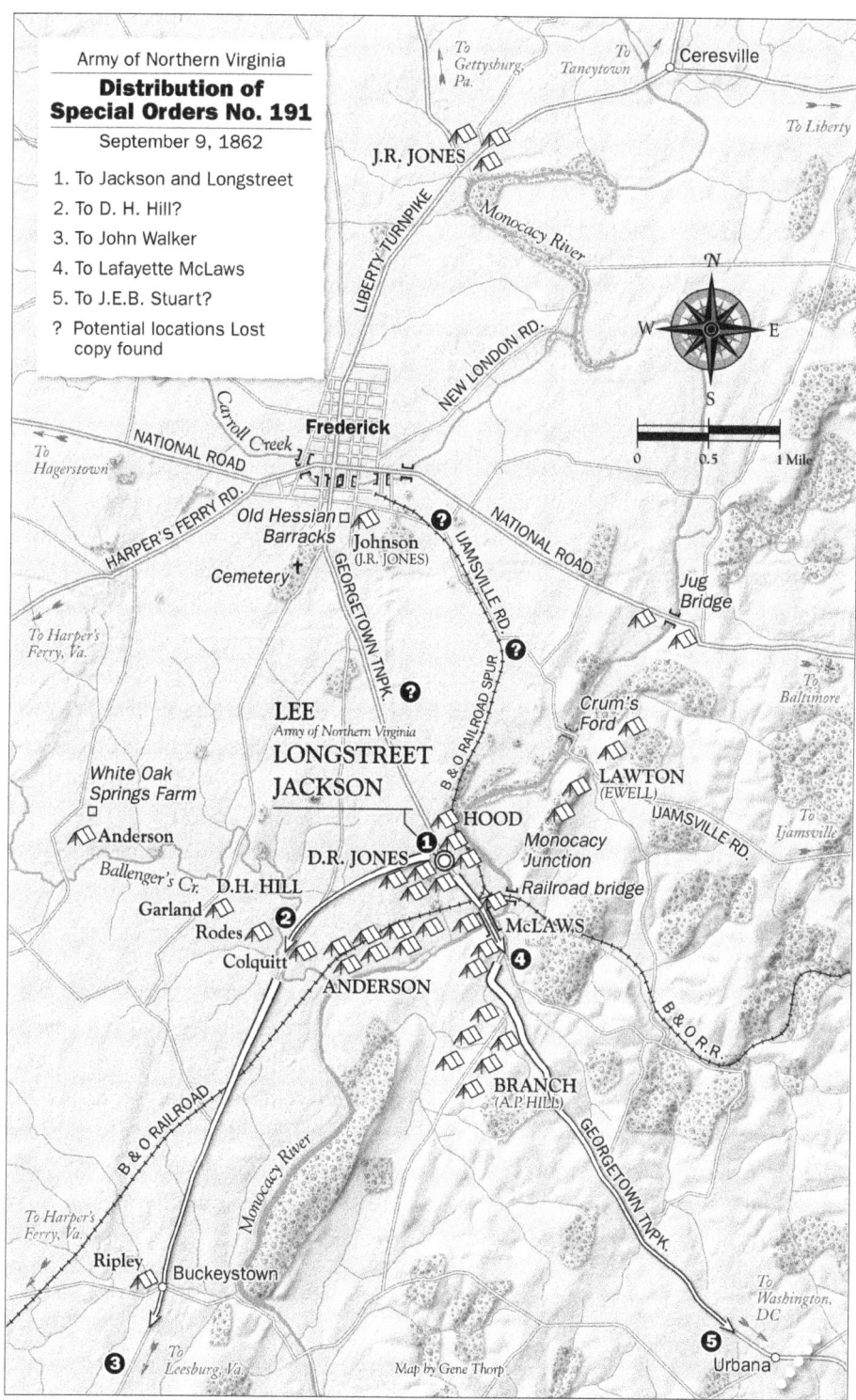

Map by Gene Thorp

of the army's imminent departure spread throughout the area within only a short time after Lee's orders had been distributed. Lieutenant Henry Kyd Douglas's mother was among these visitors. She had driven to Frederick from her home near Shepherdstown and stayed with the Markell family for a couple of days before coming to visit her son, Jackson, and Lee. According to Catherine Markell, she, Mrs. Douglas, and several other local ladies also greeted James Longstreet with a bouquet of flowers and exchanged pleasantries with Jeb Stuart, confirming his presence at headquarters that afternoon. Jackson, for his part, "said very little, but that little was of his kind, and he urged my mother to remain and spend the day with me," recalled Douglas. She declined, however, "and left with her little party, for each of whom that visit was long to be remembered."[25]

By the end of the day, copies of Special Orders No. 191 had gone out to all the commanders required to have one. This included Stonewall Jackson, James Longstreet, Jeb Stuart, John Walker, Lafayette McLaws, and Daniel Harvey Hill. Jackson, Longstreet, and Stuart were of course senior commanders, while Walker and McLaws commanded divisions that would operate on detached duty against Harpers Ferry. Lee also tasked McLaws with commanding the division of Richard Anderson as part of his detached force. A key point to remember in all of this is that neither Lee's nor Jackson's headquarters officially sent a copy of the orders in the direction of Frederick City. All the copies traveled to locations near Best's Grove, or, presumably, southwest to where D. H. Hill was camped, southeast to where McLaws and Stuart were camped, and south to where John Walker struggled to destroy the Monocacy Aqueduct. This means that the copy found near Frederick, some two and a half miles *north* of Best's Farm, was an outlier which had no business being where it was found.

There is no evidence that any other division commander in the army received a copy of the orders, meaning Lee's staff distributed a total of six copies of Special Orders No. 191 on September 9. Other copies remained in the records of army headquarters or were afterward sent to Richmond. These included the draft Special Orders No. 190, the separate copies of paragraphs I and II and III through X that were forwarded to Cooper, a copy Lee ordered sent to Jefferson Davis on September 12, and the consolidated final copy that Capt. Mason wrote into the headquarters order book. Stonewall Jackson also made one copy for D. H. Hill, which Hill kept with him for the rest of his life. All told, Lee's and Jackson's staffs

---

25 Douglas, *I Rode With Stonewall*, 148-149; Markell, "Frederick Maryland in Peace and War," 107.

made twelve copies of the orders and it was one of these—a copy addressed to Hill—that went astray.

Chapter 5

Where Did Barton Mitchell Find the Lost Orders?

Determining where Corporal Barton W. Mitchell of the 27th Indiana Volunteers found the lost copy of Special Orders No. 191 on September 13, 1862, is important when attempting to identify who lost them. Research conducted in the last fifty years has proposed three locations at various distances southeast of Frederick City. Richard C. Datzmann, M.D., a radiologist from New Orleans, produced the first estimate in February 1973. Relying on the testimony of veterans who had served with the 27th Indiana, Datzmann reached the conclusion that, "The converging roads, the distance from the ford [across the Monocacy River] and Frederick, would suggest the F. Myers farm as the approximate location."[1]

This farm can be found in the *Atlas of Frederick County Maryland* published in 1873 by D. J. Lake. Located east of the road to Crum's Ford (known then as the Ijamsville Road and as Reich's Ford Road today) and the Baltimore and Ohio Railroad spur to Frederick, the Myers farm is about one mile away from the city. The farm is also visible on the 1858 *Map of Frederick County* created by Isaac Bond, although the property was at that time owned by a man named Elias J. Delashmutt, Jr. The historian Joseph Harsh made an effort to bolster Datzmann's claim in 1999 by arguing that D. H. Hill's division camped near the Delashmutt/Myers farm on

---

1 D. J. Lake, *Map of Frederick County Maryland* (Philadelphia, PA, 1873); Richard C. Datzmann, "Who Found Lee's Lost Dispatch," (Feb. 1973), 8, copy at the research library of the Monocacy National Battlefield Park (MNBP). The Delashmutt family was well-known during the war as sympathetic to the Confederate cause. See Rossino, *Their Maryland*, 110. It is likely that Delashmutt owned the farm in September 1862 before being forced to sell it after the war, possibly because of his problematic political leanings.

September 10 when congestion prevented it from marching through Frederick City. Curiously, Harsh agreed with Datzmann about the farm even though both the 1858 and 1873 maps show multiple homesteads situated between the Georgetown Pike along which Hill camped and the Delashmutt/Myers farm located farther to the east.[2]

The Frederick County historian Timothy J. Reese produced a new look at the evidence in 2004. Citing the official history of the 27th Indiana by Edmund Brown, Reese concluded that a better candidate for the location of the orders' loss is the intersection of East South Street and Franklin Street, situated between one-half and three-quarters of a mile southeast of Frederick City. This location, argued Reese, fit a statement by Brown saying that the regiment "halted in a clover field, adjoining the city on the south." The intersection is visible on the maps of Frederick County mentioned above, not far from where the National Road enters the east side of the city.[3]

The third proposed location comes from research carried out by the staff of the Monocacy National Battlefield Park. Park personnel examined soil maps created by the U.S. Geological Survey in 1919 that uncovered a network of farm lanes not recorded on the 1858 or 1873 maps. One of these tracks crossed the Monocacy at roughly the same place as Crum's Ford. It then continued west toward the Georgetown Pike, traversing the B&O rail line at a right angle. Leveraging the testimony of participants in the XII Corps' and 27th Indiana's march, the Monocacy Park staff concluded that the Hoosier skirmishers followed this farm lane due west instead of following the road that ran north to Frederick. This led the Indiana soldiers to a spot approaching the Georgetown Pike where they could go no farther because Maj. Gen. Edwin Vose Sumner's II Corps blocked their way. It is here, close to the farms of C. E. Trail and N. Kline, a vicinity which also fits Harsh's claim concerning the halt of D. H. Hill's division late on September 10, that Indiana troops discovered the lost copy of Special Orders No. 191.[4]

2 Harsh, *Taken at the Flood*, 179-180.

3 Timothy J. Reese, *High-Water Mark: The 1862 Maryland Campaign in Strategic Perspective* (Baltimore, MD, 2004), 20; Edmund R. Brown, *The Twenty-Seventh Indiana Volunteer Infantry in the War of the Rebellion, 1861 to 1865* (Monticello, IN, 1899), 228.

4 National Park Service, "An Invitation to Battle: Special Orders 191." Online at https://www.nps.gov/mono/learn/historyculture/an-invitation-to-battle.htm.

John McKnight Bloss after the war. Despite writing soon after the Battle of Antietam that Barton Mitchell had discovered the Lost Orders, Bloss later attempted to take credit for the find himself. *Oregon State University, Special Collections & Archives Research Center*

If they cite any location at all, and many do not, histories of the campaign typically mention one of these three places—the Delashmutt/Myers farm, the intersection of East South and Franklin Streets near Frederick, or farmland near the Georgetown Pike, as the spot where Barton Mitchell discovered the lost copy of Special Orders No. 191. The analysis offered here argues that according to the available evidence, including the testimony of Sergeant John M. Bloss, a participant in the discovery, the location close to Frederick City proposed by Edmund Brown and mentioned by Tim Reese is the best possibility. A second possible location suggested by Gene M. Thorp, my friend and co-author of *The Tale Untwisted*, is also considered. This spot identified by Thorp is a small field on the west side of the Ijamsville Road before it meets the Baltimore and Ohio spur line that runs from Monocacy Junction to Frederick.

The sources record how around mid-morning on September 13 troops with the Federal XII Corps, under the command of Brig. Gen. Alpheus S. Williams, waded across the Monocacy River at Crum's Ford about three miles southeast of Frederick. Cannon fire from the spirited fight taking place atop the Catoctin range west of town echoed across the valley as three regiments of Federal cavalry under Brig. Gen. Alfred Pleasonton clashed with the Confederate rear guard under Brig. Gen. Wade Hampton and Jeb Stuart. Troops with Brig. Gen. Jacob D. Cox's Kanawha Division, a part of the IX Corps under Maj. Gen. Jesse L. Reno, had entered Frederick late the day before, driving out Hampton's cavalry, but the commanders of the XII Corps did not know this. The booming cannon encouraged them, therefore, to expect an engagement, and so Brig. Gen. George H. Gordon's Third Brigade of the First Division shook out a line of skirmishers from its leading regiment, the 27th Indiana, as a precaution. The line consisted of Company F, which the commander of the 27th Indiana, Col. Silas Colgrove,

Where Did Barton Mitchell Find the Lost Orders? | 65

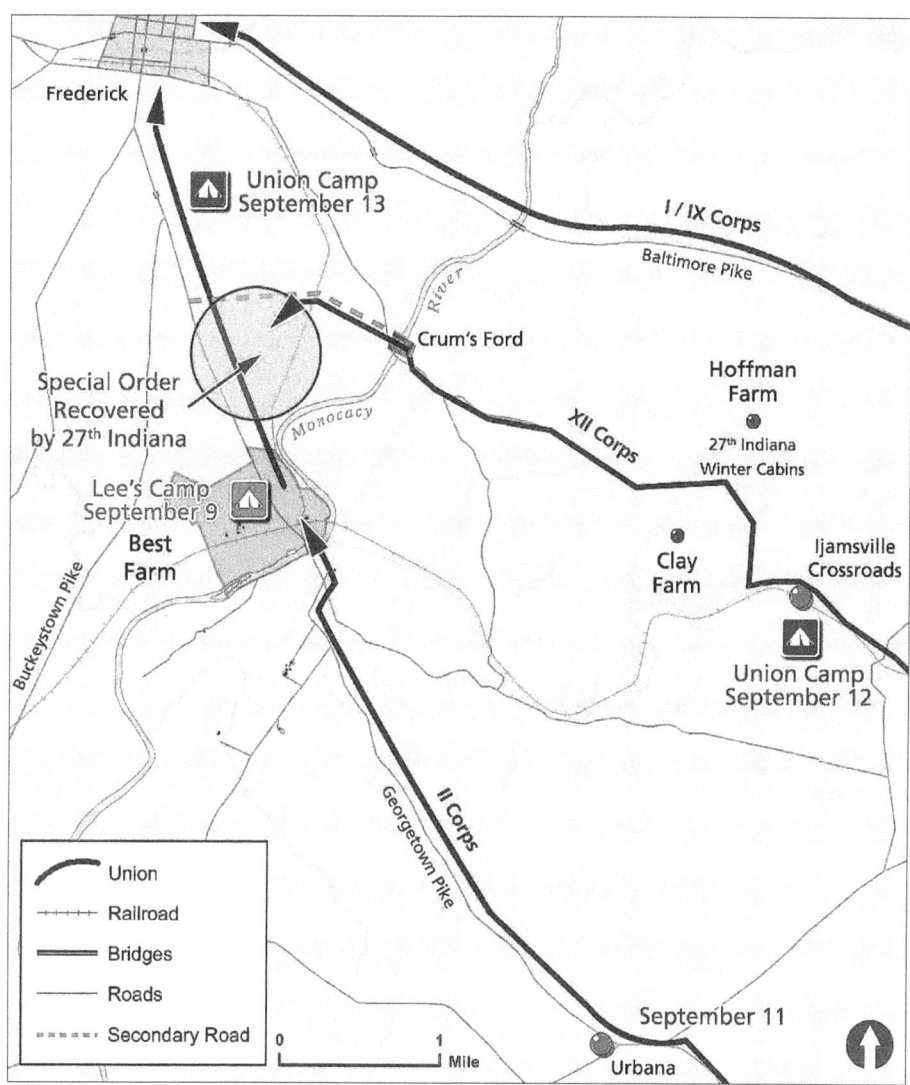

A map of the Lost Orders discovery site produced by the staff at the Monocacy National Battlefield Park. The path of the 27th Indiana depicted here is based on the identification of a forgotten farm lane running from Crum's Ford in the direction of the Georgetown Pike. The discovery site shown is highly unlikely given eyewitness testimony placing it much closer to Frederick City. *National Park Service*

divided into two platoons under the command of Capt. Peter Kopp. One platoon deployed on the left (west) side of the Ijamsville Road, followed shortly afterward by the second platoon, which deployed on the right (east) side of the road.[5]

Company F sending out two platoons of skirmishers suggests that Col. Colgrove, followed the procedure detailed in William Hardee's 1855 book *Rifle and Light Infantry Tactics*. This book served as the standard infantry instruction manual for both the Northern and Southern armies during the war, although the U.S. Army also published an abridged version for non-West Point officers called *The Volunteers Hand Book*. Article I, Section 17 of Hardee states, "Whenever a company is to be deployed as skirmishers, it will be divided into two platoons."[6]

Ten companies designated A through K, and consisting of 100 men apiece, made up a full-strength regiment of 1,000 soldiers during the war, but on September 13 the 27th Indiana counted only 440 men in its ranks. The regiment was therefore understrength at the time. This meant roughly 44 men made up each company instead of the standard 100. Two platoons then comprised each company. These platoons consisted of 50 men apiece under ideal conditions, but with the 27th Indiana counting only 440 troops across ten companies it meant that each platoon included only 22 men. Upon forming its skirmish line, Capt. Kopp's two platoons divided into five groups of four to five men apiece, with each group arranged approximately 15 feet apart. This resulted in Kopp's skirmish line stretching perpendicularly across the Ijamsville Road for a distance of 300 to 400 feet.[7]

---

5 "Our Regiment was in the advance and I had the first Plattoon off our Company as skirmishers. Afterwards, Capt. Kop with the Second Plattoon was deployed on the right of the road," John McKnight Bloss, "Letter written from the barn hospital at Antietam," Sept. 25, 1862, in Bloss Family Papers, MNBP, cited hereafter as "Letter."

6 William J. Hardee, *Rifle and Light Infantry Tactics for the Exercise and Manoeuvres of Troops when Acting as Light Infantry or Riflemen*, 2 vols. (Philadelphia, PA, 1855), 1:171-173.

7 Civil War regiments did not contain a "Company J," hence the 1,000 man estimate of a regiment at full strength. See the 27th Indiana Volunteer Infantry Monument at the Antietam National Battlefield for the strength estimate. https://www.nps.gov/anti/learn/historyculture/mnt-in-27-inf.htm. For information on the size of Civil War platoons see https://mo21infantry.tripod.com/organize.html. The calculation is as follows: five sections separated by 15 feet apiece equals a distance of 60 feet. The four or five men of each section also separated themselves by five feet apiece for a total of 20-25 feet per section, or 100-110 feet of distance altogether. This distance plus 60 feet equals 170 feet multiplied by two platoons, resulting in 340 feet altogether. I have chosen to use a number range of 300 to 400 feet in the text to account for the fact that these are only estimates. Fred L. Frechette, "The Lost Hero of the Lost Dispatch," MNBP Library. Frechette states without citing a source that Company F had 45 men in its ranks as of Sept. 13.

Where Did Barton Mitchell Find the Lost Orders? | 67

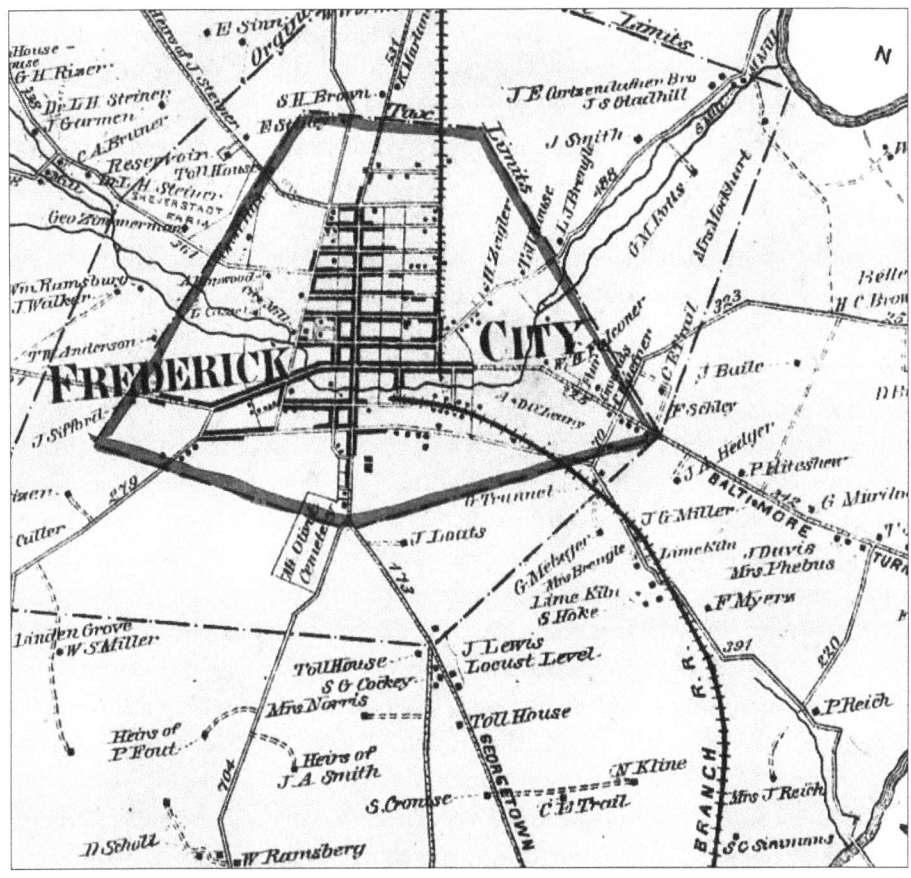

An excerpt from page 11 of D. J. Lake's 1873 *Atlas of Frederick County Maryland* showing how during the Civil War era the city limits of Frederick, MD, lay in open countryside half a mile beyond the dark lined streets of the city itself. The meadowland of Augustine D. O'Leary is clearly marked, as is the farmstead of F. Myers, previously owned by Elias Delashmutt, Jr., approximately one mile southeast of Frederick. *D. J. Lake*

The Hoosier skirmishers advanced up the road, crossed the Baltimore and Ohio Railroad spur line twice, and continued toward Frederick under the distant rumble of Alfred Pleasanton's guns. At last, with the hour approaching noon, Kopp's men came to "a meadow near the city limits," also described by Ezra Carman as "the outskirts of the city," where they received an order to halt. An important dimension of the history at this point involves the Army of the Potomac's columns on the left and right of the XII Corps. The presence of these columns helps establish where the men of Company F presumably stopped. Eight days after he was wounded at Antietam, Sgt. Bloss noted in a letter from the hospital that "Ours and Sumners Corps advanced on Frederick from the N. E. [sic]

direction. Somebody else was on our left." He then repeated this memory in 1892 during a talk before the Kansas Commandery of the Military Order of the Loyal Legion of the United States. Stating that his platoon "soon reached the suburbs of the city, where the converging lines of other divisions and corps caused us to halt," Bloss confirmed that on September 13, 1862, he had known the other columns were there.[8]

Bloss's understanding of the situation most likely developed after Col. Colgrove had given the order to halt. Whatever the case may have been, Bloss could almost certainly see and hear the column of troops marching into Frederick on his right. A "bird's eye view" lithograph of Frederick produced in 1854 by Edward Sachse of Baltimore contains a panel looking southeast from the center of town. This panel shows open countryside dotted with farmhouses, fences, trees, and even the B&O spur line heading south to Monocacy Junction. Some of the things depicted are out of proportion, such as the B&O rail line, which ran farther east before turning south, so Sachse's illustration should not be considered the equivalent of a photograph. It does at least confirm that open fields and meadows stretched away from the southern edge of town for a considerable distance. This detail provides substance to the descriptions where the 27th Indiana's skirmish line may have halted; either in a "wheat field," as Bloss described it, or in a clover field "adjoining the city on the south," as Edmund Brown's history of the regiment states, or in "a meadow near the city limits."[9]

General Sumner's II Corps came up on the 27th Indiana's left, and at noon on September 13 its various regiments were marching north into Frederick on South Market Street with multiple brass and drum bands playing. Sergeant Bloss and his companions could surely hear this martial clamor from their position less than half a mile to the east. The possibility also exists that Bloss learned about the II Corps's presence later in the afternoon and recounted it as one of the "converging columns" in his Sept. 25 letter without mentioning that detail. General Reno's IX

---

8 Bloss, "Letter," Sept. 25, 1862; John M. Bloss, "Antietam and the Lost Dispatch," Jan. 6, 1892, in Kansas Commandery of the Military Order of the Loyal Legion of the United States (MOLLUS), eds., *War Talks in Kansas* (Kansas City, MO, 1906), 84; also see Ezra A. Carman, *The Maryland Campaign of September 1862*, 3 vols., Thomas G. Clemens, ed. (El Dorado, CA, 2010), 1:279. "On the morning of the 13th [the Twelfth Corps] marched in the direction of Frederick and, at early noon, reached the outskirts of the city, where the converging columns of other commands caused it to halt in a meadow." Bloss misidentified the corps on his right as Sumner's. It was actually Reno's IX Corps. Sumner's II Corps approached Frederick on the left of Bloss's skirmish line.

9 Edward Sachse, *Bird's Eye View of Frederick, Md.* (Baltimore, MD, 1854).

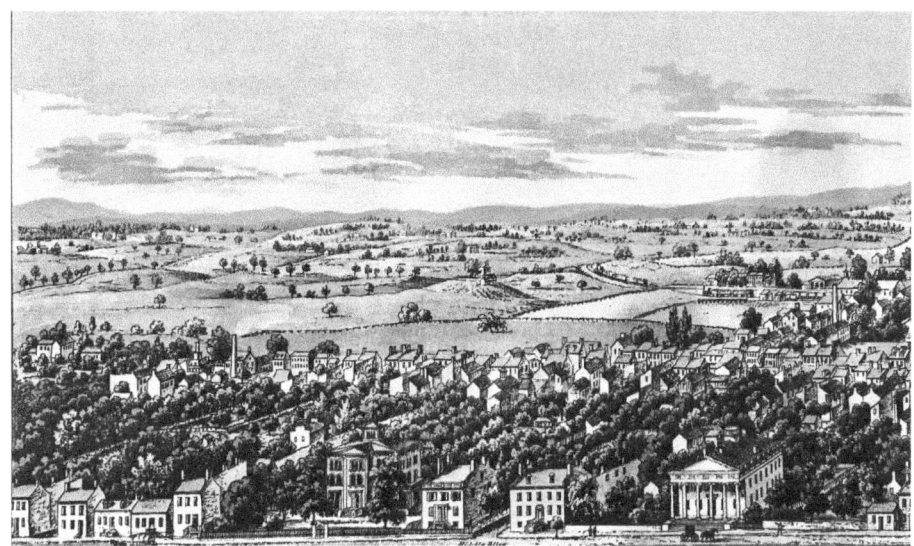

A close-up of the panel of Edward Sachse's 1854 "Bird's Eye View of Frederick City" depicting the southeastern quadrant of town and the countryside beyond. Sachse's image shows how half a mile of farm fields and meadowland made up the terrain from the houses in town all the way to the city limits. Augustine D. O' Leary's home is in the center of the image near the B&O rail depot. On the left, a row of trees lining Franklin Street can be seen running to the intersection with Ijamsville Road. A tree is depicted at the intersection. Could it be the locust tree that Hoosier skirmishers were resting under when Barton Mitchell discovered the Lost Orders?
Heritage Frederick

Corps, minus the Kanawha Division, which had already marched to a position west of Frederick, advanced into town on the 27th Indiana's right. These troops entered Frederick using the National Road, which became East Patrick Street as it crossed the city limits. The National Road followed the top of a low, east-west ridge line that even today is plainly visible from the intersection of the Ijamsville Road/East South Street/Franklin Street intersection. This means that Bloss could see the IX Corps' column from the intersection when he and his men reached it.[10]

---

10 "On reaching the city of Frederick we marched through with colors flying and bands playing"; Robert S. Robertson, 93rd New York Infantry, Sept.13,1862, entry in "Diary of the War," *Old Fort News*, Vol. XXVIII, No. 1 (Jan.-Mar. 1963), 53. "As the column passed through the town, regimental flags flying and Lambert and the rest of the boys in the band playing loudly"; Nancy N. Baxter, *Gallant Fourteenth: The Story of an Indiana Civil War Regiment* (Carmel, IN, 1980), 97. "We marched through Frederick at 10 a.m. with banners flying and bands playing"; Calvin G. Zon, ed., *The Good Fight That Didn't End: Henry P. Goddard's Accounts of Civil War and Peace* (Columbia, SC, 2008), 56–57.

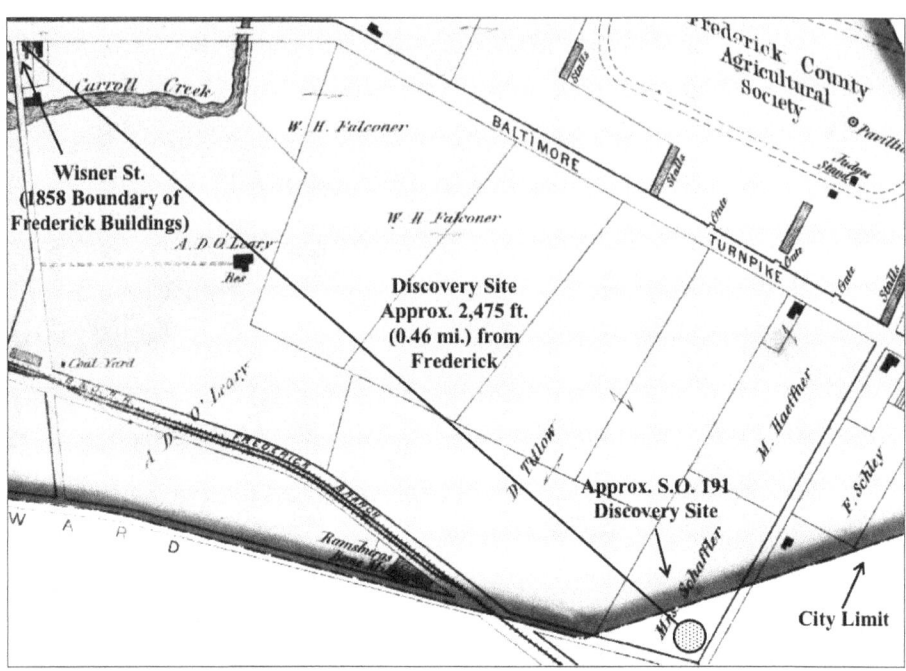

An edited excerpt from pages 52-53 of D. J. Lake's 1873 *Atlas of Frederick County Maryland* showing the site roughly one-half mile from Frederick where Barton Mitchell presumably discovered the dropped copy of Special Orders No. 191. The location fits eyewitness statements saying the meadow was next to the city, in the suburbs, on the city limits, and on the left side of the road. *D. J. Lake, Alexander B. Rossino*

These streets, no more than secondary dirt roads at the time, came together at the southeastern corner of a meadow owned by a woman named Anna Barbara Schaffler. Franklin Street, on Bloss's right, ran about 1,000 feet north from the East South Street intersection until it met the National Road. East South Street, meanwhile, stretched off to the left, running approximately one half-mile west to South Market Street. When considered from Bloss' perspective at the head of the XII Corps' column, the corps would have needed to take one of these two roads to continue its advance. However, with infantry from the II and IX Corps occupying them, it must have appeared to Bloss that there was nowhere else for the XII Corps to go. This would explain his later claim that "the converging lines of other divisions and corps caused us to halt." Therefore, it is likely in the meadow just on the north side of this intersection, on the land of Mrs. Schaffler, "adjoining the city on the south," and due to the converging army columns on the left and right blocking their path ahead, that Bloss and his comrades came to a stop. The platoon on the right of the Ijamsville Road, which had been trailing Bloss's platoon on the left of the road, then halted in the portion of the field southeast of Franklin Street on Bloss's right.[11]

According to the earliest record of the event, the letter Bloss wrote on September 25, 1862, the terrain at the location was a "wheat field." Bloss also later described the place as a "meadow" where he and his comrades "threw ourselves upon the grass to rest." The sworn testimony of others present at the time concurs with Bloss's characterization of the place. Enoch G. Boicourt of Company F was among these individuals. Signing a sworn affidavit concerning the event in 1906, Boicourt testified that he and his comrades went "forward as a skirmish line, when near Frederick City the line stopped to rest in an old meadow." Boicourt's use of

The maturing hay shown here looks similar to wheat before it is cut and dried, perhaps explaining why Sgt. Bloss referred to the location where Barton Mitchell found the Lost Orders in his September 25, 1862, letter as a "wheat field." *Alexander B. Rossino*

11 Lake, *Map of Frederick County Maryland*, 52-53. Schaffler's name is recorded in some local records as Schuffler and Schaeffler. For example, see U.S. Census Bureau, Schedule 1 Census in Frederick City, Maryland, Aug. 15, 1850, 101. The possibility exists that Bloss's men could have halted on the left side of the Ijamsville Road before the South Street and Franklin Street intersection, but this is doubtful for three reasons. First, the open ground between the B&O rail line and the road was too narrow to be called a "meadow." Second, the land there is not adjacent to the city limits. Third, none of the testimony of participants in the event mentions the railroad even though it must have been close to the left side of Bloss's skirmish line.

the adjective "old" is informative in this regard as by it he probably meant uncultivated or lying fallow, in which case the uncut grass would have been tall.[12]

George W. Welch of Company F recalled for his part how "in an old meadow, we stopped to rest," and David B. Vance, also of Company F, who like Bloss was wounded at Antietam, testified to the fact that the company's skirmish line "advanced across a field to where there had been a fence, but at that time only a row of weeds, grass and some small shrubs or bushes [was present]. The men lay down, Sergeant Bloss at the head of the company, Barton W. Mitchell next to Bloss, and on Bloss's left; I next to Mitchell, and so on." These testimonies, despite being written four decades after the war, match the description of a "wheat" field offered by Bloss in 1862 if one considers that mature hay, especially if it was timothy grass, looks like wheat to the untrained eye before it is cut and dried. Even Edmund Brown's history of the 27th Indiana added that the men "lay down upon the clean grass."[13]

It appears to have been here, then, in a grassy meadow adjoining Frederick City, under a "locas" tree, as Bloss called it, near where a fence line once ran, and close to the road, that Cpl. Mitchell spotted a folded document. He picked up the packet and opened it, at which point two cigars fell out. Mitchell, who was not illiterate as some authors have claimed, read through at least a part of the document with a comrade named John Campbell looking over his shoulder before Bloss asked to see it. Bloss then climbed to his feet and took the order to Col. Colgrove. Colgrove read the papers and carried them to Gen. Gordon, the commander of the Third Brigade. So on up the chain of command the orders eventually passed to Gen. McClellan.[14]

---

12 Bloss, "Letter," Sept. 25, 1862; Bloss, "Antietam and the Lost Dispatch," 84; Affidavit of Enoch G. Boicourt, July 30, 1906, MNBP.

13 Affidavit of George W. Welch, July 24, 1906; Affidavit of David B. Vance, Sept. 15, 1903, MNBP; Brown, *The Twenty-Seventh Indiana Volunteer Infantry*, 228.

14 Confusion about the men involved in the discovery of the orders has accumulated over the years to include Capt. Peter Kopp. John Bloss himself contributed to the muddiness by describing Kopp's involvement in a speech he gave in 1892: "I carried it (i.e., the orders) back to Captain Kopp, of our company, and together we took it to Colonel Colgrove, commanding the regiment." In Bloss's Sept. 1862 letter he wrote, "I was with him [Barton Mitchell] when he found it and read it first. I seen its importance and took it to the Col. (i.e., Colgrove)." Based on this earlier description, it is unlikely that Kopp was involved in either the orders' discovery or their delivery to Colgrove; see Bloss, "Letter," Sept. 25, 1862, and Bloss, "Antietam and the Lost Dispatch," 84; Affidavit of John Campbell, Mar. 4, 1889, MNBP: "I was with him (i.e., Mitchell) the time he picked up the Genl. Order of Genl. Lee to Gen. D. H. Hill. I looked over his shoulder and read it with him."

The only known photograph of Cpl. Barton Mitchell, the man who discovered the Lost Orders. Before his untimely death from illness in January 1868, Mitchell tried unsuccessfully to collect a monetary reward for his find. *Fred Frechette*

The process of discovering and reading the orders described by the veterans from Company F provides a clue as to the deployment of the 27th Indiana at the time. According to Hardee, regiments throwing out skirmishers were to position a company reserve "behind the centre of the line of skirmishers . . . at one hundred and fifty [paces]," or about 300 feet, from the skirmish line. Colonel Colgrove appears to have deployed all of Company F, suggesting that if he also deployed a company-strength reserve he would have needed to select another company from his regiment for the job. Assuming for the sake of argument that he did so means, according to Hardee, the "principal reserve then occupied another position "at four hundred paces," or about 1,200 feet, behind the company reserve. This principal reserve would have consisted of the balance of the 27th Indiana.[15]

According to the evidence, it appears that Colonel Colgrove shook out his skirmishers by the book. It makes sense to assume, therefore, that he conducted the rest of the procedure by the book. If so,

---

15 Hardee, *Rifle and Light Infantry Tactics*, 172; Silas Colgrove to William A. Mitchell, Dec. 3, 1879, Barton Mitchell File, MNBP: "Our troops were halted in lines and stacked arms."

74 | *Calamity at Frederick*

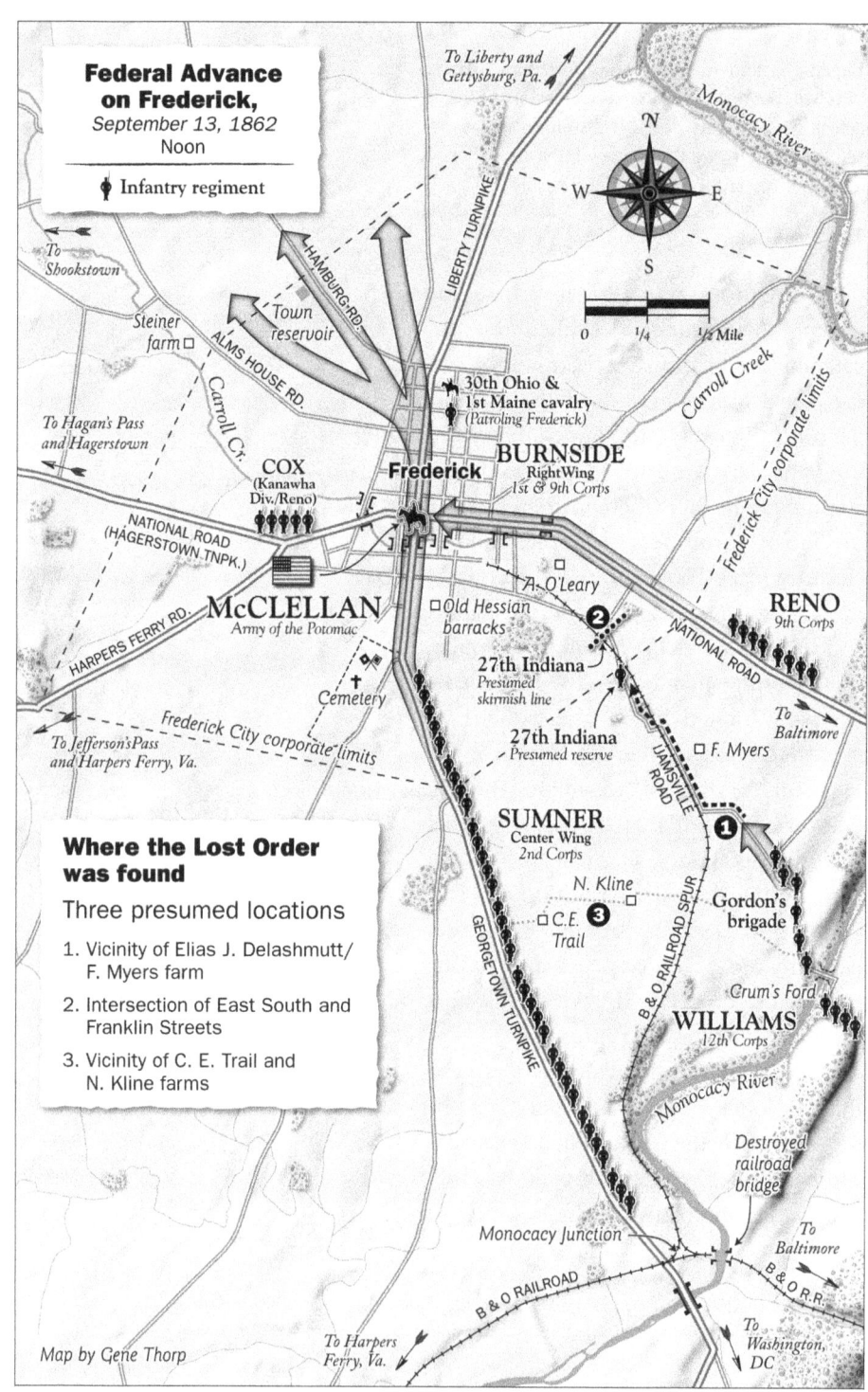

this means that Colgrove's men, from the platoons stationed at the front, to the main body of the regiment behind it, stretched a maximum distance of 1,500 feet, or close to one-quarter of a mile, from front to back. This distance makes sense given estimates of the locations where other regiments of the First Division's Third Brigade halted. Charles Mills of the 2nd Massachusetts Infantry recorded in a letter home, for example, that he and his comrades stopped in "a field about half a mile from Frederick." Alonzo Quint, also of the 2nd Massachusetts, and the regiment's chaplain, recalled similarly in a memoir published only five years after the event that he and his comrades "camped half a mile south of Fredericktown." These estimates are reasonably consistent with Company F's skirmish line halting on the southern edge of Schaffler's land because the intersection of East South Street and Franklin Street was close to a half-mile southeast of Frederick City in 1862.[16]

The Delashmutt/Myers farmhouse stood just over one-half of a mile to the rear of the intersection of Franklin and East South Streets, and according to the sources it is where the other regiments of Gen. Gordon's Third Brigade stopped their march. The Cronise farm, meanwhile, is farther away, suggesting that the location proposed by the Monocacy Park staff is unlikely to have been the place where Mitchell discovered the lost copy of Special Orders No. 191. If the testimonies presented above are accurate, it strongly suggests that researchers have looked too far afield when attempting to identify where Mitchell discovered the Lost Orders. Bloss said it took place just on the outskirts of Frederick close to the city limits.[17]

One perplexing dimension of these events remains to be addressed—the absence of any mention of the Baltimore & Ohio Railroad spur line by the

---

16 Gregory A. Coco, ed., *Through Blood and Fire: The Civil War Letters of Major Charles J. Mills, 1862-1865* (Gettysburg, PA, 1982), 29; Alonzo H. Quint, *The Record of the Second Massachusetts Infantry, 1861-1865* (Boston, MA, 1867), 130. General Williams, the commander of the XII Corps, recalled as well that on Sept. 13 "We forded the Monocacy and encamped about a mile east of the city"; Milo M. Quaife, ed., *From the Cannon's Mouth: The Civil War Letters of General Alpheus S. Williams* (Lincoln, NE, 1995), 122.

17 Consider also the testimony offered in Regimental Committee, eds., *History of the One Hundred and Twenty-Fifth Regiment Pennsylvania Volunteers, 1862-1863* (Philadelphia, PA, 1906), 51. "We waded the Monocacy on the double-quick, and reached Frederick City at noon, where we halted in a field on its outskirts"; also see Miles C. Huyette, *The Maryland Campaign and The Battle of Antietam* (Buffalo, NY, 1915), 17: "The afternoon of September 13th, we—of First Division, 12th Corps—crossed the Monocacy River and bivouacked in a stubble-field south of the Baltimore Pike, about half distance from the river and Frederick City." Huyette served with the 124th Pennsylvania Infantry, a part of Crawford's First Brigade. The 124th Pennsylvania "halted about a mile from Frederick City at 1 p.m." Diary of Sgt. C. D. M. Broomhall, 124th Pennsylvania, Sept. 13, 1862. Transcribed by Carolyn Ivanoff (Janes family papers).

participants in the orders' discovery. As it moved northwest toward Frederick City, Capt. Kopp's skirmish line would have crossed the railroad tracks twice. The balance of the regiment under Col. Colgrove also must have traversed the rails. If this is the case, why did no one write about seeing the tracks in the years after the war?

An answer to this question could be that none of the men involved in the orders' discovery thought the rail line worth mentioning. Fixated instead on the place where Mitchell found the orders, other landmarks did not figure into their memories of the event. The available maps from the era also show several houses in the path of the 27th Indiana, yet no one in the regiment mentioned their presence, either. Similarly, none of the skirmishers commented on other ordinary features, such as livestock, orchards, wells, and farmers' outbuildings. Edward Sachse's "bird's eye view" shows some of these features, suggesting that they probably still existed in September 1862. Nevertheless, no one involved in the incident commented on them. To the men of the 27th Indiana, an outhouse, a stable, or even a railroad were simply too commonplace to be of note unless something special happened near one of them, such as when David Vance testified that their company "advanced across a field to where there had been a fence."

Another answer could be that Mitchell discovered the orders before he and his fellow skirmishers encountered the rails. This implies that Mitchell found the document one mile from Frederick. Arguing for such a distance requires discarding John Bloss's comment that Mitchell found the orders in a meadow close to Frederick City. Rejecting Bloss's testimony then leaves us with no estimate of the discovery site's distance from Frederick by any of the participants in the event.

Bloss's memory of the event was admittedly not perfect 30 years later. When he described the discovery in 1892, Bloss also stated that he took the order to Capt. Kopp first, that he and Kopp then walked the document to Col. Colgrove, and that the event took place prior to 10:00 a.m. All of these details are incorrect based on other sources and the content of Bloss's own letter from September 1862. Yet, Bloss also described the discovery site as in the "suburbs of the city" and "near the city limits." These observations, when taken in tandem with Edmund Brown's comment that the 27th Indiana "halted in a clover field, adjoining the city on the south," and with William Hostetter of Company A's affidavit that the regiment "halted near the city limits," suggest that Mitchell's discovery took place closer to Frederick than the Delashmutt/Myers farm. Put simply, Bloss's testimony is the only source we have describing the place where Cpl. Mitchell found the orders. We are therefore compelled to rely on it.[18]

Lastly, Bloss stated that he and his comrades received the order to halt because to him it seemed as if the XII Corps' column could go no farther. Had Mitchell found the orders one mile from Frederick, the column still could have proceeded for a good distance. If we accept the testimony of those who witnessed Mitchell finding the orders as generally accurate, then the most likely location for the discovery remains the meadow near the intersection of Franklin and East South Streets. Situated half a mile away from Frederick, consisting of a large meadow that adjoined the city, and not permitting the XII Corps to proceed without running into the converging columns of the II and IX Corps, it appears to fit Bloss's description of the place where Barton Mitchell discovered the lost copy of Special Orders No. 191.

None of what is written here should be taken to imply that the 27th Indiana camped at the spot where Mitchell found the orders. It suggests only that Mitchell found the orders well ahead of the rest of his regiment. He and his comrades could have easily walked back to the 27th Indiana's campsite closer to the rest of the Third Brigade. We simply do not know what happened because to date no one has uncovered evidence proving it. This scenario is possible because, as Gene Thorp has noted to me, the balance of the XII Corps would have closed up with its leading elements; the 27th Indiana and the 2nd Massachusetts, if we deem the testimonies of Charles Mills and Alonzo Quint credible. This means most of the 7,600 men of its ranks could have camped closer to the Delashmutt/Myers farm one mile from Frederick. The discovery location then being just across (or west of) the Ijamsville Road from the farm before the B&O rail line thus becomes a viable alternative if we disregard the details provided by John Bloss.[19]

---

18 Affidavit of William H. Hostetter, Dec. 18, 1905, MNBP.

19 The XII Corps' strength estimate comes from Carman, *The Maryland Campaign of September 1862*, 2:583.

Chapter 6

Who Lost Lee's Orders?

Having established with as much certainty as possible where Federal troops found the lost copy of General Lee's orders, it is time to consider who might have lost the document. Daniel Harvey Hill claimed until the end of his life that he never saw the copy of the orders supposedly sent to him from army headquarters, yet for more than a century scholars and others investigating the saga have accused Hill of losing the document. They have also taken it for granted that Hill's men camped at the place where the orders were found because Hill's name appears on the lost copy, and because Col. Silas Colgrove published an article in *The Century Magazine* in the mid-1880s stating, "We stacked arms on the same ground that had been occupied by General D. H. Hill's division the evening before."[1]

The testimony of the men examined in Chapter Five of this study provides no supporting evidence for Colgrove's claim. Not a single man who participated in or witnessed the discovery of the orders described a former Confederate encampment. The only other source that mentions a Confederate presence in the area is the diary of Milton S. Lytle. A soldier with the XII Corps' 125th Pennsylvania, Lytle wrote, "On Saturday, Sept. 13th we reached Frederick. The Rebels had been driven from the city the day before, and we encamped on ground

---

1 Silas Colgrove, "The Finding of Lee's Lost Order," in Johnson and Buel, eds., *B&L*, 2:603. Colgrove's account is riddled with errors, including the mention of three cigars when Bloss made it clear in his letter written 13 days after the event that Mitchell found two cigars wrapped in the document, not three.

Maj. Gen. Daniel Harvey Hill. Commander of an unattached division during the Maryland Campaign, Hill has long been blamed for losing Lee's orders due solely to the appearance of his name on the dropped document. Hill attempted to clear his name until his death in 1889. *University of South Carolina Libraries*

which had been in their possession." What Lytle meant by "in their possession" has been lost to history. He may have meant a place that Lee's Confederates had held before they marched off. We simply cannot know for sure.[2]

Based on the other sources describing Confederate encampments, it is reasonable to expect that if the thousands of men with Hill's division had camped on the spot for the better part of a week one would find reports of refuse lying about, of butchered animal carcasses, of campfire pits, of broken equipment, etc. Take for example the recollection of James M. Stone when he and his comrades in the 21st Massachusetts (IX Corps) stopped for the evening on September 12: "we filed into a great pasture on the east side of the Monocacy River and went into camp. Lights were beginning to glimmer across the river and we were told they were in the city of Frederick. Camp refuse lying about indicated that the field had been used as a camp ground for troops in the immediate past, and inquiry brought out the fact that some of Stonewall Jackson's troops had camped on the identical field the night before." There is no such description for the place where Barton Mitchell found the Lost Orders because D. H. Hill's division did not camp there. It actually camped along Ballenger's Creek about four miles south of Frederick, not where Colgrove said it did.[3]

None of the available Confederate sources, in fact, offer evidence of any infantry camping near the intersection of East South and Franklin Streets before

---

[2] Milton S. Lytle, Civil War Era Diaries, 1860-1866, Diary 5, The Pennsylvania State University, Special Collections Library. Online at https://digital.libraries.psu.edu/digital/collection/pccolls/id/1190/rec/2.

[3] James M. Stone, *Personal Recollections of the Civil War* (Boston, MA, 1918), 83. Rossino, *Their Maryland*, 104-105, 120n20.

Lee's army left Frederick. The 1st Battalion Virginia Infantry and the 42nd Virginia camped the closest from September 6-10 when they were detailed to provost duty, but those units occupied the grounds of the old Hessian Barracks three-quarters of a mile to the west. The absence of evidence placing General Hill's division on the spot raises the obvious question why Barton Mitchell found orders addressed to Hill lying in a meadow there. It stands to reason that if Hill did not camp anyplace near where the orders were found then no courier would have been sent to that spot to deliver the orders or to lose them. The three primary culprits in the mystery so far, Daniel Harvey Hill, a member of Hill's staff, or a headquarters courier, thus begin to look more and more like improbable suspects, particularly since the only fact that implicates Hill is his name on the document. But if none of these individuals lost the orders, how did they end up at the place where Mitchell found them?

Thinking beyond D. H. Hill, a Hill staffer, or a courier leaves three possible explanations for the loss of Special Orders No. 191: 1) someone intending for the orders to be found placed them in the path of the Indiana troops approaching Frederick; 2) General Lee or a member of his staff gave the lost copy to an individual visiting army headquarters and that person dropped the orders; or 3) someone took (or made) the lost copy of the orders and then misplaced them. Each of these scenarios will be explored, proceeding from the least probable to the most probable based on the available evidence. This approach will gradually eliminate baseless speculation in favor of a source-based interpretation that suggests the likeliest culprit.

The notion of the orders being deliberately placed where Federal troops were sure to find them is the least likely possibility. Visitors from Frederick besieged Lee's and Jackson's headquarters on the afternoon of September 9. The opportunity existed, therefore, for someone with malicious intent to have slipped into the tent of one of the generals, or of his adjutant, and steal the copy of the order written for General Hill; yet no member of Lee's staff who later commented on the loss of the orders ever mentioned theft as a possibility. No member of the staff noticed that a copy of the order was missing, either. This proves nothing, of course, but it must be considered when weighing the possibility that a visiting civilian could have taken the document.

One of the headquarters slaves could be considered a viable suspect as well, but there is again no evidence of an enslaved person's involvement, or of any of the headquarters slaves being punished for the offense. Any convincing explanation offered must account, moreover, for the presence of the two cigars found by Barton Mitchell. A slave spiriting away the orders would have needed to steal the cigars, too, unless he purchased them in Frederick while on business for the staff. There is, however, no evidence of any such thing taking place, so the entire scenario must be considered purely theoretical.

This raises the possibility that Lee himself could have tasked someone, either a man in his army or a local Confederate sympathizer, with taking Hill's copy and ensuring it fell into Federal hands as a "ruse of war." This scenario also lacks supporting evidence. More importantly, there are several sources that firmly disprove it. In the first place, the idea of Lee plotting to ensure a copy of his operational plan fell into the enemy's hands smacks of treason, even if that plan was intended to be a ruse. If there is one aspect of Robert E. Lee's character that remained consistent throughout his life it was his devotion to duty. Subterfuge of the sort suggested by the deliberate transfer of his plans into the hands of a Federal commander simply does not comport with everything we know about General Lee. The man never resorted to schemes involving the deliberate placement of false information at any time during the war. It seems highly unlikely, therefore, that he would have done so during the campaign in Maryland.[4]

There is, in addition, the unnecessary complexity of such a plan. If Lee wanted a copy of his orders found by McClellan he could have left the document with one of the well-known sympathetic families in Frederick and asked for it to be handed to a local unionist anonymously. That person could have then given the document to McClellan. It is irrelevant if the Federal commander would have trusted information received in such a way because he still would have needed to pursue Lee's army west over the mountains, and he would have done exactly what he ended up doing with the orders when they fell into his hands—compare the content with what he already knew and thereby validate the information in the document. It would have been a much safer thing for Lee to have given the orders to a local conspirator and ensure the orders got to a useful unionist than to tell a conspirator to drop them in an obscure location ahead of approaching Federal soldiers.

Furthermore, if deliberately dropping the orders was the plan then why not leave them on the side of either the National Road or the Georgetown Pike, the two main routes into the city, and not in a meadow of tall grass near a nondescript, out of the way track? Doing so would have increased the odds of a Federal soldier

---

4 This thesis is proposed by the L.A.-based attorney Joseph Ryan. See https://joeryancivilwar.com/Special-Order-191/resources/Special-Order-191-Position-Paper-Joseph-Ryan.html. For comments on Lee's sense of duty see Freeman, *R. E. Lee*, 1:453.

finding the document and sending it up the chain of command. Leaving the document in the grass near a secondary road created a serious risk that the orders would be overlooked, which is something Lee surely could not countenance had his objective been to deliberately dupe McClellan.

The presence of the two cigars also militates against the orders being deliberately planted. One could argue they were intended to weight the document so it did not blow away in the wind, and there was a light breeze on the day of their discovery. Still, the orders were dropped in tall grass, or a "wheat field," as John Bloss described it, meaning the tall grass would have held the packet in place. It seems rather a waste of cherished tobacco by the perpetrator, who could have easily dropped the packet in the middle of the paved National Road where an enemy soldier finding it was more certain.[5]

The notion of Lee purposely giving away his plans makes even less sense when one considers his thinking within the context of the events. Lee wrote in August 1863 that he had intended to draw McClellan after him by moving toward Hagerstown and threatening Pennsylvania. This move alone was sufficient for the general to have accomplished his objective without resorting to subterfuge. Paragraph IX of Special Orders No. 191 also makes it clear that Lee hoped to bring his army back together "at Boonsborough or Hagerstown" for a clash with the enemy. He did not identify a specific location because as of the orders' dictation on September 9 Lee did not yet know where he wanted to fight his decisive engagement. He would not finalize this decision until September 12, when he chose the heights behind Beaver Creek, located between Boonsboro and Hagerstown, after he had seen them with his own eyes.[6]

Writing to D. H. Hill in February of 1868, Lee confirmed that "at the time the order fell into Genl. McClellan's hands, I considered it a great calamity and subsequent reflection has not caused me to change my opinion." To this he added, "When they were issued (9th Sept.) I supposed there would have been time for

---

5 Admiral Sir Francis Beaufort of Great Britain developed the method of measuring wind widely utilized in the mid-nineteenth century. His scale ran from Force 0 (calm) to Force 12 (stormy). The recorded wind speed in Frederick on Sept. 13 at 2:00 p.m. was Force 3. See H. Wallbrink and F. B. Koek, "Historical Wind Speed Equivalents of The Beaufort Scale, 1850-1950," at "https://icoads.noaa.gov/reclaim/pdf/Hisklim13.pdf; Joseph L. Harsh, Sounding the Shallows: A Confederate Companion for the Maryland Campaign of 1862 (Kent, OH, 2000), 15.

6 Alexander B. Rossino, "Lee's Beaver Creek Plan: The September 1862 Battle He Never Had the Chance to Fight and Why That Matters," in *North & South*, Series II, Vol. 3, No. 1 (June 2022), 19-28.

Col. Thomas L. Rosser. Commander of the 5th Virginia Cavalry during the Maryland Campaign, Rosser conducted speaking tours across the South after the war to raise money for Confederate memorials. A comment Rosser uttered in Raleigh, NC, in 1897 placed the blame for losing Lee's orders on a member of Stonewall Jackson's headquarters staff, fueling speculation the cuplrit was Henry K. Douglas. *Library of Congress*

their accomplishment and for the army to have been reunited before Genl McClellan could cross the South Mountains." This statement lines up with the other evidence for Lee's plan. To argue that Lee would write comments such as these if he had intended to plant Special Orders No. 191 beggars belief.[7]

Writing after the war "that he (Genl. Lee) had been much surprised at the sudden change in McClellan's tactics," Rev. Edward C. Gordon, a librarian at Washington College in Lexington, Virginia, confirmed following a discussion with the general that McClellan's surprising advance had caught Lee off balance. The general politely characterized this in his August 1863 campaign report as the enemy advancing "more rapidly than was convenient." Charles Marshall later expanded on this sentiment in an unpublished manuscript, writing, "General Lee did not become aware of the cause that led to the sudden advance of the Federal army after he had left Frederick until the official report of General McClellan was published some months later, when he learned for the first time that the movement of General McClellan had been caused by the loss of the order." These comments decisively refute the notion that Lee ordered the lost copy of Special Orders No. 191 deliberately planted so that they would fall into enemy hands.[8]

This raises the possibility of a yet unidentified individual having taken or made a copy of the orders before losing them. Colonel Thomas L. Rosser, the

---

7 Lee to Hill, Feb. 21, 1868, D. H. Hill Papers #2035-z, SHC, UNC.

8 R. E. Lee to E. C. Gordon, Feb. 15, 1868, in Freeman, *Lee's Lieutenants*, 2:718; OR 19:1, 140; Maurice, ed., Lee's *Aide-De-Camp*, 160. McClellan's final report appeared in print in February 1864.

commander of the 5th Virginia Cavalry during the Maryland Campaign, described such a scenario during a lecture tour in 1897. Claiming without elaboration that the culprit "was one of Jackson's staff," Rosser said "when it [the order] was handed to him to deliver [to General Hill], he said, 'O, we have that order,' and so, carelessly, wrapped it round his cigars, placed it in his pocket, and lost it." Rosser added a tantalizing clue about the identity of this individual, stating, "he hoped this man would tell his connection with it before he died." At the time Rosser made this comment, Joseph G. Morrison and Henry K. Douglas, both of whom had been aides on Jackson's staff in September 1862, were still alive. We also know from his memoirs that Douglas smoked cigars, although we do not have similar information for Morrison.[9]

The lost copy of the orders addressed to D. H. Hill could have come from Jackson's headquarters. Old Jack, after all, wrote out a copy of the orders for Hill based on the copy he received from army headquarters. It is not known, however, if Jackson wrote this copy at his headquarters or if he made it in the adjutant's tent at Lee's headquarters and sent it to Hill from there. These details are unknowable unless new evidence comes to light. It remains possible, therefore, that a member of Jackson's staff, such as Morrison or Douglas, could have mishandled the order and lost it, but there is no evidence to suggest it beyond Tom Rosser's allusion to a man who still lived in 1897. The specificity of Rosser's comment also casts doubt on his allegation. As of September 9, when the orders were distributed, Rosser and his men occupied a position several miles east of Frederick City. How Rosser could have known what the perpetrator said (and did) when he was handed the orders is incomprehensible because Rosser was not present. If someone told him about it later then the information is little more than hearsay and cannot be considered reliable.

The final possibility is that someone visiting Lee's encampment or Jackson's headquarters procured the copy (or a copy of the copy) intended for Hill and lost it afterward. Indulging this scenario means that the individual who received the copy must have had a reason for possessing it otherwise neither Lee, nor Jackson, nor any of their staff would have given it to him. Brigadier General William Nelson

---

9 Thomas J. Arnold, "The Lost Dispatch—A War Mystery," in *Confederate Veteran*, Vol. 30, No. 8 (August 1922), 317; Douglas, *I Rode With Stonewall*, 74, 265. Morrison died in 1906. Douglas died in 1903. See Wilbur D. Jones, "Who Lost the Lost Orders? Stonewall Jackson, His Courier, and Special Orders No. 191," in *Civil War Regiments: A Journal of the American Civil War*, Vol. 5, No. 3 (1997), 1-26, for a lengthy and entirely speculative accusation that Douglas lost the orders.

Brig. Gen. William N. Pendleton. Commander of the Reserve Artillery during the campaign in Maryland, Pendleton had access to and a reason for carrying a copy of Special Orders No. 191. There is, however, no hard evidence he lost the copy found by Barton Mitchell. *Library of Congress*

Pendleton, the commander of the army's Reserve Artillery, and the former Rector of All Saints Episcopal Church in Frederick, fits this description. As is noted in Chapter Three, Pendleton reported to Lee upon his arrival in the area on September 8. Although this visit took place before Lee had dictated the orders to Charles Marshall, Pendleton wrote in a letter to his wife on September 10, "To-day we go farther inward; I must not indicate where lest my letter fail and give some clue where I would not have information gotten. Suffice it [to say] that General Lee seems well to understand what he is about."[10]

This statement makes it clear that Pendleton possessed at least a broad understanding of Lee's plans. Lee could have explained these to his artillery chief on September 8, or he could have ordered a copy of Special Orders No. 191 sent to Pendleton after their creation on the morning of September 9. Yet much like the possibility of Morrison or Douglas having lost the orders, there is no evidence that Pendleton received a copy of the document. One of the staff at Jackson's headquarters also could have handed it to the aging preacher.

Pendleton and Jackson maintained a close personal relationship, so it is possible that the artillery commander visited Old Jack after reporting to Lee. He may have procured a copy of the orders at that time, but it is unknown if this happened since there is no evidence for it. The most substantial thing that can be said in favor of Pendleton possessing a copy of the orders is that his command is mentioned in the same paragraph as Hill's division. Pendleton, therefore, had a reason to be carrying the orders if he was given a copy. He could have then lost the document while visiting Frederick to see friends, which he admitted in a letter to his wife is precisely what he did after reporting to Lee. Absent new evidence, this is

10 Lee, *Memoirs of William Nelson Pendleton*, 211.

Maj. Gen. James Ewell Brown "Jeb" Stuart, commander of the Army of Northern Virginia's cavalry division. Stuart had access to Special Orders No. 191, a reason for carrying them, mentioned possessing the orders in his campaign report, and established his headquarters outside of Frederick on Sept. 11 within 1,500 ft. of the presumed discovery site. These circumstances make Stuart a prime suspect for losing the orders. *Library of Congress*

the most that can be concluded about Pendleton's possible involvement in the loss of Special Orders No. 191.[11]

Major General Jeb Stuart is the final individual to consider. Stuart visited Frederick frequently between September 6 and 12, and in the context of the orders' loss his activities on the dates September 9 and 12 stand out. Chapter Four of this study quotes the diary of Catherine Markell in Frederick, who wrote on September 9 that "General Pryor called, [and] also General J. E. B. Stuart." The general then returned to his headquarters in Urbana later that day. As Maj. Heros von Borcke recalled in his postwar memoir, "General Stuart and myself were invited to dine with the doctor of the place [S. G. Cockey in Urbana], at whose pleasant dwelling we passed a few hours most delightfully. The universal verandah looked out upon the same beautiful landscape that we had admired from other points, and afforded us a cool retreat for cigars and conversation."[12]

We know that Stuart used the Georgetown Pike to travel to and from his headquarters because Catherine Markell mentions seeing the cavalier at army headquarters on the afternoon of September 9. Stuart thus had the opportunity to take (or be given) the extra copy of the orders lying around for Hill. This scenario is

---

11 Ibid., 211. "I spent the day in calling on my old friends in Frederick." The notion of Pendleton possessing a copy of the orders is explored in Rossino, *Their Maryland*, Appendix B. This speculative discussion is based on the possibility that Pendleton lodged at the Delashmutt/Myers farm since Elias Delashmutt was part of a family sympathetic to the Confederate cause. Subsequent research conducted for this study casts doubt on that speculation.

12 Markell, "Frederick Maryland in Peace and War," 107; Von Borcke, *Memoirs*, 1:199.

not far-fetched. There is, after all, no record of a copy of the orders being sent to Stuart, which is unusual given his rank, and yet Stuart's Maryland Campaign report refers specifically to Special Orders No. 191, indicating that he did possess a copy. To reiterate, Stuart reported, "on the 11th, the enemy advanced in force with infantry. Having maintained the present front even longer than was contemplated by the instructions covering the investment of Harper's Ferry (found in the orders appended to this report), the cavalry was withdrawn to within 3 miles of Frederick."[13]

These appended orders have never been found. They are not in the *Official Records*, nor have they turned up elsewhere. Admittedly, the *Official Records* are an imperfect collection, with asterisks denoting missing documents in many of the volumes. The absence of Stuart's appended copy of Special Orders No. 191 nevertheless raises the question whether he still had the copy in February 1864, or if he added the comment to cover for having lost them outside of Frederick in September 1862. This latter scenario is not beyond the realm of possibility. Stuart's command withdrew to the Monocacy River on September 11 in "[a] steadily falling rain," according to Heros von Borcke. The Southern horsemen then "took up a new position on the opposite [western] bank, [with] the greater part of our cavalry encamped between that point and Frederick. About half a mile from the latter place we fixed our headquarters at the farmhouse of an old Irishman."[14]

A glance at the 1873 D. J. Lake map of Frederick County shows the farm of Augustine D. O'Leary southeast of Frederick City. Could this have been the place where Jeb Stuart established his headquarters? There is credible evidence revelant to Von Borcke's brief entry to suggest it was. In the first instance, there is the distance from Frederick. The meadowland around O'Leary's house intersects with the plots owned by W. H. Falconer, Daniel Titlow, and Anna Barbara Schaffler close to the intersection of East South Street, Ijamsville Road, and Franklin Street about half a mile southeast of town, depending on the place from which the distance is measured. This vicinity would have made a perfect spot for cavalry to camp given the tall grass described by the men who found the Lost Orders and the

---

13 OR 19:1, 815.

14 Von Borcke, *Memoirs*, 1:200-202. O'Leary owned valuable land. The 1860 Census records his occupation as "Farmer" and the "Value of Real Estate" as $10,000, which is a large sum for the time; see Records of the 1860 U.S. Census. Online at https://www.archives. gov/research/census/1860.

location of the meadow on the southwestern side of Fredrick City, where Jeb Stuart established his defensive line.

In the second instance, there is Von Borcke's description of the farm's owner being "an old Irishman." Born in Ireland in 1807 (the same year as Lee), O'Leary turned 55 years old in 1862. Fifty-five is not considered old age in the present day, but it was in 1862. Lee's hair and beard, for example, had turned almost completely white by September of that year and the members of his staff sometimes referred to him as "the old man" behind his back. Add to this a third point, Von Borcke's observation that their Irish host "amused us very much with his 'buthiful brogue'." According to his obituary in the *Frederick News*, dated July 31, 1900, O'Leary immigrated to the United States "when he was about 15 years of age," and reached Frederick in 1840. Fifteen years living in Ireland would have been more than long enough for O'Leary to acquire the accent of his homeland, and to retain it for the rest of his life.

Fourth, Von Borcke added the detail that O'Leary's "pretty daughters" entertained the Southern cavaliers with a "lively little dance at night." Census records show that as of 1860 O'Leary had three daughters living with him named Mary, Martha, and Susan, aged 26, 22, and 20, respectively. Fifth, according to the diary of William R. Carter, the 3rd Virginia Cavalry of Fitz Lee's command fell back west of the Monocacy River on September 10, camped near Frederick, and then "moved & encamped near a mill" on September 11. A large mill owned by a man named Delashmutt stood adjacent to the property of Daniel Titlow at the time, approximately three-quarters of a mile from Frederick. This mill occupied two acres of ground that also shared a property line with the land of Augustine O'Leary and that of Anna Schaffler. Those plots and the mill stood right next to each other, meaning the mill would have been a prominent and visible landmark to anyone camped in the area.[15]

Sixth, a strangely detailed report appeared in the *Washington Evening Star* on September 15 stating, "About 4 o'clock in the afternoon [of September 12] the approach of the Federal advance, consisting of Gen. Cox's division of the Army of [the] Gauley, was announced, when the Rebel cavalry hastily mounted, and

---

15 U.S. Census Bureau, Schedule 1 Census in Frederick City, Maryland, Jun 15, 1860, 77; Frederick News, July 31, 1900; Swank, ed., *Sabres, Saddles, and Spurs*, 13. Carter makes it clear that the 3rd Virginia Cavalry remained close to Frederick until early September 12. The owner of the mill could have been Elias Delashmutt, Jr., but this is not confirmed. By 1873, and possibly as early as 1868, Delashmutt had sold the mill to John S. Ramsburg, who used it as a bone mill to manufacture fertilizer from slaughterhouse waste; see Thomas J. C. Williams and Folger McKinsey, *History of Frederick County*, 2 vols. (Hagerstown, MD, 1910), 2:753.

prepared for departure. At 5 o'clock a messenger rode up to the Rebel General Stuart, who was with his cavalry near the railroad depot, and informed him that he heard the Federal column was entering the city by the Baltimore turnpike. He immediately sent an order to Colonel Hampton, of the Hampton Legion, to attack the head of the advancing Federal column, which was done directly in the streets of Frederick." Frederick's rail depot at the time stood on the west side of Augustine O'Leary's property south of the city. It was, in fact, directly adjacent to O'Leary's property, suggesting that a local bystander witnessed Stuart receiving the message about Cox's force and then giving Wade Hampton the attack order.[16]

Seventh, and finally, Catherine Markell revealed in her diary that Jeb Stuart knew the O'Leary family. Writing on September 12 that General Stuart "dined here" during the afternoon before the Confederate cavalry retreated through Frederick in the face of advancing Federal IX Corps troops, Markell noted that "the O'Leary's were there." An entry in Markell's diary from four days earlier confirms that these were the same O'Learys who hosted Jeb Stuart and at least a portion of his command on their farm. "Captain Green of North Carolina, Captain Drish, Major Kennedy. Major McIntosh of South Carolina here also," recorded Markell. "Martha O'Leary gave her pretty gold necklace to Captain Green in exchange for his sleeve buttons. She never saw him again."

As is noted above, Augustine O'Leary had a twenty-four-year-old daughter named Martha living with him. The O'Leary's Confederate sympathies are confirmed by an entry in the diary of Jacob Engelbrecht, another local Fredericktonian, albeit a Union man, noting that Jerome O'Leary, the oldest son of Augustine O'Leary according to the 1860 census, "left town following the [Rebel] army towards Hagerstown" as a new recruit on September 11. These seven pieces of evidence support the conclusion that the pro-Confederate O'Leary family hosted the headquarters of Jeb Stuart, including his large entourage, a part of Wade Hampton's command, and at least the 3rd Virginia Cavalry of Fitz Lee's command, on the southern end of their farm on the night of September 11-12.[17]

Establishing the total number of men included in this mix cannot be worked out with complete accuracy. It is possible, however, to arrive at an informed estimate. Research on Stuart's staff completed by Robert Trout, for example, leads

---

16 *Washington Evening Star*, Sept. 15, 1862.

17 Markell, "Frederick Maryland in Peace and War," 107-108; William R. Quynn, ed., *The Diary of Jacob Engelbrecht, 1840-1882* (Frederick, MD, 2001), 949; U.S. Census Bureau, Schedule 1 Census in Frederick City, Maryland, Jun 15, 1860, 77.

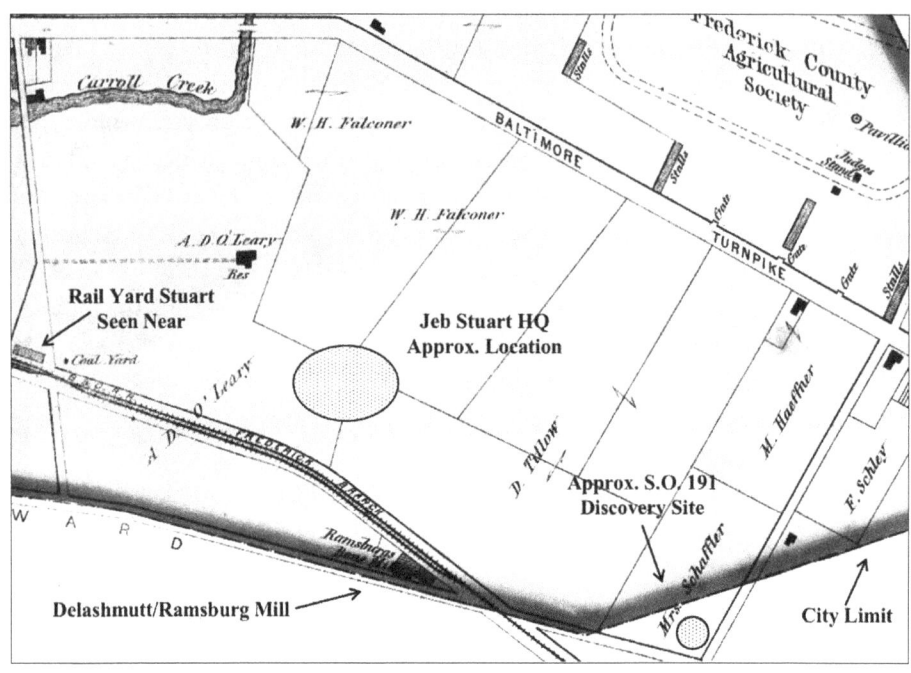

An edited excerpt from pages 52-53 of D. J. Lake's 1873 *Atlas of Frederick County Maryland* showing the approximate site of Maj. Gen. Jeb Stuart's headquarters overnight from Sept. 11 to 12. Seven pieces of evidence put Stuart's headquarters on or close to this spot. The proximity to the place where Barton Mitchell probably discovered the Lost Orders is unmistakable.

D. J. Lake, Alexander B. Rossino

---

to the conclusion that 18 or so officers served with Stuart's headquarters in September 1862. This figure does not count teamsters, enslaved persons, and other supporting staff, so the actual size of Stuart's entourage could have been much larger. As for the 3rd Virginia Cavalry, one estimate of its strength at the end of August 1862 puts 223 men in its ranks. Combining these two estimates leads to the conclusion that as many as 300 men with Stuart's command may have camped overnight on the O'Leary farm on September 11. Identifying O'Leary's farm as Stuart's headquarters is important because it means that Stuart, carrying a copy of Special Orders No. 191, camped with a portion of his command only a short distance from the intersection of East South Street and Franklin Street where

Barton Mitchell is presumed to have found the lost copy. Can this be a coincidence?[18]

If Jeb Stuart lost Lee's orders, two questions need to be answered. The first is why he was carrying a copy addressed to D. H. Hill and not to himself. The second is how he lost them. Concerning D. H. Hill's name on the lost copy, Chapter Four recounts how Lee considered Hill's division subordinate to Stonewall Jackson until Wednesday, September 10. It was only when the army marched out that day that Hill's command became formally detached. Lee, therefore, ordered a copy of paragraphs III through X of the orders made for Hill, but since Jackson had already sent Hill a copy, and probably communicated that to army headquarters, the extra, now unneeded, copy for Hill remained in the adjutant's tent until someone such as Jeb Stuart took them. The possibility also exists that someone at army headquarters sent the Hill copy to Jackson. That copy then remained at Jackson's headquarters until the unidentified individual picked them up and took them with him.

There is evidence to support the assumption that Hill never saw the copy of Special Orders No. 191 made for him at Lee's headquarters. Seeking to clear his name after the war, Hill pursued an investigation of his own by writing to the former members of Lee's staff for any information they might possess concerning the incident. Colonel Robert H. Chilton, whose signature allegedly appears at the bottom of the lost document, was one of these men. Chilton responded to a letter from Hill in June 1867 by writing that no one noticed anything had gone awry when the orders were distributed. "This order was . . . marked confidential," claimed the colonel, and "sent to the Major Genls of the army by couriers, whose standing orders were to bring back . . . some written evidence of delivery. This order was so important, that violation of this rule would have been noticed, and I think I should certainly recollect [if] its delivery had been omitted in any case."[19]

---

18 Robert J. Trout, *They Followed The Plume: The Story of J.E. B. Stuart and His Staff* (Mechanicsburg, PA, 1993), 328-329; John Owen Allen, "The Strength of the Union and Confederate Forces at Second Manassas," Unpublished Master's Thesis, George Mason University (Fairfax, VA, 1993), 184. According to a witness in Frederick, Stuart's command included a large number of wagons and livestock, supporting the idea of a relatively large encampment on the O'Leary farm: "[Sept. 11] There is a great noise tonight and rumors of Stuart's cavalry preparing to leave. Wagon's rumbling through the streets mingled with the lowing of the cattle they take with them"; Ann R. L. Schaeffer, *Records of the Past: Civil War Diary, September 4-23, 1862* (Frederick, MD, no date).

19 Robert H. Chilton to Daniel Harvey Hill, June 27, 1867, in D. H. Hill Papers #2035-z, Southern Historical Collection, The Wilson Library, University of North Carolina at Chapel Hill.

Hill also wrote to Charles Marshall. Marshall echoed Chilton's memory in his reply dated November 11, 1867. Writing that orders "were sent out by orderlies who were required in cases of moment to bring back the envelopes or some other receipts from the officers to whom they were sent," Marshall added, "If a copy of the order in question was addressed to you, we had nothing to call our attention to any irregularity in its transmission, nor did we ever suspect that there had been, until we learned what had taken place from McClellan's report."[20]

The process described by Chilton and Marshall makes it reasonable to conclude that D. H. Hill never saw the orders because no one at army headquarters sent them to him. This unneeded copy then sat in the adjutant's tent (or at Jackson's headquarters) until Jeb Stuart arrived on September 9. A staff member either gave Stuart the Hill copy of the orders at that point or he wrote out another copy for the cavalry commander based on the Hill copy. Robert Chilton's "signature" on the lost copy of the orders provides a tantalizing clue that events may have unfolded in the latter direction.

Multiple examples from official documents bearing the colonel's name, including Special Orders No. 190, the two-paragraph copy of Special Orders No. 191, and the final, complete copy of Special Orders No. 191, show that Chilton tended to run together his initials and the first letter of his last name in a single, sweeping scrawl. He never signed documents by printing out those letters separately, and yet the signature on the copy of the orders found by Barton Mitchell displays exactly that characteristic—Chilton's first and middle initials printed out separately in front of his last name.

The reason for this discrepancy is easy to explain. Chilton did not sign the document. An analysis of the handwriting (see Appendix A) leads instead to the conclusion that Lee's military secretary, Col. Armistead L. Long, probably wrote out the lost copy, including Chilton's signature. Why Long would have copied the order originally written out for Hill is a mystery. We know only from an analysis of the handwriting that it appears to match Long's penmanship from other documents he is known to have written. Jeb Stuart could have then procured this copy for his use and gone back to Urbana where he spent the balance of the

---

20 Charles Marshall to Daniel Harvey Hill, Nov. 11, 1867, in D. H. Hill Papers, Accession 32032, Barcode 5627792, Location 4/B/21/1/5, Box 4, Folder 11, Library of Virginia, Richmond, VA.

afternoon lounging on the porch of the Cockey house enjoying cigars with Heros von Borcke.[21]

Explaining from this point how Jeb Stuart could have lost the orders is relatively straightforward. The sources show that pressure from the Army of the Potomac grew to such an extent on September 11 that it forced Stuart to withdraw his command from the New Market—Urbana—Barnesville line to a new defensive position on the west bank of the Monocacy River. They also confirm that upon reaching the vicinity of Frederick, Stuart ordered Wade Hampton to position some of his cavalry on the National Road east of the city and some at Monocacy Junction where the Georgetown Pike crosses the river. Stuart then retired to his new headquarters on the farm of Augustine D. O'Leary.[22]

Now for the speculative part of the scenario. After waking on the next morning, Friday, September 12, Stuart could have used the orders to wrap up and secure the two cigars given to him in Urbana by S. G. Cockey before he rode out to check his line. The most direct route for Stuart to take to Monocacy Junction, where Hampton had posted two squadrons of cavalry from Cobb's Legion, entailed riding across the meadowland owned by O'Leary, Titlow, and Anna Schaffler to the Ijamsville Road. This route would have taken Stuart directly past the spot where Barton Mitchell found the dropped orders.[23]

The key feature here is the B&O rail spur leading out of Frederick. The Ijamsville Road and the B&O spur line run roughly parallel until the railroad diverges south to Monocacy Junction. This rail bed would have provided Stuart

---

[21] Chilton's signature being a forgery means Brig. Gen. Alpheus Williams's Assistant Adjutant General, Lt. Samuel E. Pittman, stated incorrectly that he recognized Chilton's signature from having done business with him in Detroit before the war. Williams took Pittman at his word and ordered the document sent to McClellan with the following note on the reverse side: "General, I enclose a General Special Order of Gen. Lee commanding Rebel Army which was found on the field where my corps is encamped. It is a document of interest & is no doubt genuine." Thomas G. Clemens confirms that "Pittman never served with Chilton [because he] did not join the U.S. military until [after] Chilton had resigned"; see Carman, . . . *The Maryland Campaign of September 1862*, 1:279-280n5. Pittman may have known Chilton from other connections outside of the army, but this is not clear. Whatever the case may have been, McClellan acted on information of dubious authenticity, which was a bold move on his part.

[22] According to David Waldhauer, "The Affair at Frederick City: A Correction of General Johnson's Account," in *SHSP*, Vol. 13 (Richmond, VA, 1885), 417-418: "When General Hampton came along after the brigade had passed, he, in person, ordered me to gather my men and take the rear. It was sharp work from that time, for a squadron of the Second South Carolina, that had been on picket at the Monocacy Bridge, retreated hastily through the city."

[23] OR 19:1, 815; Von Borcke, *Memoirs*, 1:200; Harriet Bey Mesic, *Cobb's Legion Cavalry: A History and Roster of the Ninth Georgia Volunteers in the Civil War* (Jefferson, NC, 2011), 22.

with the most direct route to Hampton's men, whom Stuart admitted in his campaign report "it was of great importance" to withdraw as enemy columns approached on the National Road that afternoon. After visiting the troopers at Monocacy Junction, Stuart would have then needed to travel back up the B&O spur line and Ijamsville Road to return to Hampton's command guarding the National Road. The words "back up" are used here because if Stuart had first traveled south to the Junction, then this is the route he would have known to take.

Stuart riding north from the Junction would have once again carried him past his headquarters, where he could stop if it was necessary. The Ijamsville Road also leads to Franklin Street, which runs a short distance to the National Road. This scenario suggests that Stuart could have ridden past the location where Mitchell found the lost orders at least twice on the morning of September 12. At some point during one of these rides the orders, probably stuffed into a vest or coat pocket where they did not fit properly (perhaps because of the cigars), could have been jarred loose by the gait of Stuart's horse and fallen out. They then landed in the tall grass on the roadside where Cpl. Mitchell found them.[24]

In addition, there is evidence at least some of Stuart's men knew about the road from Urbana to Frederick that passed through Ijamsville to Crum's Ford across the Monocacy River. According to the diary of a trooper named Harvey Davis, he and his comrades in Company D of the 1st North Carolina Cavalry left Urbana, "On the 11th . . . and passed Ijamsville on the B&O R[ailroad] and went to Frederick City, Md." Presumably, Jeb Stuart took the Georgetown Pike from Urbana to Frederick, but the possibility also exists that he may have traveled the route through Ijamsville. If he did, it suggests that Stuart took the Ijamsville Road to Frederick from Crum's Ford, providing yet another opportunity for the orders to fall from his pocket or saddlebag in the vicinity of where Mitchell found them.[25]

The rain on September 11 is potentially important in this context. Referred to by Von Borcke as steady, J. P. Rawl of the 2nd South Carolina confided in a letter that this was no light shower: "We arrived at Frederick, a small town where we

---

24 Stuart ended up back in Frederick City for more socializing that afternoon; see Markell, "Frederick Maryland in Peace and War," 108. "12th. Fred left on Billy this morning for Hagerstown. Generals Jeb Stuart, Fitz Lee, Wade Hampton, and all their aids with Dr. Davis Thompson, dined here." A search of all the available sources did not turn up information confirming Stuart riding to Monocacy Junction the morning of September 12. OR 19:1, 815, 822.

25 Francis B. Dedmond, "Harvey Davis's Unpublished Civil War 'Diary' and the Story of Company D of the First North Carolina Cavalry," in *Appalachian Journal*, Vol. 13, No. 4 (Summer 1986), 391.

Who Lost Lee's Orders? | 95

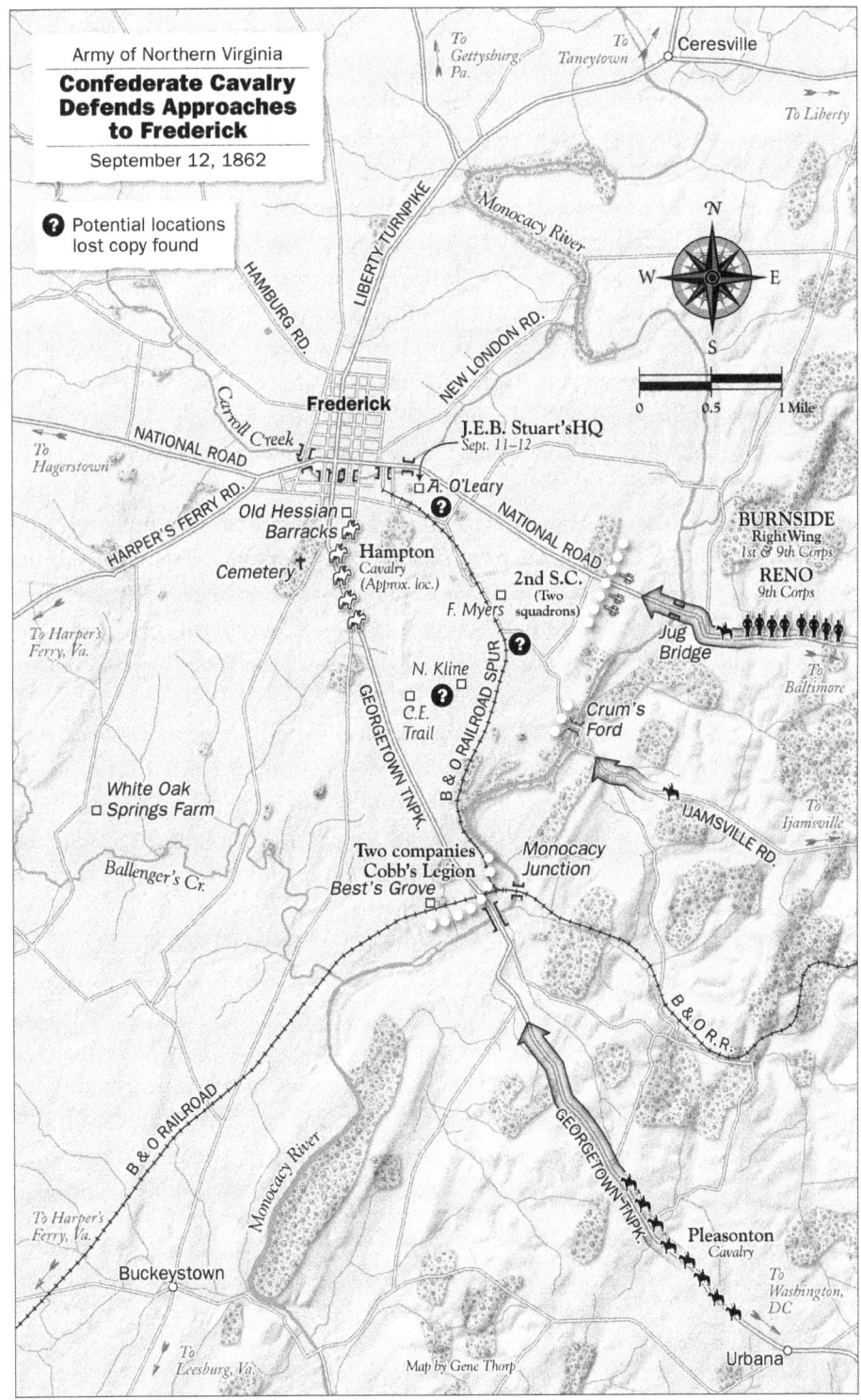

remained during the night," wrote Rawl. "Our bed was in the cornrows, and the downpour of rain ran around our sides." It rained heavily overnight from September 11 to September 12, therefore, and yet there is no sign of water damage on the lost copy of the orders given to McClellan. Why this is the case can be explained in three ways. Either the locust tree, shrubs, and bushes near which the orders were found protected the paper from saturation; the paper used for the orders proved to be resilient to water; or the carrier of the document dropped them after the downpour had stopped. The orders then lay in the grass for approximately twenty-four hours before Barton Mitchell found them on September 13.[26]

The possibility that Jeb Stuart may have lost Lee's orders is stunning to consider. Of all the men in the Army of Northern Virginia it was Stuart who best understood the importance of guarding critical information. Longstanding confusion about where Barton Mitchell found the orders, as well as D. H. Hill's name on the document, has led researchers to look at other suspects and in other directions than Jeb Stuart. It was the rollicking Confederate cavalier, however, who had ready access to Lee's headquarters, making it easy for him to take a copy of the orders, even if that copy was originally addressed to D. H. Hill. Identifying the location of Stuart's Frederick headquarters as the O'Leary farm then places the general—and a copy of Special Orders No. 191—in the same meadow where Mitchell probably found the document.

What is more, Stuart seems to have occasionally smoked cigars. The historical record shows that he enjoyed one with Heros von Borcke and S. G. Cockey in Urbana before ordering his command's retreat to Frederick. This makes it reasonable to suggest that Cockey gave Stuart the two cigars found wrapped in the orders as a parting gift when the general left his house. Stuart put the cigars in the orders for safekeeping. He then lost both the orders and the stogies due to carelessness, a hole in his pocket, or just plain bad luck. That Barton Mitchell found them in the out of the way place where they were dropped is nothing short of a miracle.

The scenario outlined above does not prove that Jeb Stuart lost the errant copy of Special Orders No. 191. It does, however, provide an informed hypothesis based upon the facts: that Stuart had the means to have procured Hill's copy of the orders, had a reason to be carrying a copy of the orders, and had situated his Frederick headquarters close to the spot where Cpl. Mitchell found the dropped

---

26 J. P. Rawl, "Maryland Raid," in United Daughters of the Confederacy, eds., *Recollections and Reminiscences 1861-1865 through World War I*, 12 vols. (Charleston, SC, 2001), 11:180.

document. Jeb Stuart is the only senior commander whose movements in the days immediately before September 13 fit the location where the orders were discovered.

Stuart's conduct late on September 13 is also curious if it is examined in this context. Well after dark, Stuart sent Lee a message about a "gentleman of Maryland" having been present when McClellan received a paper that caused him to throw his hands in the air and exclaim, "Now I know what to do!" This civilian then allegedly rode through Federal lines to report the event to the Confederate army.

The truthfulness of this story is suspect. It is, for one thing, not confirmed by any other contemporary source—Federal or Confederate. Lee does not mention the incident in his campaign report, for example, which is a point worth dwelling on because the general did report a remarkably similar occurrence during the Gettysburg campaign.

Writing of that latter incident, "information was received from a scout that the Federal Army, having crossed the Potomac, was advancing northward," Lee referred to Henry T. Harrison, a spy employed by James Longstreet to gather intelligence. Lee, according to Longstreet, declined to see Harrison after sentries brought him to army headquarters. He also "expressed [a] want of faith in [the] reports of scouts" until Longstreet convinced Lee to listen to the man. The fact that Lee would recall this incident during the Gettysburg Campaign in an official document, but not its equivalent during the Maryland Campaign, seems incongruous.27

Stuart also did not mention the helpful citizen in his campaign report. This is very curious for such an unusual and, one would think, significant event. Comparing Stuart's situation in 1862 with Longstreet's in 1863 brings into sharp

---

27 Freeman, *Lee's Lieutenants*, 2:718, 721. Lee also described the incident in a letter to D. H. Hill that he wrote the week after making the comments to Edward Gordon and William Allan that are described by Freeman: "Early on the morning of the 14th inst. at Hagerstown a dispatch from him (i.e., Stuart) stating that he had fallen back to the South Mountains; that Genl. McClellan was pressing forward on the roads to Boonsborough and Rohrersville gaps, and that he had learned from a citizen of Maryland, that he was in possession of the order directing the movement of our troops"; Lee to Hill, Feb. 21, 1868, D. H. Hill Papers #2035-z, SHC, UNC. Ezra Carman mentioned the incident in his then unpublished history of the campaign, but by the 1890s William Allan's earlier writing about it was already well known; see Carman, *The Maryland Campaign of September 1862*, 1:293. OR 27:2, 307; also see *Edward P. Alexander, Military Memoirs of a Confederate: A Critical Narrative* (New York, NY, 1907), 230; Longstreet, *From Manassas to Appomattox*, 346-347; Harsh, *Sounding the Shallows*, 168-175 contains a long discussion of this incident.

relief the differences between how each man handled the events. Writing in his Gettysburg Campaign report, "On the night of the 28th, one of my scouts came in with information that the enemy had passed the Potomac, and was probably in pursuit of us," Longstreet thought Harrison's arrival important enough to cite. Jeb Stuart allegedly had a similar experience, but unlike Longstreet he concluded that his civilian source did not merit a mention in his report. Add to this the fact that none of Stuart's staff commented on the "gentleman of Maryland" in any of their writings, either. Lieutenant Price did not refer to a visit by a civilian in any of his letters during the campaign; Heros von Borcke did not describe the incident in his 1866 memoir; William Blackford, another of Stuart's aides, did not comment on a civilian visiting camp; and John Esten Cooke never mentioned it in his numerous postwar publications.[28]

A unique occurrence such as this deserved at least a single line. This is particularly the case because a civilian should not have been able to simply walk up to the tent of a major general without being challenged by a sentry or a member of the general's staff. There is no record of such a challenge happening. Once again it is worth comparing this incident to the arrival of Henry Harrison at Longstreet's headquarters in June of 1863. According to Old Pete,

> A young man had been arrested by our outlying pickets under suspicious circumstances. He was looking for General Longstreet's head-quarters, but his comfortable apparel and well-to-do, though travel-stained, appearance caused doubt in the minds of the guards of his being a genuine Confederate who could be trusted about head-quarters. So he was sent up under a file of men to be identified. He proved to be Harrison, the valued scout. He had walked through the lines of the Union army during the night of the 27th and the 28th, secured a mount at dark of the latter day to get in as soon as possible, and brought information of the location of two corps of Federals at night of the 27th, and approximate positions of others.

Neither Stuart nor his staff described anything like this, which is highly perplexing unless we consider the possibility that Stuart may have contrived the tale to alert Lee to the threat generated by the loss of the orders without admitting his responsibility. Writing a private note that he sealed and sent to Lee via courier

---

28 William Allan and Edward C. Gordon, Feb. 15, 1868, in Freeman, *Lee's Lieutenants*, 2:718, 721; *OR* 27:2, 358.

would have allowed Stuart to implement the scheme without anyone else knowing about it, hence the lack of corroborating information from the general or his staff.[29]

The behavior of George McClellan described by the "gentleman of Maryland" is also suspect. McClellan knew by noon on September 13 that Lee's army occupied Middletown Valley and the Cumberland Valley beyond it. He also knew that Southern troops had been seen crossing back into (West) Virginia at Williamsport and that no Confederate force had entered Pennsylvania. This left only Washington County, Maryland, and the western portion of Frederick County, as the places where Lee's army could be found. McClellan did not know that Lee had split his forces, nor did he know the strength of the Confederates around Harpers Ferry, but he did suspect that Lee was threatening the ferry because General-in-Chief Henry Halleck had given him command over the cut-off garrison on September 12.

Informed that Col. Miles had been out of telegraphic communication since one day earlier, Little Mac immediately ordered Alfred Pleasonton to send riders toward the ferry firing their guns every so often to alert the garrison to their approach. This act suggests that McClellan knew Harpers Ferry was in danger even before the lost copy of Special Orders No. 191 confirmed it. Having known this at the time there was little reason for McClellan to have shouted "Now I know what to do!" upon reading the document.[30]

McClellan also understood the need for operational security, and there is no record of him discussing the lost copy of Special Orders No. 191 with anyone immediately around him on September 13 other than Brig. Gen. John Gibbon, who visited army headquarters late in the day. During that conversation, recounted Gibbon after the war, "General McClellan expressed himself freely in regard to his movements and taking from his pocket a folded paper, he said: 'Here is a paper with which if I cannot whip 'Bobbie Lee,' I will be willing to go home.' He spoke

---

29 Longstreet, *From Manassas to Appomattox*, 346-347. A member of Longstreet's staff did write about the Harrison incident: "At night I was roused by a detail of the provost guard bringing up a suspicious prisoner. I knew him instantly; it was Harrison, the scout, filthy and ragged, showing some rough work and exposure. He had come to 'Report to the General, who was sure to be with the army,' and truly his report was long and valuable. I should here say that in every respect it was afterwards fully confirmed by events and facts"; G. Moxley Sorrel, *Recollections of a Confederate Staff Officer* (New York, NY, 1905), 164.

30 The War Department received the last telegram from Miles, timestamped 1:50 p.m., on Sept. 11. President Lincoln noted in a telegram to McClellan sent at 5:45 p.m. on Sept. 12 that the War Department had received "nothing from Harper's Ferry or Martinsburg to-day"; See OR 19:2, 266, 270. For a detailed discussion of what McClellan knew before noon on Sept. 13 see Thorp & Rossino, *The Tale Untwisted*, Chapters Two and Three.

cheerfully and confidently and added, 'I will not show you the document now but there (turning down one of the folds) is the signature (showing 'R. H. Chilton Adjt. Gen.') and it gives the movement of every division of Lee's Army."[31]

If McClellan would not show the document to a trusted friend, or discuss it in any detail after revealing he possessed it, how likely is it that he would have yelped enthusiastically to a collection of staff officers and a visiting stranger about reading the orders earlier in the day? The answer is unlikely. It is even less likely that such an incident would have gone unnoticed. The Army of the Potomac leaked information like a sieve. Reports containing damning details about anti-administration talk among senior officers, for example, appeared routinely in print throughout the campaign. Few secrets, no matter how sensitive, remained undisclosed for long.

Indeed, newspapermen traveling with the army learned about the discovery of Lee's orders only a short time after it occurred. This is no surprise as one publication alone, the *New York Herald*, had embedded reporters with the army's main headquarters and five of its corps headquarters. Predictably, then, the *Herald* published a column dated September 14—less than 24 hours after the orders' discovery—which stated, "Officers who left Frederick this morning report that a general order of General Lee was found there." The September 15 edition of the *Washington Evening Star* added even more detail, writing, "A member of Colonel Colgrove's regiment found a paper purporting to be Rebel order No. 119." Neither of these reports mentioned McClellan shouting with glee upon receiving the document even though the correspondents involved surely would have included that detail had they learned about it. That is unless it never happened.[32]

McClellan's alleged reaction to reading Lee's orders is so out of character for the general that it is quite unbelievable. What is more, given the flow of information at the time, and the importance of the event, it seems improbable that any of the staff present would have let such a dramatic incident pass without later mentioning it in a letter or memoir, particularly after multiple newspapers publicized it. Add to

---

31 McClellan did mention the orders in his telegraphic communications with the War Department in Washington, DC; John Gibbon, *Personal Recollections of the Civil War* (New York, NY, 1928), 73.

32 *Washington Evening Star*, Sept. 15, 1862; *New York Herald*, Sept. 15, 1862. The *Herald's* column is dated Sept. 14. *The Baltimore Sun*, Sept. 16, 1862, also published the *Star's* account, but added even more details, including a summary of Lee's directive for the army to reassemble at Hagerstown following the surrender of Harpers Ferry. For the names of the reporters embedded with the army see Louis M. Starr, *Bohemian Brigade: Civil War Newsmen in Action* (New York, NY, 1954), 136.

this the failure of a swarm of Northern reporters to learn about McClellan shouting "Now I know what to do!" and the truthfulness of Stuart's tale becomes dubious. The circumstances surrounding the event strongly suggest that Stuart contrived the story. The question, if he did, is why.[33]

Situated near Boonsboro on the night of September 13, Stuart likely received word of the enemy's campfires spread across Middletown Valley, on the eastern side of South Mountain. This confirmed that McClellan had pursued him in force and stood poised to strike D. H. Hill's command the next morning. Interpreted from the perspective of Stuart losing Special Orders No. 191, it is easy to envision him worrying that the document he mislaid had somehow made its way into the Federal commander's hands. Stuart then fretted about his blunder and may have felt it necessary to fabricate the story of the Maryland gentleman so that he could warn Lee without disclosing his responsibility for the orders' loss. This would explain why Stuart's note reached Lee at nearly the same time as D. H. Hill's alarming report about the presence of a heavy enemy force on his front. McClellan's aggressive advance confirmed Stuart's suspicion that the Federal commander had seen Lee's lost plans.[34]

The evidence that Jeb Stuart may have lost Lee's orders is circumstantial. There is, however, more of this circumstantial evidence for his culpability than there is for any other individual in the Army of Northern Virginia, so the possibility that he lost the orders must be taken seriously. At the very least, Stuart had the means to both procure the document and the opportunity to lose it ahead of the Army of the Potomac's occupation of Frederick. The same cannot be said for any other senior officer in Lee's army. This does not make Jeb Stuart the man who lost the orders, but it does make him the most promising suspect, particularly if one applies the same standard of proof to Stuart's culpability that has been applied to D. H. Hill's over the years.

It is a low bar. Silas Colgrove claimed that his men found the lost orders at the campsite of Hill's division, and so investigators of the incident have routinely declared Hill guilty of the document's loss. This is despite a lack of corroborating evidence that Hill's division had camped at that location. Jeb Stuart's name is not on the orders, but sufficient evidence exists to show that his headquarters group,

---

33 Stuart making up the story about the "gentleman of Maryland" also could be what lay behind Lee's 1868 comment that after hearing about the orders' loss during the war, "Genl. Stuart and other officers in the army were very indignant about the matter"; Freeman, *Lee's Lieutenants,* 2:719.

34 Harsh, *Taken at the Flood,* 248.

and at least one regiment of his cavalry, did camp within shouting distance of where Barton Mitchell found the orders and their mysterious cigars. If the proximity of a campsite can be counted as evidence for one general's guilt then it is only right to apply it to the other.

Chapter 7

The Importance of the Lost Orders to Wrecking Confederate Operations in Maryland

Debate about the importance of the loss of Special Orders No. 191 to the outcome of the Maryland Campaign has long revolved around the response of Maj. Gen. George B. McClellan to reading the discovered document. To those in agreement with the thesis proposed by Stephen W. Sears, the Lost Orders provided McClellan with potentially war-winning intelligence that he squandered through excessive indecision. Conversely, to those who prefer the interpretation of Joseph L. Harsh, McClellan gained little useful information in the orders, particularly because the Federal commander had already begun pushing troops west from Frederick in pursuit of Lee's army before the document passed into his hands.[1]

The merits of these arguments notwithstanding, neither takes into account the impact that McClellan's actions had on Confederate operations from September 14 onward. When considered from this point of view, it becomes clear that his assault on the South Mountain gaps had three significant effects: it ruined Lee's plan for the campaign after the capture of Harpers Ferry; it forced Lee to take up a less than favorable *ad hoc* defensive position at Sharpsburg; and it weakened the Army of Northern Virginia's combat strength in the days leading up to the clash there on September 16-17.

---

1 Stephen W. Sears, *Landscape Turned Red: The Battle of Antietam* (Boston, MA, 1983), 114-118; Sears, *George B. McClellan: The Young Napoleon* (New York, NY, 1988), 280-284; Harsh, *Taken at the Flood*, 241; Stotelmyer, *Too Useful to Sacrifice*, 11-12.

104 | *Calamity at Frederick*

Early morning march
September 14, 1862
3 a.m. to noon

Cavalry regiment
Infantry brigade

Map by Gene Thorp

According to Paragraph IX of Special Orders No. 191, Lee desired that following the fall of the Federal garrison at Harpers Ferry, "The commands of Generals Jackson, McLaws, and Walker, after accomplishing the objects for which

The Importance of the Lost Orders

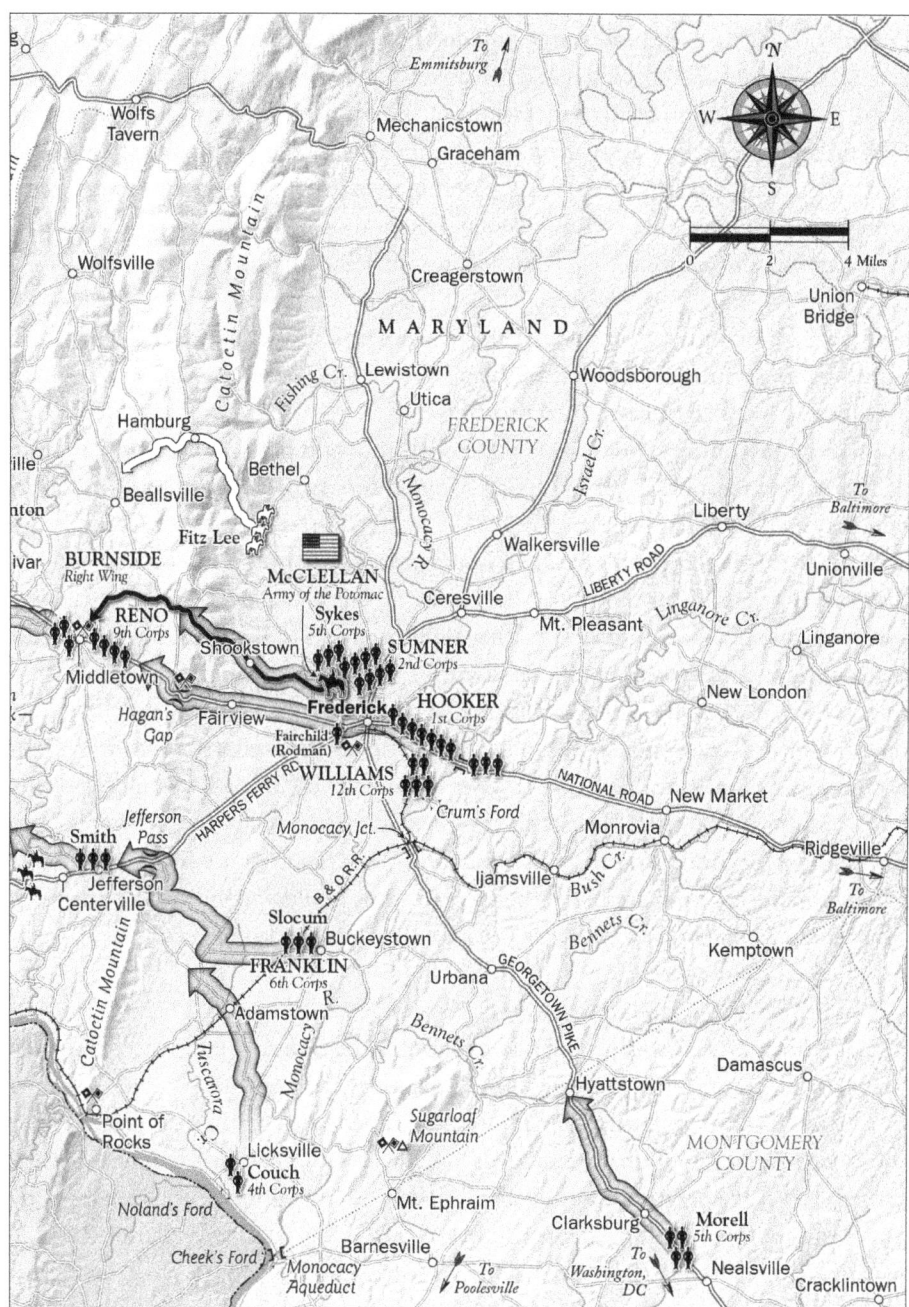

they have been detached, will join the main body of the army at Boonsborough or Hagerstown." Why Lee envisioned reassembling his army in the middle of Washington County, Maryland, is explained by his overall strategy for waging war in the state. After initially seeking to instigate a popular rebellion north of the

Potomac River, Lee learned from Confederate sympathizers in Frederick City that it was likely no uprising would take place until martial law in the state had been lifted. The arrest of prominent secessionists and the seizure of private property by Federal authorities had convinced those aligned with the South that they could never successfully resist the national government's occupation forces unless Lee's army could defend them. The general noted this belief in his August 1863 campaign report, writing, "The difficulties that surrounded them [Maryland's secessionists] were fully appreciated . . . [and] we expected to derive more assistance . . . from the just fears of the Washington Government than from any active demonstration on the part of the people, unless success should enable us to give them assurance of continued protection."[2]

A second source echoes Lee's statement, this one penned by a British army officer named Garnet Joseph Wolseley. Visiting the Army of Northern Virginia in mid-October 1862, Wolseley wrote, "It is generally stated that the Confederate authorities calculated upon a rising in Maryland directly [when] their army entered that state. Everybody to whom I spoke on the subject ridiculed the idea . . . that any such rising would take place, until either Baltimore was in their hands, or they had at least established a position in that country." Wolseley's comment confirms two things. First, it reinforces the conclusion that the policy of entering Maryland to test the strength of secessionist sentiment came from "Confederate authorities" in Richmond. This means that Robert E. Lee did not act on his own when he took his army across the Potomac. He was carrying out an official policy of the Confederate government. Second, Wolseley's comment makes it clear that many of the officers with whom he spoke shared Lee's belief their army could encourage an uprising in Maryland only if it won a victory (i.e., "established a position in the country") or if it marched on Baltimore.[3]

In response to the reluctance of Maryland's people to rise up, Lee took steps to reassure those who might be inclined to support the South. He instructed Charles Marshall to compose a proclamation explaining the reasons for the Army of Northern Virginia's presence in the state and, after learning on September 8 that the Federal garrison remained in place at Harpers Ferry, he designed Special Orders No. 191 to capture it. Lee also learned on September 8 that a new army under the command of McClellan had begun advancing toward Frederick. In view

---

2 OR 19:2, 604 and OR 19:1, 144.

3 James A. Rawley, ed., *The American Civil War: An English View. The Writings of Field Marshal Viscount Wolseley* (Mechanicsburg, PA, 2002), 32.

of this oncoming threat, Lee hoped that Jackson and the others detached for the operation could quickly seize the ferry and then rejoin Longstreet's command for a decisive battle with McClellan's force. A slight alteration Lee made to this plan on September 11 included marching a portion of the army toward Hagerstown (and Pennsylvania) to "induce the enemy to follow" west of South Mountain. This maneuver substantiated a statement attributed to Lee that appeared in the September 12 issue of the *Philadelphia Inquirer* which held that "the battle ground must hereafter be in Maryland" if the state's people failed to rebel.[4]

Once he arrived west of South Mountain, Lee intended to confront McClellan on ground of his choosing. There he could crush the Army of the Potomac far from the protection of the Washington defenses and achieve the potentially war-ending victory that had eluded him at Second Manassas. Lee therefore chose the heights along a small watercourse called Beaver Creek as his preferred battleground. Anchored in the southwest by rough terrain along Antietam Creek, and ranging as tall as 560 feet in elevation, this undulating ridge line runs east-northeast nearly to the base of South Mountain. The Beaver Creek heights offered Lee a strong position that would be difficult, although not impossible, for an enemy to flank if it was occupied by a determined defender.

Multiple sources confirm the general's desire to defend the Beaver Creek line. These include a dispatch Lee sent to Maj. Gen. Lafayette McLaws on the evening of September 13, after he learned from D. H. Hill that a powerful enemy column had appeared at the eastern foot of South Mountain. Telling McLaws, "General Longstreet will move down [from Hagerstown] to-morrow," Lee added that Longstreet's men would "take position on Beaver Creek this side of Boonsborough."[5]

On the following morning, according to the war reminiscences of Angela Kirkham Davis, a New York-born woman residing in Funkstown, Maryland, Lee issued a warning to the people of her village, located some four miles behind Beaver Creek. Lee advised them to flee from the fight he believed was about to take place in their midst. Then Lee spoke to his artillery chief, Brig. Gen. William N. Pendleton, about the Beaver Creek position later that day. Pendleton recalled this in his campaign report, stating that on "Sunday morning, 14th, we were summoned to return toward Boonsborough, the enemy having advanced upon General D. H.

---

4 OR 19:2, 601-602, 605; OR 19, 1:145; *Philadelphia Inquirer*, Sept. 12, 1862. For more details see Rossino, "Lee's Beaver Creek Plan," in *North & South*, Series II, Vol. 3, No. 1 (June 2022).

5 OR 19:2, 607.

Hill. When I arrived and reported to you [General Lee] a short distance from the battle-field, you directed me to place in position on the heights of Beaver Creek the several batteries of my command." Pendleton's report demonstrates that even as the Battle of South Mountain raged Lee hoped to fall back to his chosen position along Beaver Creek.[6]

Sources also show that contrary to claims made by Lee and Longstreet after the campaign about departing from Hagerstown at daybreak to reinforce Hill at South Mountain, Longstreet's reduced command of eight brigades (Brig. Gen. Robert Toombs's brigade remained at Hagerstown) and the independent brigade of Brig. Gen. Nathan "Shanks" Evans did not get on the road until after the fighting at South Mountain began around 8:00 a.m. Lee clinging stubbornly to his Beaver Creek plan would account for this delay because, as the general himself later wrote, "It had not been intended to oppose its [the Federal army's] passage through the South Mountains, as it was desired to engage it as far as possible from its base."[7]

McClellan's army "advancing more rapidly than was convenient from Fredericktown," wrecked these plans for Lee by forcing him to defend the South Mountain passes. Doing so placed the Confederate commander in a difficult position. Unfamiliar with the terrain atop the mountain, and too disabled by injuries incurred during an accident at the end of August to ride a horse, Lee could not personally direct his army's defense of the mountain passes. The situation five miles south at Crampton's Gap proved even more headache-inducing as its defense remained entirely beyond the general's control. Consequently, three major outcomes resulted from McClellan using the information he learned in the Lost Orders. He attacked the South Mountain gaps, he forced Lee to abandon the favorable defensive position he had chosen, and he compelled Lee to defend ground on South Mountain that the Confederate general neither knew nor planned on defending in the first place.[8]

The rapidity of McClellan's unexpected advance knocked Lee off balance. Not only did the defeat at South Mountain then force Lee to fall back in the direction of

---

6 Letter of Angela K. Davis in S. Roger Keller, *Crossroads of War: Washington County, Maryland, in the Civil War* (Shippensburg, PA, 1997), 25; OR 19:1, 830; also see David G. Martin, *The Fluvanna Artillery* (Lynchburg, VA: H. E. Howard, 1992), 49.

7 OR 19, 1:145; also see Alexander B. Rossino, "Confederate Defeat at South Mountain: Robert E. Lee's Moment of Hesitation on the Morning of September 14, 1862," *The Antietam Journal*, Vol. IV (March 2023).

8 Messages from J. E. B. Stuart and D. H. Hill alerting Lee to the Federal advance arrived just after dark on September 13; Freeman, *Lee's Lieutenants*, 2:721; OR 19:1, 140.

Virginia, it also called into question where, or even if, the general could salvage his plan to fight north of the Potomac. After all, Jackson's siege of Harpers Ferry remained underway with Lee ignorant of when it might be concluded. Lee had hoped that Jackson could compel the garrison's surrender by Sunday, September 14, at the latest, but on the morning of September 15 he found himself still oblivious to the operation's progress. For a short time overnight on September 14, Lee even considered returning to Virginia, writing to McLaws after learning of the Federal victory at Crampton's Gap that "The day has gone against us and this army will go by Sharpsburg and cross the river."[9]

Then, at around 8:00 a.m. on September 15, a note from Jackson finally made its way to Lee, stating that he anticipated the enemy would surrender Harpers Ferry in short order. Receiving this note in the vicinity of Keedysville breathed new life into Lee's faltering operation and he quickly sought ground on which to fight the battle he had envisioned fighting at Beaver Creek. This ground he found on the far side of Antietam Creek, and although Lee did not say it the terrain there resembled the Beaver Creek position to a degree. With heights standing as tall as 500 feet above sea level between the creek and Sharpsburg, Lee found a position closer to Jackson in (West) Virginia that was on the flank of Lafayette McLaws's position in Pleasant Valley, and which looked similar to the one he had originally intended to occupy several miles to the north.

Yet unlike the Beaver Creek position, Antietam Creek and the heights in front of Sharpsburg anchored only the center and far right of the Confederate line. Rolling countryside bisected by low ridges and peppered with woodlots characterized the terrain on the Confederate left flank. This ground proved to be defensible, but South Mountain did not hem in the position there as it did along Beaver Creek. Putting numbers to this equation, the distance between the eastern end of the Beaver Creek heights and the western slope of South Mountain near the small community of San Mar is approximately 1,056 yards, or 0.6 miles. This distance equals a battlefront just under three Civil War era brigades in length. North of Sharpsburg, the distance from the creek to farmer David Miller's soon-to-be-immortal cornfield, where the bulk of Maj. Gen. Joseph Hooker's attack fell the morning of September 17, is 2,816 yards, or 1.6 miles. This distance equals a front line more than one division long, meaning McClellan could

---

9 Longstreet, *From Manassas to Appomattox*, 206; also see OR 19:1, 816, and McLaws, "The Maryland Campaign," Rawley, ed., *Wolseley*, 32: "Harper's Ferry . . . held out two days longer than was expected"; OR 51:2, 618-619.

maneuver a larger number of troops against the Confederate left than he would have been able to had Lee managed to defend the Beaver Creek heights. The resulting stand-up fight at Sharpsburg thus proved to be less to the benefit of the smaller, numerically weaker Army of Northern Virginia and more to the advantage of the larger Army of the Potomac.[10]

Fighting at the Beaver Creek position would have also provided Lee with a battlefield accessible by multiple entry and exit points. With only a single road and a rocky ford across the Potomac behind him at Sharpsburg, even Lee himself judged the position to be "a bad one" by comparison. Arguably, therefore, this secondary field on which Lee chose to fight proved to be substantially less favorable to his army and more favorable to the enemy than the position he had initially hoped to take. Although he did not know it, McClellan's attack at South Mountain, informed by what he had learned in Special Orders No. 191, effectively negated the battlefield advantage that Lee had sought to achieve in Washington County.[11]

McClellan's attack on the South Mountain gaps created yet another knock-on effect detrimental to the Army of Northern Virginia—it compelled Lee to reassemble his army before either he or it was prepared. This resulted in a loss of combat strength when the fight at Sharpsburg broke out. The experiences of Longstreet's command on September 14 and, to a lesser extent, of McLaws's command on September 16-17 are instructive here. Informed estimates put Longstreet's effective strength at approximately 7,800 men when his command made its forced march from Hagerstown on the morning of September 14. This march, made mostly on the quick, and even the double-quick (i.e., jogging), proved too taxing for many men to take, particularly those of Old Pete's troops who lacked footwear. Consequently, when Longstreet reached the top of South Mountain, D. H. Hill estimated that his command "did not exceed four thousand men." It is unknown how many of these men later caught up with the army on its march to Sharpsburg, but they were not available for at least the defense of Turner's and Fox's Gaps, clashes that caused significant casualties and resulted in a decisive

---

10 For the combat fronts referenced see Dave Powell, "A Matter of Tactics" (Sept. 3, 2014), *Emerging Civil War*, online at https://emergingcivilwar.com/2014/09/03/ a-matter-of-tactics/.

11 OR 19:1, 142; Lee's decision to fight at what he knew was a bad position also reinforces the argument that he did so in the hope that "military success might afford us an opportunity to aid the citizens of Maryland in any efforts they might be disposed to make to recover their liberties"; OR 19:1, 144.

Confederate reverse. Their experience illustrates the chaos into which McClellan's sudden advance threw the Army of Northern Virginia.[12]

McLaws's situation provides a similar example. Detached from the rest of the army with Richard H. Anderson's division to besiege Harpers Ferry on the Maryland side of the Potomac River, McLaws's division suffered severe losses from straggling in the run-up to Sharpsburg. According to one strength estimate provided by John Owen Allen, 7,337 men comprised the four brigades of McLaws's division as of September 2. By September 13, this number had dropped to an estimated 3,778 men available for duty, meaning that while in Maryland, and even before the engagement at Crampton's Gap on the following day, 48.5% of McLaws's men had abandoned the army.[13]

The fights atop Maryland Heights and at Crampton's Gap further depleted McLaws's strength by another 929 men and officers killed, wounded, or missing/captured. Then, on the afternoon of September 16, Lee, scrambling desperately to reassemble his scattered army so that he could fight above the Potomac and achieve the "military success" that he hoped would encourage Marylanders to rebel, called McLaws from Harpers Ferry to Sharpsburg. The Georgian made a forced march that night which further reduced his strength by another 7.7%, or 220 men (probably an underestimate), leaving McLaws with only 2,629 effectives for the battle on September 17.[14]

This overnight march must have been severe. To quote McLaws himself, "The straggling of men, wearied beyond further endurance, and of those without shoes and of others sick was very great, which accounts for the small force carried into action. But by the evening of the 18th most of the absentees had joined and my force was nearly as large as that I had carried into action on the 17th, although I had lost heavily in killed and wounded." Brigadier General William Barksdale, whose four regiments of Mississippians marched with McLaws, recalled similarly, "a portion of my men had fallen by the wayside from loss of sleep and excessive fatigue, having been constantly on duty for five or six days, and on the march for

---

12 Longstreet's strength estimate comes from Hartwig, *To Antietam Creek,* 339; Daniel Harvey Hill, "Address Before the Reunion of the Virginia Division, Army of Northern Virginia," in *SHSP* (1885), 13:268.

13 Allen, "The Strength of the Union and Confederate Forces at Second Manassas," 202-203; McLaws's Estimate, OR 19:1, 860.

14 OR 19:1, 144, 860-862.

almost the whole of the two preceding nights . . . I went into the fight with less than 800 men."¹⁵

Brigadier General Joseph Kershaw, a South Carolinian commanding a brigade in McLaws' division, reported that his men "were also under arms or marching nearly the whole of the nights of Monday and Tuesday, arriving at Sharpsburg at daylight on Wednesday morning, September 17. . . . [M]any had become exhausted and fallen out on the wayside, and all were worn and jaded." An unidentified soldier with the 8th Alabama, a part of Col. Alfred Cummings's brigade in R. H. Anderson's division agreed, calling the march to Shepherdstown "trying in the extreme." Lastly, recalled James Dinkins of the 18th Mississippi:

> About daylight we reached Shepardstown on the Potomac river, and crossed over to the Maryland side, but we crossed with a small proportion of the command which began the march. We remember that Company 'C,' Eighteenth Mississippi, left Harper's Ferry with over sixty men and three officers, but we went into the battle of 'Sharpsburg' with sixteen men and one officer. Other companies, of course, suffered similar diminution. The march was one of the severest ever made by infantry troops.¹⁶

One cannot help but wonder what a difference it would have made to the Battle of Antietam/Sharpsburg if Lee had possessed more time to reassemble his army. Licensed Antietam battlefield guide Russell Rich argues in a 2022 study of Confederate straggling during the campaign that the loss of so many troops prior to Antietam did not diminish the combat effectiveness of Lee's army on the battlefield. This conclusion seems to say more about the fighting prowess of veteran Confederate troops than it does about the army's thin ranks. It cannot be ignored that Lee sought multiple times to launch an attack on the Federal right flank both during and after the fight at Antietam. A lack of available space due to a bend in the Potomac River and McClellan's massing of artillery on that flank

---

15 Lafayette McLaws, "The Capture of Harper's Ferry," in *Philadelphia Weekly Express*, Vol. XXXI (Sept. 19, 1888); OR 19:1, 883.

16 OR, 19:1, 864-865; Wolseley learned much the same thing in October 1862, writing, "owing to the hurried marches Lee and Jackson had made before the battle, nearly one-half of their men were scattered over the country in their rear, unable to get up in time from sore feet occasioned by want of shoes or boots," Rawley, ed., *Wolseley*, 31; James Dinkins, *1861 to 1865: Personal Recollections and Experiences in the Confederate Army by an "Old Johnnie"* (Cincinnati, OH, 1897), 57; "A Short History of the 8th Ala. Regt." Edward Porter Alexander Papers, 1852-1910, #1-4485 (7), SHC, UNC.

contributed to the maneuver's failure, but Lee scarcely being able to muster 5,000 men for the endeavor also proved to be a key deficiency.[17]

At no point on September 17 were Lee's men able to recover the ground they lost in the early hours of the struggle. Counterattack certainly, and this Lee did, but recover their original lines or drive the Federals back to Antietam Creek, never. The battle thus ended as a Confederate defeat precisely because Lee did not have the men he required for an effective offensive, and he did not have the men because straggling significantly reduced the number present for action. This material weakness then persisted until the following day when Lee retired to Virginia because McClellan's army had received reinforcements while Lee's had not. The general summarized this situation in his campaign report, writing, "As we could not look for a material increase in strength, and the enemy's force could be largely and rapidly augmented, it was not thought prudent to wait until he should be ready again to offer battle." Systemic weakness caused by straggling, and exacerbated by high combat losses, forced Robert E. Lee to abandon his campaign and the effort to bring Maryland into the Confederate fold.[18]

Even before McClellan's unanticipated advance on September 13-14, Lee had complained to Jefferson Davis about straggling's devastating effect on his army: "One great embarrassment is the reduction of our ranks by straggling, which it seems impossible to prevent with our present regimental officers. Our ranks are very much diminished I fear from a third to one-half of the original numbers." The threat posed by McClellan's advance then intensified the problem by causing Lee's men to engage in a series of forced marches to rejoin the army in Maryland. By the time the clash erupted at Sharpsburg, Lee's army, numbering between 50,000 and 70,000 men at the campaign's outset, according to some estimates, had lost a crippling number of stragglers.[19]

---

17 Russell Rich, "Very Much Diminished: Straggling in the Army of Northern Virginia in the Maryland Campaign," *The Antietam Journal,* Vol. III (Sept. 2022), 34-60.

18 OR 19:1, 151; Histories of the Maryland Campaign have long judged the Battle of Sharpsburg/Antietam to be a tactical draw. This characterization needs to be re-evaluated. The clash at Gettysburg is considered a Union victory even though it achieved exactly the same outcome. On both fields the two armies slugged it out, stopped fighting, stared at each other for a while, and Confederate forces withdrew. If judged by the same criteria, Antietam/Sharpsburg should be considered a Confederate defeat. Either that or Gettysburg should be considered a drawn fight and not a Union victory.

19 OR 19:2, 606; OR 19:1, 143; Gene Thorp, "In Defense of McClellan at Antietam: A Contrarian View," in *The Washington Post* (September 2012) puts Lee's initial strength at 63,800. Available online at https://www.washingtonpost.com/lifestyle/style/in-defense-of-

Straggling during the campaign angered Lee so much, in fact, that he complained about it in a missive to Jackson and Longstreet on September 22. Implementing a series of reforms at this point, including daily roll call, the creation of a permanent provost guard, and increased efforts by field officers to observe and account for the presence of their men, General Lee made sure that service in the Army of Northern Virginia became much more rule-bound after Antietam/Sharpsburg than it had been up to that point.[20]

Quantifying the full extent to which men falling out of the ranks weakened the Army of Northern Virginia is probably impossible, although we can arrive at a reasonable estimate. To quote Darrell L. Collins's summary of Confederate strength on September 30, less than two weeks after the fight at Antietam/Sharpsburg, Lee's army counted 52,189 men in its ranks. Compared to the fewer than 40,000 men with which Lee and others claimed to have fought the battle one can only imagine what the outcome might have been had the Confederate commander possessed this additional 12,000 troops on September 17. It is doubtful that elements of the Federal II Corps would have penetrated the Confederate center as they did at the Sunken Road if Longstreet had another 5,000 men to throw into the fight. Similarly, Ambrose Burnside probably would not have been able to drive in Lee's right flank if Jacob Cox's IX Corps had faced 3,000 men defending the heights of Antietam Creek instead of Col. Henry L. Benning's "little over four hundred." Possessing an additional 4,000 men would have also given Lee the men he needed for the attack on the Federal right for which he ached so badly.[21]

The examples of Longstreet on September 14 and McLaws on September 17 suggest that the hard marches forced by McClellan's rapid advance contributed to reducing the number of combat effectives available to Lee by a sizable margin. D. H. Hill shared this viewpoint, stating, "Had all our stragglers been up, McClellan's army would have been completely crushed or annihilated." Combine the army's decimation with it being compelled to fight on ground more favorable to the Federals than the position Lee first chose and a more urgent sense of the damage caused to the Confederate operation by the loss of Special Orders No. 191

---

mcclellan-at-antietam-a-contrarian-view/2012/09/06/79a0e5cc-f131-11e1-892d-bc92fee603 a7_story.html. Also see Harsh, *Taken*, 39 for an estimate of around 75,500 and Hartwig, *To Antietam Creek*, 679-680 for his estimate of 73,305.

20 OR 19:2, 618-619.

21 Darrell L. Collins, *The Army of Northern Virginia: Organization, Strength, Casualties, 1861-1865* (Jefferson, NC, 2016), 154-157. The numerical estimate for Benning's strength comes from Brig. Gen. Robert Toombs; *OR* 19:1, 889.

The Importance of the Lost Orders | 115

becomes clear. Writing to Hill in February 1868, Lee referred to the loss of the orders as "a great calamity and subsequent reflection has not caused me to change my opinion." From ruining Lee's plan to fight along Beaver Creek and forcing him to defend the South Mountain passes, which itself caused significant casualties, to giving the Federals a more advantageous place to fight and reducing Confederate strength by pressing the army to reassemble on the quick, one cannot help but agree with Lee's characterization of the orders' loss as a disaster.[22]

On February 15, 1868, the general himself told William Allan, a veteran of the Army of Northern Virginia and one of its earliest historians, "Had the Lost dispatch not been lost, and had McClellan continued his cautious policy for two or three days longer, I would have had all my troops reconcentrated on [the] Md. side, stragglers up, [and] men rested." Charles Marshall echoed this sentiment, writing in his war memoir that "Instead of being united and fresh as it would have been had General McClellan continued his slow rate of advance for twenty-four hours longer, as there is reason to believe he would have done but for the loss of the order . . . it [the army] had to engage the enemy at great disadvantage." Longstreet's men and those under D. H. Hill, continued Marshall:

> went into the battle [at Sharpsburg] under the disheartening effects of the disaster at Boonsboro', and considerably reduced in number by that engagement, while those of General Jackson had to make a long march in intensely warm weather and go into battle without opportunity for necessary repose and refreshment. In considering the Maryland campaign, it is proper to take into account the effect of the accident of the lost order upon the result—a misfortune that was not incident to the plan of campaign, although it had a most important influence upon the result. . . . The effect of the loss of that order does not show any want of wisdom or prudence in the policy of the invasion of Maryland in 1862. But for that, no battle need have been fought at Sharpsburg, or at South Mountain, or anywhere except at a time and upon terms of General Lee's own selection.[23]

Supposing Marshall is correct, and taking into account Robert E. Lee's own estimate of the harm caused to his operation by the loss of Special Orders No. 191, one cannot reasonably conclude other than to say that the discovery of the mislaid document by Barton Mitchell around noon on September 13 contributed mightily to the Confederate defeat in Maryland. For that the credit must go to George

---

22 OR 19:1, 1026, OR 19:2, 618-619; Lee to Hill, Feb. 21, 1868, D. H. Hill Papers #2035-z, SHC, UNC.

23 Freeman, *Lee's Lieutenants*, 2:718; Maurice, ed., *Lee's Aide-de-Camp*, 160-161.

Brinton McClellan, whose actions forced Lee into a difficult situation for which he was ill prepared, and who by doing so saved the Republic when it faced the possibility of a terrible defeat that might have ended it for good.

Conclusion

The loss of Special Orders No. 191 set the stage for a reversal of Confederate fortunes in Maryland. Whereas General Lee had begun the campaign with optimism, and the expectation that he had an extended period of time to operate on what he called the Confederacy's "northern frontier," it rapidly deteriorated into a bloody struggle for survival. The populace did not rise up in rebellion during the two weeks that Lee's army spent in Maryland and this caused some in the army to wonder if they had been given enough time. This lingering doubt, along with the belief that Maryland remained too "tightly tied" by geography and Federal occupation forces, caused Lee to look on the state with sympathy and regret. He had tried his best to carry out Richmond's policy of bringing a Southern border state into the fold and in the end he had failed. The loss of Special Orders No. 191 proved to be a key factor contributing to this disappointing outcome.[1]

There is no source that names the person who lost the orders. This makes it necessary to analyze the circumstantial evidence surrounding who might have dropped the document. It appears after completing such an examination that Jeb Stuart may have been that man. This hypothesis is based on three considerations: that Stuart had access to the orders, that he had a reason to be carrying a copy of the orders, and that there is evidence placing him close to the place where Barton Mitchell presumably discovered the orders. Other suspects, such as William Pendleton, had access to the orders and a reason to be carrying them, but there is no evidence placing them or him near where the document was discovered. Henry K. Douglas, another name often bandied about in connection with the event, also had access to the orders. He did not have a reason to be carrying them, however, and, like Pendleton, there is no evidence for him ever being near where Mitchell

---

1   OR 19:2, 644.

found the document. Only Jeb Stuart fits the bill when all three criteria are applied to the historical circumstances.

Stuart would never be blamed for failing to guard a key military secret at a critical time, but one wonders if he did not feel some guilt for it by claiming to have "appended" a copy of the orders to his February 1864 campaign report and by sending Lee his message about the alleged "gentleman of Maryland" witnessing Union commander George McClellan reading the lost orders on September 13. Questioning the connection between these things is merely speculation. With luck, however, new evidence will be unearthed someday that provides some clarity.

In the interim, we must be satisfied with the light this study sheds on several other subjects related to the Lost Orders. Among these is the unexpectedly rapid end of Lee's plan to operate north of the Potomac until winter closed out the 1862 campaigning season. The Confederate commander had set out on his "expedition" with visions of invading Pennsylvania for food and forage. Yet by mid-morning on September 8, news of the enemy's advance from Washington, and word that Federal troops remained at Harpers Ferry, had disabused Lee of the delusion he had time to carry out his operation. Lee decided, therefore, to march west of South Mountain, where he hoped his veteran troops could meet the allegedly "demoralized" enemy on ground of his own choosing.

These events evolved much more quickly than Lee had anticipated, resulting in the Army of Northern Virginia's expulsion from Maryland only fourteen days after the first troops from D. H. Hill's command crossed the Potomac on September 4. The brevity of this timespan represents something akin to a lightning campaign in nineteenth century terms, when the speed of a man on foot dictated the pace of military operations. It certainly does not fit the longstanding characterization of a campaign extended to an unreasonable length by dawdling or procrastination by George McClellan.

Indeed, the evidence shows that McClellan's advance put pressure on Lee much earlier than the Confederate general had expected or was willing to later admit. So much so, in fact, that by the time his army moved out on September 10, Lee probably felt the enemy already nipping at his heels. The general later claimed that when leaving Frederick, he had believed the pace of the enemy's advance would be slow enough for the detached commands under Jackson, Walker, and McLaws to capture Harpers Ferry and rejoin the balance of the army near Hagerstown. He also stated to Rev. E. C. Gordon and William Allan in 1868 that if McClellan had "continued in his cautious policy for two or three days longer" it would have provided sufficient time to concentrate the Army of Northern Virginia for battle.[2]

These claims sound like a man rationalizing his own miscalculations. The vanguard of the Army of the Potomac's Second Corps had nearly reached Hyattstown, a point only 12 miles from Frederick, by September 10. Seasoned troops could march twice that distance in a single day if no enemy stood in their path. Even Jeb Stuart managing to delay McClellan's advance for 24 hours, which he did by holding his defensive position at Urbana until the afternoon of September 11, added only another day of distance between the Federals and Lee's scattered force. In short, the buffer of two or three days that Lee says he thought he had amounted to little more than an illusion. Barton Mitchell's discovery of the Lost Orders only worsened the already tenuous situation in which Lee had put himself.

The steady increase of pressure by McClellan on September 13 then shattered Lee's hope that Stuart's cavalry could prevent the Federals from advancing to South Mountain before Jackson had compelled the surrender of Harpers Ferry. Once enemy troops appeared in number at the eastern base of the mountain, Lee surely began to suspect that time had run out on his operation. He nevertheless waited for word from Jackson on the morning of September 14, and held up Longstreet's return to Boonsboro, which helped to cripple his army's defense of the South Mountain gaps. It was only on the morning of September 15—one day late, according to Lee's own estimate—that Jackson finally reported Harpers Ferry's capitulation. When that news came, Lee returned to his plan and stood his ground in Washington County, Maryland.

Light has also been shed on the generation of Lee's orders. Commonly thought to have been dictated by Lee on September 9 immediately after his conference with Generals Jackson and Longstreet, this study presents evidence showing instead how the orders developed over the course of two days. This process began on September 8 with a verbal instruction from Lee for Jackson to take command of the Harpers Ferry operation and to arrange for the army's rear guard when it departed from Frederick on September 10. Clarity has also been provided concerning the timeframe when Lee dictated the orders on September 9 and the involvement of the hitherto unacknowledged participant in the drama, Maj. Richard C. Taylor.

---

2 See Freeman, *Lee's Lieutenants*, 2:721.

The one man missing from this saga is Col. Robert H. Chilton. Long maligned for being the incompetent administrator who failed to spot the loss of Special Orders No. 191, and identified as a central player in the disaster by having his name on the lost copy, the results of this study suggest that Chilton made no mistakes. The colonel appears to have been responsible for doing nothing more than signing the official copies of Lee's orders and, perhaps, of using the inexperienced Dick Taylor as a temporary headquarters adjutant. If the analysis of the document's handwriting offered in Appendix A of this study is reasonable, it suggests that Chilton did not even sign the lost copy of Special Orders No. 191, thereby absolving him of responsibility. To this historian's eye, it appears that Armistead Long was the man who copied Chilton's signature from the official copy of the document. The colonel cannot be faulted for that.[3]

The evidence presented also provides a firmer understanding of where Barton Mitchell found the lost copy of Special Orders No. 191. Most estimates of the distance from Frederick City have caused researchers to look farther away than they should have, with the result that no one has been sure where the orders were found. This understandable confusion has in turn made it impossible to name the culprit who lost the orders. Identifying the place of their discovery as close to where Jeb Stuart camped on September 11-12 provides significantly more reason to believe that he, and not the long-maligned D. H. Hill, may have dropped the document and its two cigars.

Stuart's potential involvement also forces a re-evaluation of his performance during the Maryland expedition. General Lee considered it exemplary, writing in his campaign report that the cavalry's "vigilance, activity, and courage were conspicuous, and to its assistance is due, in a great measure, the success of some of the most important and delicate operations of the campaign." Learning that Stuart had dropped the copy of Special Orders No. 191 handed to McClellan surely would have changed Lee's outlook. One can only speculate what impact this might have had on operations later in the war. Would Lee have trusted Stuart to the extent that he did if he knew the Virginian was responsible for one of the war's worst intelligence failures? This question is unanswerable, but one cannot help thinking it would have shaken Lee's faith in Stuart to the core.[4]

Orders falling into the hands of the enemy occurred more than once during the war. As Steven Stotelmyer insightfully points out in his study of McClellan's

---

3 See Appendix A.

4 *OR* 19:1, 152-153.

generalship, the opposing forces in the war lost and found each other's orders no fewer than five times, yet it is only the loss of Special Orders No. 191 that has earned the moniker of THE Lost Orders. This is because many scholars writing about the event have deemed it to have been a "once in a lifetime" opportunity for the Federal commander. The argument offered here is that while the orders' loss and transfer to McClellan was not a potentially war-winning event, it did materially alter the outcome of the Maryland Campaign in the U.S. Army's favor. Lee seems to have thought so as well and for months after the campaign's disappointing end he puzzled over what had prompted McClellan to change his tactics.[5]

Learning from the later publication of McClellan's campaign report that the discovery of the lost copy of Special Orders No. 191 had motivated the transformation of the Federal commander's effort, Lee at last had his answer. It was also on this occasion that Lee learned the copy had been addressed to D. H. Hill. Lee's bewilderment about the matter represented a form of self-deception. Thinking until September 8 that he had weeks to plan his next move, and waiting for Maryland's people to respond to his proclamation while believing the enemy crippled from the recent defeat at Second Manassas, Lee surely felt blindsided by the news that McClellan had begun marching his army toward Frederick. This unanticipated movement forced General Lee to put his own army in motion well before he was ready. Barton Mitchell's discovery of the orders may have accelerated the Army of the Potomac's advance, but Lee had already felt the pressure growing five days earlier.[6]

Had the orders not been lost, and had Lee been allowed two days longer to reassemble his army on September 14 and 15, the history of the campaign, indeed the war itself, might look very different. One can only wonder at the bitterness with which Lee later received confirmation of the orders' loss, and the disappointment he must have felt at having his effort to recruit Maryland into the Southern cause stymied at the very moment when the conditions for Confederate independence seemed most promising. A Confederate victory north of the Potomac might have finally encouraged the intervention of Britain and France sought by Richmond. Secessionists in Maryland might have also erupted in rebellion, isolating Washington and forcing President Lincoln to evacuate the capital city. All of these

---

5 Stotelmyer, *Too Useful to Sacrifice*, 26-27.

6 "I do not know how the order was lost, nor until I saw McClellan's published report after the termination of the war did I know certainly that it was the copy addressed to you"; Lee to Hill, Feb. 21, 1868, D. H. Hill Papers #2035-z, SHC, UNC. Venable, *"Personal Reminiscences,"* 46.

things and many others in the South's favor might have occurred if the loss of one key document had not sent events spiraling off in a different direction. Such is the caprice of history.

Appendix A

Who Wrote the Lost Copy of Lee's Special Orders No. 191?

Many authors have written about Lee's Lost Orders over the years, but practically no one has tried to identify the document's writer by analyzing the penmanship. Since no detailed study of the orders would be complete without conducting such an examination, I decided to hire a specialist in graphology—the science of analyzing handwriting—to compare the lost copy of Special Orders No. 191 to documents written by seven individuals who could have had access to the orders. The graphologist who completed the work concluded that the submitted writing samples shared too many similarities to easily determine if one of the individuals was the author. She therefore declared the results of the study inconclusive.[1]

Not satisfied with this result, I decided to conduct the same analysis myself, starting with Robert Chilton's signature. Before going any further, and at the risk of stating the obvious, I am not a graphologist. Older readers, however, will surely remember being able to recognize the handwriting of close friends and family members, people whose penmanship they used to see on a regular basis before the advent of computer keyboards and smart devices. I believe that after working with the original documents for months on end, such as I did for this study, one can acquire a similar type of familiarity with the writing of historical figures. It is the results of this experience that I share here. I offer the observations below in the hope that readers will at least find them interesting, if not also

---

1 The lone exception is Los Angeles-based attorney, Joseph Ryan, who reviewed the handwriting in the Lost Orders and declared it not to be Chilton's. Ryan does not focus on Chilton's signature as part of his analysis. More importantly, he mars the importance of his finding by arguing without evidence that Robert. E. Lee conspired to have Jeb Stuart "lose" the order on purpose to draw McClellan into a fight along Antietam Creek. See Joe Ryan, "Special Order 191: Ruse of War" at https://joeryancivilwar.com/Special-Order-191/Ruse-of-War.html. The seven individuals in question are: Charles S. Venable, Armistead L. Long, Robert H. Chilton, Henry K. Douglas, Elisha F. Paxton, Richard C. Taylor, and James E. B. Stuart. The analyst is Beverley East of the Washington, DC, firm Strokes and Slants.

convincing. I hope as well that the conclusions I have reached will inspire further exploration of the subject.

As is discussed in Chapter Six, the signature at the bottom of the Lost Orders does not match Chilton's signature on other headquarters documents. What is more, when the writing in the Lost Orders is compared to that of other documents written in Chilton's hand it becomes abundantly clear that the colonel did not write the lost copy, either.

The graphic below shows the signature at the bottom of the Lost Orders (Ex. 1) along with four other known examples of Chilton's name. An aspect of the writing in Ex. 1 that quickly jumps out are the printed capital letters "R," "H," and "C." These are important to note when comparing the Chilton signatures excerpted from the other documents. Another point worth mentioning is the fact that the letters from "h" onward are not connected to the "C" at the beginning of Chilton's surname. This is also significant for reasons that will be explained.

The second excerpt (Ex. 2) comes from a letter written by Chilton to D. H. Hill in June of 1867. In it, Chilton responded to questions posed by Hill concerning the orders and how they might have been lost. Hill sent this letter to get information that might help him refute the growing chorus of accusations he had lost the orders and cost Robert E. Lee a victory in Maryland. This example of Chilton's signature clearly does not match the example from the Lost Orders (Ex. 1). Not only is the structure of the "R" different, the structure of the "H" and the "C" do not match, either. Moreover, although Chilton did at least put periods after his first and second initials on this occasion, the angle of the penmanship is not the same.[2]

To be thorough, and to see if the 1867 example might be an outlier, I sought out other examples of Chilton's signatures from official wartime documents. The first of these I located in a letter from Robert E. Lee to Jefferson Davis that Chilton penned on September 20, 1862 (Ex. 3). It is easy to see that this version of the signature matches the 1867 Chilton signature (Ex. 2) but does not match the signature from the Lost Orders (Ex. 1). This is particularly the case as far as the structures of the "R," the "H," and the "C" in Ex. 2 and Ex. 3 are concerned. Examples 2 and 3 show that Chilton tended to run together his initials and the first letter of his last name in a single, sweeping scrawl. He did not sign documents by printing out those letters separately.[3]

Lastly, I decided to compare Chilton's Lost Orders signature with the copies of his name he wrote on Special Orders No. 190 (Ex. 4) and the two-paragraph version of Special Orders No. 191 (Ex. 5). In these documents, which Chilton signed on or about September 9, 1862, we can see that the colonel elected not to use periods after his first and second initials. He nevertheless wrote those initials and his last name in the usual fluid motion that linked all three of them together. The

---

2 Robert H. Chilton to Daniel Harvey Hill, June 22, 1867, D. H. Hill Papers, 1848-1951, #2035-z, in SHC, UNC.

3 Robert H. Chilton to William N. Pendleton, Sept. 16, 1862, William N. Pendleton Papers, 1798-1889, #1466, Folder 27b, in SHC, UNC. Robert E. Lee to Jefferson Davis, Sept. 20, 1862, in Personal Papers, Robert E, Lee Letters, 1862-1865, Accession 25786, Box 7420595, Location 4/B/13/5/7, Library of Virginia, Richmond, VA

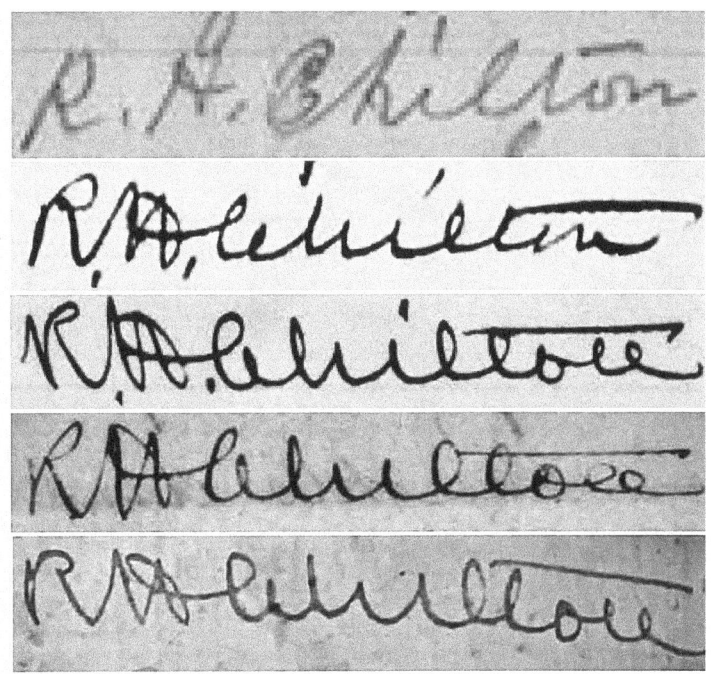

Four examples of Robert H. Chilton's official signature and one forgery (Top). Chilton always joined his initials and the first letter of his last name in one motion. The forged version does not display this characteristic. Note as well that while Chilton also did not use periods when signing Special Orders No. 190 and the two paragraph version of Special Orders No. 191 periods can be seen in the forged version of his signature at the bottom of the lost copy. *Library of Virginia, National Archives, Library of Congress*

---

signatures look very much like the others displayed from other Chilton-signed documents. By contrast, the Chilton signature on the lost copy of Lee's orders does not have this characteristic. In fact, it bears no resemblance to any of the other examples shown, making it an outlier.

Finding four examples of Chilton's signature that match each other, but do not match the signature on the McClellan copy of Special Orders No. 191, leads to the conclusion that the colonel did not sign the lost copy found by Barton Mitchell. The difference becomes even more stark when longer examples of the handwriting are compared. These are shown below.

Even a cursory examination of these excerpts leads to the conclusion that the handwriting in Ex. 2 and Ex. 3 does not match the handwriting in Ex. 1, which is the McClellan copy of the orders. This evidence renders it an inescapable fact that Col. Robert H. Chilton neither wrote nor signed the copy of the orders discovered outside of Frederick, Maryland.

If Chilton did not write and sign the orders, who did? Hoping to answer this question, I designed my own method of comparing words, letters, and numbers so a statistical result could be developed to measure the likelihood that a given individual might have written the Lost Orders. This approach starts with identifying words in the Lost Orders that also appear in other documents, including

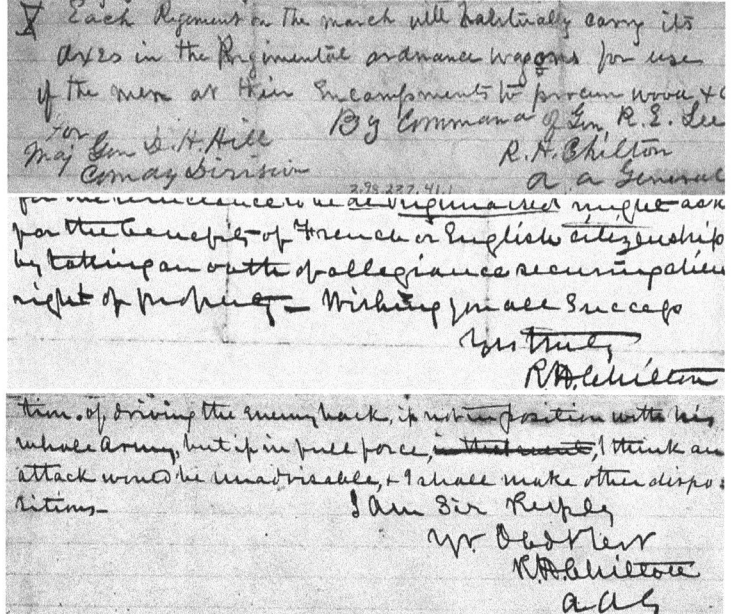

Chilton Signature, McClellan Copy of Lost Orders (Ex. 1)

Chilton Signature, Letter to D. H. Hill, June 22, 1867 (Ex. 2)

Chilton Signature, Lee to Davis, Sept. 20, 1862 (Ex. 3)

Longer examples of Chilton's penmanship compared with a portion of the Lost Orders, illustrating that the colonel neither wrote nor signed the lost copy of the orders. *Library of Virginia, Library of Congress*

---

common words, such as "the" and "it," and unique words, such as army ranks and the names of people and places.

Taking instances of each word from the documents and placing them in a table enabled a visual comparison of the writing. I then assigned the results of the comparison to one of four categories: matching words, non-matching words, partially matching words, and words that have similar characteristics, but which also display anomalies. These words I labeled "inconclusive."

Following this step, I assigned one point to each word being compared and compiled the numbers. This method is illustrated below in a page of the analysis profile for Col. Armistead L. Long. It provides a basis for measuring the likelihood that the writing being compared belonged to the writer of the Lost Orders.

Returning to the example of Robert Chilton, after comparing words from multiple documents, I found that only one word matched one word from the Lost Orders. Another 28 words examined did not match while five words matched partially, and 10 words were inconclusive. Expressed in points this result is one (1) point for matching words, five (5) points for partially matching words, 28 points for non-matching words, and 10 points for inconclusive results. Adding together the matches and partial matches generates a total of six "positive" results and 38 "negative" results out of the possible 44 points available, making it only 13.63% likely that Chilton wrote the lost copy of Special Orders No. 191.

Category	Definition	Point Value*
Match	Words from separate documents that display the same structure or which are consistently formed in the same manner by the writer.	1
Partial Match	A portion of a word from on document that closely matches the same word from another document to which it is being compared. The formaton of the word is also similar, even if there are slight variations, such as a slant.	1
No Match	The words being compared from separate documents look different.	1
Inconclusive	A word that shows some similar characteristics to the word being compared, but which also contains differences significant enough to cause doubt.	1

* The methodology used to evaluate the similarity of words found in the Lost Orders and other documents authored by the subjects examined. *Alexander B. Rossino*

After investigating several potential candidates who may have written the Lost Orders, I ranked them from highest to lowest by percentage results. The individual with the highest percentage of matches, both full and partial, was most likely to be the person who copied the Lost Orders. The results of the analysis are shown in the table below with the percentage in the left field of the table *excluding* inconclusive results and the percentage in the right field *including* inconclusive results.[4]

I calculated inconclusive results in this manner because these words contain at least some similar characteristics and, as we all know from our own handwriting, each of us can sometimes write the same word differently. It can be useful to consider, therefore, how they affect the percentages if inconclusive results are counted as complete matches. Think of this as a second data point that can help confirm the results derived from tabulating only the matches and partial matches. The case of Robert Chilton is again useful here. Even including the inconclusive results, fewer than 40% of the examined words from his writing matched. This reinforces the conclusion reached from the signature comparison that he did not write the Lost Orders.

Col. Armistead L. Long. *National Archives*

---

4 An eBook detailing the Special Orders 191 handwriting analysis will be made available soon.

Special Orders No. 191 Handwriting Analysis of Col. Armistead L. Long, General Lee's Military Secretary

Percentage of Matching Words (Ex. Inconclusive Results): 46.66%
Percentage of Matching Words (Inc. Inconclusive Results): 73.33%
Percentage of Average Between Both: 59.99%

Long Documents	The Lost Orders	Long Documents	The Lost Orders

The analysis confirms that more words from Long-written documents match words found in the Lost Orders than words examined penned by other individuals. This supports the conclusion Long wrote the orders. Why he did is a mystery.

Observations

1. Long often formed his lower-case "d" without a stem.
This is unique to his writing and to the Lost Orders.

2. Long often misspelled "Middletown" as "Middleton," and it is misspelled in the Lost Orders.

3. Long regularly wrote his lower-case "t" with a detached crossing line.

4. Long wrote "to" uniquely, with the word always at a sharp right angle and with an open-topped "o."

Officer	% of Matching Words (Ex. Inconclusive Results)	% of Matching Words (Inc. Inconclusive Results)
Col. Armistead L. Long Military Secretary HQ ANV	44.66%	73.33%
Maj. Richard C. Taylor Temp. Aide-de-Camp, HQ ANV	31.25%	71.87%
Matching Word Results at 25% or Below		
Maj. Charles Marshall Aide-de-camp, HQ ANV	25.00%	65.38%
Lt. Col. Charles S. Venable, Aide-de-Camp, HQ ANV	24.13%	41.37%
Maj. Gen. James E. B. Stuart Commander, Cavalry Division	21.73%	54.34%
Lt. Joseph G. Morrison Aide-de-Camp, HQ Jackson	21.21%	33.33%
Matching Word Results at 20% or Below		
Lt. Henry K. Douglas Aide-de-camP, HQ Jackson	20.00%	46.66%
Brig. Gen. William N Pendleton Commander, Reserve Artillery	20.00%	25.00%
Maj. Walter H. Taylor Aide-de-Camp, HQ ANV	17.24%	44.82%
Col. Robert H. Chilton Chief of Staff & Assistant Adjutant General, HQ ANV	13.63%	36.36%
Maj. Elisha F. Paxton Assistant Adjutant General HQ Jackson	10.52%	42.10%

The results of this analysis suggest instead that Lee's military secretary, Col. Armistead L. Long, wrote the copy of Special Orders No. 191 which found its way to McClellan outside of Frederick, Maryland. Several of the words from Long-written documents are exact matches of the same words from the lost copy of Special Orders No. 191. It is for this reason that I conclude Long was the likely writer of the document and not Dick Taylor, an examination of whose handwriting resulted in the second-highest percentage of matching words. Long's composition of unique words, such as the abbreviation "Comdg" and the name "D. H. Hill," are simply too close to ignore. Taylor's writing did not match as exactly when it came to unique words. I found instead more matches of generic words along the lines of "it" and "take." These types of matches seem less convincing than unique words and names.

Why it may have been Long who wrote out the lost copy of the orders is unclear, as is the means by which the copy traveled to the location where Barton Mitchell found it. Chapter Six of this study suggests that Jeb Stuart could have taken (or was given) the unneeded copy of the orders during a visit to headquarters on September 9. This is why Cpl. Mitchell found the dropped document near the place where Stuart established his headquarters on the night of September 11, after he had withdrawn from Urbana to Frederick. A similar explanation could be concluded from Dick Taylor writing out the lost copy of the orders, too. After all, as Charles Venable noted, it was Taylor who copied the orders for distribution on September 9.

The possibility also exists that Long himself, or Taylor, or some other individual, took the orders from headquarters and lost them during a last-minute trip to Frederick before the army marched out on September 10. If the results of this analysis are convincing, then we must add to the Lost Orders mystery the question why Armistead Long wrote out the dropped copy. Did he do it at General Lee's request, did Jeb Stuart take him aside and ask him for the orders, or did Long write out a copy for himself or for someone else? Until additional information comes to light these questions will remain unanswered. It is simply impossible at this point to conclude one way or the other.

Appendix B

Comparing the Text of Special Orders No. 190 and No. 191

The argument is made in Chapter Six of this study that General Lee dictated the first copy of his orders for the operation against Harpers Ferry to Maj. Charles Marshall around mid- to late-morning on September 9, 1862. This draft, which Marshall labelled Special Orders No. 190, and which contained paragraphs III through X, preceded a second draft labelled Special Orders No. 191 that contained only paragraphs I and II. Lee's aide, Capt. Arthur P. Mason, later combined these documents into a single copy for the headquarters order book labelled Special Orders No. 191. It is this copy of the orders that then made it into the Official Records.

Why Lee generated these orders separately is unknown, although it may have had something to do with the content of paragraphs I and II. These ordered army commanders to stop their men from entering Frederick due to problems with shopkeepers and instructed Maj. Walter Taylor to meet Jefferson Davis in Virginia and keep the Confederate president from crossing the Potomac River. Unlike Special Orders No. 190, these first two paragraphs did not address military operations. The assumption is, therefore, that Lee kept them separate from paragraphs III through X because those paragraphs contained specific instructions for most of the army's senior commanders.

To this author's knowledge, a comparison of the first draft of Lee's orders with the copy dropped near Frederick and delivered to George McClellan has never been presented in print. Comparing these documents reveals numerous differences that readers might find interesting and which will hopefully encourage additional research into the orders' generation and loss. The comparison also reveals many idiosyncrasies in the writing of the copy that was lost. These may be able to help future researchers confirm or refute the conclusion reached in Appendix A that Col. Armistead L. Long wrote out the mislaid copy. By default, Long is referred to as the author in this appendix.

Paper and Document Headers

Orders No. 190 and 191 are both written on beige paper printed with blue lines to create rows for text. Because this book is printed in black and white those details will not be noticeable to readers. The paper on which Marshall wrote Special Orders No. 190 also appears to be as wide as the paper on which Long wrote the lost copy of Special Orders No. 191. Special Orders No. 190, however, contains 27 lines and a large space for the header of the document. By contrast, the lost copy of Special Orders No. 191 contains 30 lines and a large header space. We can conclude from this that each set of the orders is written on different paper stock, for what that observation is worth. Marshall also wrote Special Orders No. 190 in ink while Long, presumably, wrote the lost copy of Special Orders No. 191 in pencil.

Examining the document headers reveals several differences. The first of these is the absence of the bracketed word "Confidential" in Special Orders No. 190. This omission makes sense because No. 190 was a draft not meant for distribution. Major Richard C. Taylor, the aide in the adjutant's tent who wrote out most of the copies that were intended for distribution, added the word "Confidential" as part of the process of disseminating the orders to the army's field commanders.

As Robert Chilton noted in a postwar letter to D. H. Hill, "This order ... marked confidential, was sent to the Major Genls of the army by couriers, whose standing orders were to bring back the envelopes receipted, or some written evidence of delivery." The ten-paragraph headquarters order book copy of Special Orders No. 191 similarly does not contain the word "Confidential" because it too was not prepared for distribution. Charles Marshall commented on this process in a postwar letter to D. H. Hill, writing, "Such orders were usually copied by the staff, with another copied into the Confidential book, or retained to be copied into the general order book post factum." In short, the presence of the word "Confidential" is evidence that the writer of the lost copy of the orders made it from a previously prepared copy.[1]

Two of the three other differences between the headers and first paragraphs of Special Orders No. 190 and 191 are minor. The third difference is more consequential. Addressing the minor details first, the lost copy of the orders is numbered "191" while the draft is numbered "190." This is, of course, a function of the fact that Col. Long probably copied the lost document from the number-corrected copies produced by Dick Taylor. Long also appears to have written "No." as "Nr.," so the lost copy of the orders reads "Special Orders Nr. 191" not "Special Orders No. 191." More important is the fact that on the lost copy of the orders the date, which Marshall wrote as "September 9th," is written as "Sept. 9" with an underlined "12" where the "th" should be. Is this because Long, who had poor eyesight and went almost completely blind in the late 1860s due to combat "exposure," misread Marshall's handwriting, or is it because Long actually wrote out the lost copy at noon on September 9?

Lastly, the header of the lost copy of the orders contains several abbreviations that are not in Special Orders No. 190. There is also one clear error, with the number written before "9" being scratched out. Taken together, the abbreviations and the error hint that the writer wrote out the lost copy in bad light or in haste, which would have been the case if Generals Lee or Stuart asked Col. Long to make the copy on a busy day when the headquarters staff was preparing to leave Frederick with the rest of the army. The colonel may have tried to get the task done as quickly as possible by abbreviating several words and, potentially, by making a mistake with the date.

Paragraph III

Turning to paragraph III, there are several obvious differences between the documents. The first of these is the abbreviation of the word "General." In Special Orders No. 190, that abbreviation is written as "Genl" while in the Lost Orders it is written as "Gen" with the additional letter dropped.

---

1 R.H. Chilton to D. H. Hill, June 27, 1867, D. H. Hill Papers #2035-z, SHC, UNC; Marshall to Hill, Nov. 11, 1867 in D. H. Hill Papers, Accession 32032, Barcode 5627792, Location 4/B/21/1/5, Box 4, Folder 11, Library of Virginia, Richmond, VA.

Comparing the Text of Special Orders No. 190 and No. 191 | 133

> Head Quarters Army of No. Va.
> September 9th 1862
>
> Special Orders }
> No. 190
>
> III The Army will resume its march tomorrow taking the Hagerstown road. Genl Jackson's command will form the advance and after passing Middletown, with such portion as he may select take the route towards Sharpsburg cross the Potomac at the most convenient point and by Friday morning take possession of the Balt. & Ohio R.R. capture such of the enemy as may be at Martinsburg and intercept such as may attempt to escape from Harpers Ferry.
>
> IV Genl Longstreet's command will pursue the main road as far as Boonsboro, where it will halt, with reserve, supply and baggage trains of the Army.
>
> V Genl McLaws with his own division and that of Genl. R. H. Anderson will follow Genl. Longstreet, on reaching Middletown will take the route to Harpers Ferry and by Friday morning possess himself of the Maryland Heights and endeavor to capture the enemy at Harpers Ferry and vicinity.
>
> VI Genl Walker with his division after accomplishing the object in which he is now engaged, will cross the Potomac, at Cheek's Ford ascend its right bank to Lovettsville take possession of Loudon Heights if practicable by Friday morning, Keyes Ford on his left and the road between the end of the mountain and the Potomac on his right. He will as far as practicable co-operate with Genl's McLaws & Jackson & intercept retreat of the

The second difference is the spelling of the name "Middletown." Charles Marshall, a native Marylander, wrote out the town's name correctly. Colonel Long, a native Virginian, did not, writing instead "Middleton." Referring again to Long's poor eyesight, it is worth asking if Long's misspelling of the word is due to the colonel's already questionable vision or a result of haste or carelessness. The third noticeable difference between paragraph III of the two documents is the irregular punctuation in Special Orders No. 191. Marshall's copy of the paragraph is meticulously punctuated. The lost copy is not. It is missing periods, commas, and apostrophes in most places. One wonders again if this is a

(Confidential)

Hd Qrs Army of Northern Va
Sept 9th 1862

Special Orders
No 191

III. The army will resume its march to-morrow taking the Hagerstown road. Gen Jackson's command will form the advance and after passing Middleton with such portion as he may select take the route towards Sharpsburg. Cross the Potomac at the most convenient point & by Friday morning take possession of the Baltimore & Ohio R.R.; capture such of the Enemy as may be at Martinsburg and intercept such as may attempt to Escape from Harpers Ferry.

IV. Gen Longstreet's command will pursue the main road as far as Boonsboro where it will halt, with reserve supply and baggage trains of the army.

V. Gen McLaws with his own division and that of Gen R. H. Anderson will follow Gen Longstreet. On reaching Middleton will take the route to Harpers Ferry and by Friday morning possess himself of the Maryland heights and Endeavor to capture the Enemy at Harpers Ferry and vicinity.

VI. Gen Walker with his division

enemy

VII. Gen'l D. H. Hill's division will form the rear guard of the army pursuing the road taken by the main body. The reserve Artillery, Ordnance and Supply trains &c. will precede Gen'l Hill.

VIII. Gen'l Stuart will detach a squadron of Cavalry to accompany the commands of Gen'ls Longstreet, Jackson and McLaws, and with the main body of the Cavalry will cover the route of the army bringing up all stragglers, that may have been left behind.

IX. The commands of Gen'ls Jackson, McLaws & Walker after accomplishing the objects for which they have been detached will join the main body of the army at Boonesboro or Hagerstown.

X. Each Regiment on the march will habitually carry its axes in the Regimental Ordnance wagons for use of the men at their encampments to procure wood &c.

By Command of Gen'l R. E. Lee
R H Chilton
A. A. General

result of poor vision, haste, or simple carelessness. Finally, Long wrote out "Baltimore" when referring to possession of the railroad as one of Jackson's objectives. Charles Marshall abbreviated the name as "Balto." in his copy.

after as the object in which he is now engaged will cross the Potomac and cheeks from as cende its right bank at Louthsville take possession of London Hights if practicable by Friday morning keeps from on his left and the road between the End of Mountain and the Potomac on his right. He will as far as practicable cooperate with Gen McLaws & Genl Jackson in intercepting the retreat of the Enemy.

VII Gen D. H. Hill's division will form the rear guard of the army pursuing the road taken by the main body ~~army~~. The reserve artillery ordnance and supply trains will precede Gen Hill

VIII Gen Stuart will detach a squadron of Cavalry to accompany the commands of Gens. Longstreet Jackson and McLaws and with the main body of the Cavalry will cover the route of the army & bring up all stragglers that may have been left behind.

IX The commands of Gen Jackson McLaws & Walker after accomplishing the objects for which they have been detached will join the main body of the army at Boonsboro or Hagerstown

X Each Regiment on the march will habitually carry its axes in the Regimental ordnance waggons for use of the men at their encampments to procure wood &c

By Command of Genl R. E. Lee

R. H. Chilton
A a General

for Maj Genl D. H. Hill
Comag Division

Paragraph IV

This paragraph contains all of the differences listed for paragraph III. The abbreviation "Gen" is present as is the uneven punctuation. There are, however, no misspellings in this paragraph.

Paragraph V

This paragraph is interesting because in the lost copy of the orders Long indented the text more deeply than he did in the previous two paragraphs, especially paragraph III. Is this because he was writing on an uneven surface or for some other reason? Paragraph V of Special Orders No. 191 also contains the shorter abbreviation of the word "General," the uneven punctuation, such as between "Longstreet" and "on," which is marked with a period, not a comma, and the misspelled "Middleton" from paragraph III. In addition, this paragraph contains some strange capitalization with the word "endeavor" capitalized when it should not be.

Paragraph VI

The indentation of this paragraph in Special Orders No. 191 is even more pronounced than in paragraph V. There is also a highly unusual abbreviation of the word "accomplishing" as "ac." in Col. Long's version of the text. It also seems as if the text is becoming less legible as it proceeds. For example, the word "Keyes" in Charles Marshall's Special Orders No. 190 is written crisply and clearly. In Special Orders No. 191, the word is so poorly drafted that it looks like "Keeps." Long has at least retained some of the punctuation from the original text and on this occasion he wrote out the abbreviation for "General" as both "Gen" and "Genl." That said, Long's construction of the final sentence is different. In Marshall's copy of the orders, the last portion of the sentence reads, "He will as far as practicable cooperate with Genl's McLaws + Jackson + intercept retreat of the enemy." In Special Orders No. 191 the sentence reads, "He will as far as practicable cooperate with Gen. McLaws + Genl Jackson in intercepting the retreat of the enemy."

Paragraph VII

Colonel Long again made an error copying a sentence in this paragraph. Whereas Maj. Marshall's first sentence ends with the words "the main body," Long's sentence ends with the scratched out, and redundant, words "of the army." The ever present "Gen" abbreviation is found in this paragraph as well.

Paragraph VIII

Long's handwriting in this paragraph looks cramped compared to the earlier paragraphs, perhaps indicating that his hand had grown tired. A clue for this is the fact that the writing is now more upright than it was in the previous paragraphs when it displayed a slight rightward tilt. The text's indentation is also minimal compared to paragraph VI. Both of these characteristics appear to indicate that Long also realized he had begun to run out of space. He therefore adjusted his writing style to fit all of the text onto the paper. In terms of the text's content, Long's characteristic abbreviation of "General" is present, although he wrote "Gens" instead of "Genl's" in the sentence "the commands of Genl's Longstreet, Jackson and McLaw's" in Marshall's draft. Long also added a

"+" symbol in the portion of the sentence from Marshall's text that reads "will cover the route of the army [+] bring up all stragglers, that may have been left behind."

Paragraphs IX, X, and End

These paragraphs display most of the idiosyncrasies evident elsewhere in Col. Long's version of the orders. Major Marshall spelled Boonsboro as "Boonesboro" in paragraph IX, which Long changed in his version of the orders. Otherwise, Long's version followed Marshall's text closely. The draft copy of the orders furthermore contains the signature of Robert H. Chilton that is clearly different from the name that Long copied onto his copy of the orders. Long also added "For Maj Gen D. H. Hill Comdg Division," which is missing from Special Orders No. 190. Notably, that address does not adhere to Charles Marshall's standard for neatness. Long did not even attempt to straighten his lines, with the result that the text is crammed into the lower left corner of the document.

Conclusions

Summing up this brief analysis, several observations can be made about the lost copy of Special Orders No. 191 compared to the draft copy of Special Orders No. 190. These begin with the fact that Col. Long had a unique way of abbreviating the word "General." Long also did not take care when writing out his copy of the orders. His handwriting is sloppy, uses very little punctuation, displays uneven capitalization, is not straight, and contains spelling errors. The size of the words on page one of the orders is also larger than on most of page two, indicating that Long began to run out of space and compressed his writing to squeeze in the remaining text.

In general, the errors and sloppiness of the writing, as well as the use of a pencil, also suggest that Long wrote out the document quickly, perhaps even on a pad against his thigh, instead of upright at a desk with a pen and a well of ink. These characteristics could hint at Long writing out the copy of Special Orders No. 191 extemporaneously, as if he had been asked to write them by Lee or Jeb Stuart in the midst of his other duties. Lastly, the orders bear the hallmarks of being made from an already finalized copy, including the bracketed word "Confidential," the forged signature of R. H. Chilton, and the addition of the address for D. H. Hill.

Bibliography

Archival Sources

Antietam National Battlefield Library, Keedysville, MD
    Virginia Cavalry Vertical File
Huntington Library, San Marino, CA
    Stuart (Jeb) Military Papers
Library of Virginia, Richmond, VA
    Daniel Harvey Hill Papers
    Robert E. Lee Letters, 1862-1865
    Monocacy National Battlefield Park, Frederick, MD
    Bloss Family Papers
    Boicourt, Enoch G. Affidavit, July 30, 1906
    Hostetter, William H. Affidavit, Dec. 18, 1905
    Mitchell, Barton W. Letters and Papers
    Vance, David B. Affidavit, Sept. 15, 1903
    Welch, George W. Affidavit, July 24, 1906
State Archives of North Carolina. Raleigh, NC
    Daniel Harvey Hill Papers, 1821-1889
Union Presbyterian Seminary, William Smith Morton Library, Richmond, VA
    Robert L. Dabney Papers and Miscellaneous Papers
University of North Carolina, Southern Historical Collection, The Wilson Library, Chapel Hill, NC
    Daniel Harvey Hill Papers, 1848-1951
    Lafayette McLaws Papers, 1836-1897
    Edwin Augustus Osborne Papers, 1832-1928
    William Nelson Pendleton Papers, 1798-1889
University of Virginia, Albert and Shirley Small Special Collections Library, Charlottesville, VA
    General Thomas L. Rosser and Rosser Family Papers 1774-1983
    McDowell-Miller-Warner Papers
Virginia Military Institute, Lexington, VA
    Daniel Harvey Hill Papers, 1816-1945
Virginia Museum of History and Culture
    Robert Edward Lee Headquarters Papers, 1850–1876
Washington and Lee University, Lexington, VA
    Elisha Franklin Paxton Papers
Washington County Historical Society, Hagerstown, MD
    Angela Kirkham Davis. War Reminiscences: A Letter to My Nieces

Published Primary Sources

Alexander, Edward Porter. *Military Memoirs of a Confederate: A Critical Narrative.* New York, NY: Charles Scribner's Sons, 1907.

Allan, William. *The Army of Northern Virginia in 1862.* Boston, MA: Houghton Mifflin, 1892.

_____. "Memoranda of Conversations with General Robert E. Lee." *Lee the Soldier.* Gary W. Gallagher, ed. Lincoln, NE and London: University of Nebraska Press, 1996.

_____. "First Maryland Campaign." *Southern Historical Society Papers,* Vol. 14 (1886).

Andrews, Welburn J. *Sketch of Company K. 23rd South Carolina Volunteers, in the Civil War, from 1862-1865.* Richmond, VA: Whittet & Shepperson, Printers, 1909.

Andrews, William H. *Footprints of a Regiment: A Recollection of the 1st Georgia Regulars.* Atlanta, GA: Longstreet Press, 1992.

_____. "Hardships of Georgia Regulars." *Confederate Veteran,* Vol. 17, No. 5 (May 1909).

Arnold, Thomas J. "The Lost Dispatch—A War Mystery." *Confederate Veteran,* Vol. 30, No. 8 (August 1922).

Atkisson, George B. "Charlie 'Recruit' to Troup Artillery." *Confederate Veteran,* Vol. 19, No. 11 (November 1911).

Avery, A. C. "On the Life and Character of Lieut.-General D. H. Hill." *Southern Historical Society Papers, Vol.* 21 (1893).

Bartlett, Napier. *Military Record of Louisiana.* New Orleans, LA, 1875.

_____. *A Soldier's Story of the War.* New Orleans, 1874.

Baylor, George. *Bull Run to Bull Run or Four Years in the Army of Northern Virginia.* Richmond, VA: B. F. Johnson Publishing Company, 1900.

Beale, George W. "Maryland Campaign: The Cavalry Fight at Boonsboro Graphically Described." *Southern Historical Society Papers,* Vol. 25 (1897).

Beale, Richard L. T. *History of the Ninth Virginia Cavalry.* Richmond, VA: B. F. Johnson Publishing, 1899.

Beall, Thomas B. "Reminiscences About Sharpsburg." *Confederate Veteran,* Vol. 1, No. 8 (August 1893).

Beck, Brandon, ed. *Third Alabama! The Civil War Memoirs of Brigadier General Cullen Battle, CSA.* Tuscaloosa, AL: University of Alabama Press, 2000.

Benning, Henry L. "Notes by General H. L. Benning on the Battle of Sharpsburg." *Southern Historical Society Papers,* Vol. 16 (1888).

Bernard, George. *War Talks of Confederate Veterans.* Dayton, OH: Morningside Press, 1981.

Betts, Alexander D. *Experience of a Confederate Chaplain, 1861-1865.* Piedmont, SC, 1904.

Blackford, William W. *War Years with Jeb Stuart.* New York, NY: Charles Scribner's Sons, 1945.

Bloss, John M. "Antietam and the Lost Dispatch." *War Talks in Kansas.* Kansas Commandery of the Military Order of the Loyal Legion of the United States (MOLLUS), eds. Kansas City, MO: Franklin Hudson Publishing Company, 1906.

Booth, George W. *Personal Reminiscences of a Maryland Soldier in the War Between the States.* Baltimore, MD: Fleet-McGinley & Company, 1898.

Brooks, Ulysses. R. ed. *Stories of the Confederacy.* Columbia, SC: The State Company, 1912.

Brown, Edmund R. *The Twenty-Seventh Indiana Volunteer Infantry in the War of the Rebellion 1861 to 1865.* Monticello, IN, 1899.

Buck, Samuel D. *With the Old Confeds: Actual Experiences of a Captain in the Line.* Gaithersburg, MD: Butternut Press, 1983.

Buel, Clarence C. & Johnson, Robert U., eds. *Battles and Leaders of the Civil War*. 3 Vols. New York, NY: The Century Co., 1884-1888.

Caldwell, James F. J. *The History of a Brigade of South Carolinians Known First as "Gregg's" and Subsequently as "McGowan's Brigade."* Philadelphia, PA: Morningside Press, 1866.

Carman, Ezra A. *The Maryland Campaign of September 1862: Volume 1, South Mountain*. Thomas G. Clemens, ed. El Dorado, CA: Savas Beatie, 2010.

Carraway, D. F. "Lieutenant-General A. P. Hill: Some Reminiscences of the Famous Virginia Commander." *Southern Historical Society Papers*, Vol. 19 (1891).

Cauthen, Charles E. *Family Letters of the Three Wade Hamptons*. Columbia, SC: University of South Carolina Press, 1953.

Chamberlayne, John H. *Ham Chamberlayne – Virginian Letters and Papers of an Artillery Officer in the War for Southern Independence, 1861-1865*. Richmond, VA: Dietz Printing Co. 1932.

Charles, Robert K. "Brief Sketch of the First Maryland Campaign." *Confederate Veteran*, Vol. 14, No. 2 (February 1906).

Clark, Walter, ed. *Histories of the Several Regiments and Battalions from North Carolina in the Great War*. Wendell, NC: Broadfoot Publishing, 1982.

_____. "The Battle of Sharpsburg—Personal Incidents." *The Wake Forest Student*, Vol. 17, No. 2 (November 1897).

Cockrell, Monroe F., ed., *Gunner with Stonewall: Reminiscences of William T. Poague*. Jackson, TN: McCowat-Mercer, 1957.

Coco, Gregory A., ed. *Through Blood and Fire: The Civil War Letters of Major Charles J. Mills, 1862-1865*. Gettysburg, PA, 1982.

Colgrove, Silas. "The Finding of Lee's Lost Orders." *Battles and Leaders of the Civil War*, Vol. 2. Robert Underwood Johnson and Clarence Clough Buel, eds. New York, NY: The Century Company, 1885.

Cooke, John Esten. *Stonewall Jackson: A Military Biography*. New York, NY: D. Appleton and Company, 1866.

_____. *The Life of Stonewall Jackson: From Official Papers, Contemporary Narratives, and Personal Acquaintance*. New York, NY: Ayres & Wade, 1863.

Cox, Jacob D. *Military Reminiscences of the Civil War, Vol. 1: April 1861-November 1863*. New York, NY: Charles Scribner's Sons, 1900.

Cummings, Cully C. "Mississippi Boys at Sharpsburg." *Confederate Veteran*, Vol. 5, No. 1 (January 1897).

Curran, Robert E., ed. *John Dooley's Civil War: An Irish American's Journey in the First Virginia Infantry Regiment*. Knoxville, TN: The University of Tennessee Press, 2012.

Cutrer, Thomas W., ed. *Longstreet's Aide: The Civil War Letters of Major Thomas J. Goree*. Charlottesville, VA: University Press of Virginia, 1995.

Dabney, Robert L. *Life and Campaigns of Lieut.-Gen. Jackson*. New York, NY: Blelock, 1866.

_____. *A Memorial of Lieut. Colonel John T. Thornton, of the Third Virginia Cavalry, C.S.A*. Richmond, VA: Presbyterian Committee of Publication, 1864.

Daniel, Frederick S. *Richmond Howitzers in the War: Four Years Campaigning with the Army of Northern Virginia*. Richmond, VA, 1891.

Davis, Jefferson. "Robert E. Lee." *The North American Review*, Vol. 150, No. 398 (January 1890).

Davis, Nicholas A. *Campaign from Texas to Maryland*. Richmond, VA: Office of the Presbyterian Committee, 1863.

Dedmons, Francis B. Dedmond. "Harvey Davis's Unpublished Civil War 'Diary' and the Story of Company D of the First North Carolina Cavalry." *Appalachian Journal*, Vol. 13, No. 4 (Summer 1986).

Dickert, D. Augustus. *History of Kershaw's Brigade*. Dayton, OH: Morningside Books, 1973.

Dinkins, James. *1861 to 1865: Personal Recollections and Experiences in the Confederate Army*. Dayton, OH: Morningside Press, 1975.

_____. "The Griffith-Barksdale-Humphrey Brigade, and Its Campaigns." *Southern Historical Society Papers*, Vol. 32 (1904).

Douglas, Henry K. *I Rode with Stonewall*. Chapel Hill, NC: University of North Carolina Press, 1940.

_____. "Stonewall Jackson in Maryland." *Battles and Leaders of the Civil War*, Vol. 2. Robert Underwood Johnson and Clarence Clough Buel, eds. New York, NY: The Century Company, 1885.

Dowdey, Clifford & Manarin, Lewis H., eds. *The Wartime Papers of R. E. Lee*. Boston, MA: Little Brown & Co., 1961.

Dozier, Graham T., ed. *A Gunner in Lee's Army: The Civil War Letters of Thomas Henry Carter*. Chapel Hill, NC: The University of North Carolina Press, 2014.

Dunaway, Wayland F. *Reminiscences of a Rebel*. New York, NY: The Neale Publishing Company, 1913.

Durkin, Joseph T., ed. *John Dooley Confederate Soldier, His War Journal*. Washington, DC: Georgetown University Press, 1945.

Early, Jubal A. *Autobiographical Sketch and Narrative of the War Between the States*. Philadelphia, PA: Lippincott, 1912.

_____. "Letter from Jubal A. Early." *Southern Historical Society Papers*, Vol. 7 (1879).

Edwards, W. H. *A Condensed History of Seventeenth Regiment S.C.V. From Its Organization to the Close of the War*. Columbia, SC: R. L. Bryan Co., 1906.

Eggleston, George. *A Rebel's Recollections*. Bloomington, IN: Indiana University Press, 1959.

Evans, Clement A., ed. *Confederate Military History*. 12 Vols. Atlanta, GA: Confederate Publishing Company, 1899.

Evans, Robert G., ed., *The 16th Mississippi Infantry: Civil War Letters and Reminiscences*. Jackson, MS: University Press of Mississippi, 2002.

Folsom, James M. *Heroes and Martyrs of Georgia*. Baltimore, MD: Butternut and Blue, 1995.

Fonerden, Clarence A. *A Brief History of the Military Career of Carpenter's Battery*. New Market, VA: Henkel & Co. 1911.

Forsyth, Charles. *History of the 3d Alabama Regiment, C.S.A.* Montgomery, AL: Confederate Publishing Co. 1866.

Gallagher, Gary, ed. *Fighting for the Confederacy: The Personal Recollections of General Edward Porter Alexander*. Chapel Hill, NC: University of North Carolina Press, 1989.

Gibbon, John. *Personal Recollections of the Civil War*. New York, NY: G.P. Putnam's Sons, 1928.

Giles, Valerius C. *Rags and Hope: The Recollections of Val C. Giles, Four Years with Hood's Brigade, Fourth Texas Infantry*. New York, NY: Coward-McCann, 1961.

Goldsborough, William W. *The Maryland Line in the Confederate States Army*. Baltimore, MD: Kelly, Piet & Co., 1869.

Goldsmith, Washington L. "Crucial Test for General S. D. Lee." *Confederate Veteran*, Vol. 3, No. 5 (May 1895).

Gordon, John B. *Reminiscences of the Civil War*. New York, NY: Charles Scribner's Sons, 1904.

Govan, Gilbert E. & Livingood, James W., eds. *The Haskell Memoirs*. New York, NY: G. P. Putnam's Sons, 1960.

Haines, Jr., Joseph D. ed. *The Diary of Col. John Henry Stover Funk of the Stonewall Brigade, 1861-1862*. Columbia, SC: Shotwell Publishing, 2022.

Hamilton, J. G. De Roulhac, ed. *The Papers of Randolph A. Shotwell*. 3 Vols. Raleigh, NC: The North Carolina Historical Commission, 1929-1936.

Hardee, William J. *Rifle and Light Infantry Tactics for the Exercise and Manoeuvres of Troops when Acting as Light Infantry or Riflemen*, 2 Vols. Philadelphia, PA: Lippincott, Grambo & Co., 1855.

Hassler, William H., ed. *The Civil War Letters of William Dorsey Pender to Fanny Pender*. Chapel Hill, NC: University of North Carolina Press, 1962.

Haynes, Draughton S. *Field Diary of a Confederate Soldier*. Darien, GA: Ashantilly Press, 1963.

Hill, Daniel Harvey. "The Lost Dispatch." *The Land We Love*, Vol. IV. Charlotte, NC: Hill, Irwin & Co., 1868.

_____. "The Lost Dispatch—Letter from General D. H. Hill." *Southern Historical Society Papers*, Vol. 13 (1885).

_____. "Address Before the Reunion of the Virginia Division, Army of Northern Virginia." *Southern Historical Society Papers*, Vol. 13 (1885).

Hood, John B. *Advance and Retreat: Personal Experiences in the United States and Confederate States Armies*. New Orleans, LA: Hood Orphan Memorial Fund, 1880.

Hopkins, Luther W. *From Bull Run to Appomattox: A Boy's View*. Baltimore, MD: Fleet-McGinley & Company, 1908.

Hough, Franklin B. *History of Duryee's Brigade During the Campaign in Virginia Under Gen. Pope and in Maryland Under Gen. McClellan in the Summer and Autumn of 1862*. Albany, GA: J. Munsell, 1864.

Hubbs, G. Ward, ed. *Voices from Company D: Diaries by the Greensboro Guards, Fifth Alabama Infantry Regiment*. Athens, GA: University of Georgia Press, 2003.

Hughes, William E., ed. *The Civil War Papers of Lt. Colonel Newton T. Colby, New York Infantry*. Jefferson, NC: McFarland & Company, 2003.

Hunter, Alexander. "A High Private's Account of the Battle of Sharpsburg." *Southern Historical Society Papers*, Vol. 10 (1882).

Hurst, Marshall B. *History of the Fourteenth Alabama Vols*. Richmond, VA, 1863.

Huyette, Miles C. *The Maryland Campaign and the Battle of Antietam*. Buffalo, NY: The Hammond Press, 1915.

Johnson, William A. "The Capture of Harper's Ferry." *Confederate Veteran*, Vol. 5, No. 6 (June 1897).

Johnston, David E. *The Story of a Confederate Boy*. Ann Arbor, MI: University Microfilms, 1972.

Johnston, J. S. "A Reminiscence of Sharpsburg." *Southern Historical Society Papers*, Vol. 8 (1880).

Kittrell, Warren. *History of the Eleventh Georgia Volunteers*. Richmond, VA: Smith, Bailey & Co., 1863.

Lang, David. "Civil War Letters of Colonel David Lang." *Florida Historical Quarterly*, Vol. LIV (1976).

Ledford, P. L. *Reminiscences of the Civil War, 1861-1865*. Thomasville, NC: News Print House, 1909.

Lee, Fitzhugh. *General Lee*. New York, NY: D. Appleton and Company, 1898.

_____. "Letter from General Fitz Lee." *Southern Historical Society Papers*, Vol. 4 (1877).

Lee, Laura E. *Forget-Me-Nots of the Civil War, A Romance Containing Original Letters of Two Confederate Soldiers*. St. Louis, MO: A. R. Fleming Printing Co. 1909.

Lee, Robert E., Jr. *Recollections and Letters of General Robert E. Lee*. New York, NY: Archibald, Constable & Co., Ltd., 1904.

Lee, Susan P. *Memoirs of William Nelson Pendleton*. Philadelphia, PA: Hess Publications, 1893.

Long, Armistead L. *Memoirs of Robert E. Lee*. New York, NY: J. M. Stoddart and Company, 1886.

Longstreet, James. *From Manassas to Appomattox*. Bloomington, IN: Indiana University Press, 1960.

———. "The Invasion of Maryland." *Battles and Leaders of the Civil War*, Vol. 2. Robert Underwood Johnson and Clarence Clough Buel, eds. New York, NY: The Century Company, 1885.

McCarthy, Carlton. *Contributions to a History of the Richmond Howitzer Battalion*. Baltimore, MD: Butternut and Blue, 2000.

———. *Detailed Minutiae of Soldier Life in the Army of Northern Virginia, 1861-1865*. Richmond, VA: B. F. Johnson Publishing Co., 1899.

McClellan, Henry B. *The Life and Campaigns of Major-General J. E. B. Stuart*. Boston, MA: Houghton, Mifflin and Company, 1885.

———. *Campaigns of Stuart's Cavalry*. Edison, NJ: Blue and Gray Press, 1993.

McClendon, William A. *Recollections of War Times by an Old Veteran While Under Stonewall Jackson and Lieut. General James Longstreet*. Montgomery, AL: The Paragon Press, 1909.

McDaniel, J. J. *Diary of the Battles, Marches and Incidents of the Seventh S. C. Regiment*. (1862).

McDonald, Archie P., ed. *Make Me a Map of the Valley: The Civil War Journal of Stonewall Jackson's Topographer*. Dallas, TX: Southern Methodist University Press, 1973.

McLaws, Lafayette. "The Maryland Campaign." Savannah, GA: Confederate Veterans Association, 1896.

———. "The Capture of Harper's Ferry." *Philadelphia Weekly Press*, Vol. XXXI (1888).

McMurray, Richard, ed. *Footprints of a Regiment: A Recollection of the 1st Georgia Regulars*. Atlanta, SGA: Longstreet Press, 1992.

Maurice, Frederick, ed. *An Aide-de-Camp of Lee: Being the Papers of Colonel Charles Marshall*. Boston, MA: Little, Brown and Co., 1927.

Military Order of the Loyal Legion of the United States (MOLLUS), eds. *War Talks in Kansas*. Kansas City, MO: Franklin Hudson Publishing Company, 1906.

Mills, George H. "Supplemental Sketch Sixteenth Regiment." *Histories of the Several Regiments and Battalions from North Carolina*, Vol. 4. Walter Clark, ed. Goldsboro, NC: Nash Brothers, Book and Job Printers, 1901.

Mixson, Frank M. *Reminiscences of a Private*. Columbia, SC: The State Company, 1910.

Moore, Frank, ed. *The Rebellion Record: A Diary of American Events*. 8 Vols. New York, NY: G. P. Putnam, 1864.

Moore, Edward A. *The Story of a Cannoneer Under Stonewall Jackson*. New York, NY: The Neale Publishing Company, 1907.

Moore, Robert A. & Silver, J. W., eds. *A Life for the Confederacy, as Recorded in the Pocket Diaries of Pvt. Robert A. Moore. Co. G. 17th Mississippi Regiment, Confederate Guards, Holly Springs, Mississippi*. Wendell, NC: Broadfoot Publishing Company, 1987.

Morgan, William H. *Personal Reminiscences of the War of 1861-5*. Lynchburg, VA: J. P. Bell Company, 1911.

Morrison, Joseph G. "Jackson at Harper's Ferry." *Philadelphia Weekly Press*, Dec. 22, 1883.

Myers, Frank M. *The Comanches: A History of White's Battalion, Virginia Cavalry*. Baltimore, MD: Kelly, Piet, & Co., Publishers, 1871.

Neese, George. *Three Years in the Confederate Horse Artillery*. New York, NY: The Neale Publishing Company, 1911.

Nisbet, James C. *Four Years on the Firing Line*. Chattanooga, TN: The Imperial Press, 1914.

Oeffinger, John C., ed. *A Soldier's General: The Civil War Letters of Major General Lafayette McLaws*. Chapel Hill, NC: The University of North Carolina Press, 2002.

Oldaker, Glenn C., ed. *Centennial Tales: Memoirs of Colonel "Chester" S. Bassett French, Extra Aide-de-Camp to Generals Lee and Jackson, The Army of Northern Virginia, 1861-1865*. New York, NY: Carlton Press, 1962.

Otey, William Mercer. "The Story of Our Great War." *Confederate Veteran,* Vol. 7, No. 8 (August 1899).

Owen, William M. *In Camp and Battle with the Washington Artillery.* Boston, MA: Ticknor and Company, 1885.

Park, Robert E. *Sketch of the Twelfth Alabama Infantry of Battle's Brigade, Rodes' Division, or Early's Corps of the Army of Northern Virginia.* Richmond, VA: W. M. Ellis Jones, Book and Job Printer, 1906.

Parks, Leighton. *Turnpikes and Dirt Roads.* New York, NY: Charles Scribner's Sons, 1927.

_____. "What a Boy Saw of the Civil War." *The Century Magazine,* Vol. 70, No. 2 (1905).

Philpot, G. B. "A Maryland Boy in the Confederate Army." *Confederate Veteran,* Vol. 24, No. 7 (July 1916).

Polley, Joseph B. *A Soldier's Letters to Charming Nellie.* New York, NY: The Neale Publishing Company, 1908.

_____. *Hood's Texas Brigade: Its Marches, Its Battles, Its Achievements.* Dayton, OH: Morningside Bookshop, 1976.

Ramsay, John A. "Additional Sketch Tenth Regiment. Light Batteries A, D, F and I." *Histories of the Several Regiments and Battalions from North Carolina,* Vol. 1. Walter Clark, ed. Goldsboro, NC: Nash Brothers, Book and Job Printers, 1901.

Rawl, J. P. "Maryland Raid." *Recollections and Reminiscences 1861-1865 through World War I,* 12 Vols. United Daughters of the Confederacy, eds. Charleston, SC: UDC, 2001.

Rawle, William B. *History of the Third Pennsylvania Cavalry in the American Civil War, 1861-1865.* Philadelphia, PA: Franklin Printing Company, 1905.

Rawley, James A. *The American Civil War: An English View. The Writings of Field Marshal Viscount Wolseley.* Mechanicsburg, PA: Stackpole Books, 2002.

Ray, Neill W. "Sixth Regiment." *Histories of the Several Regiments and Battalions from North Carolina in the Great War, 1861-'65,* Vol. 1. Walter Clark, ed. Goldsboro, NC: Nash Brothers, Book and Job Printers, 1901.

Rea, D. B. "Cavalry Incidents of the Maryland Campaign." *The Maine Bugle,* Campaign II, Call II (April 1895).

Reese, James. "Private Soldier Life—Humorous Features." *Confederate Veteran,* Vol. 16, No. 4 (April 1908).

Robertson, Robert S. "Diary of the War." *Old Fort News,* Vol. XXVIII, No. 1 (Jan.-Mar. 1963).

Robson, John S. *Reminiscences of the Civil War.* Durham, NC: The Educator Co. Printers and Binders, 1898.

Schiller, Herbert N. *A Captain's War: The Letter and Diaries of William H. S. Burgwyn 1861-1865.* Shippensburg, PA: White Mane Publishing Co., 1994.

Sheeran, James B. *Confederate Chaplain.* Milwaukee, WI: The Bruce Publishing Company, 1960.

Sieburg, Evelyn R. & Hansen II, James E., eds. *Memoirs of a Confederate Staff Officer from Bethel to Bentonville.* Shippensburg, PA: White Mane Publishing Co., 1998.

Skock, George & Perkins, Mark W., eds. *Lone Star Confederate: A Gallant and Good Soldier of the Fifth Texas Infantry.* College Station, TX: Texas A&M University Press, 2003.

Sloan, John A. *Reminiscences of the Guilford Grays.* Washington, DC: R. O. Polkinhorn, Printer, 1883.

Smith, James P. "With Stonewall Jackson in the Army of Northern Virginia." *Southern Historical Society Papers,* Vol. 43 (1920).

Smith, N. S. "Additional Sketch Thirteenth Regiment." *Histories of the Several Regiments and Battalions from North Carolina,* Vol. 1. Walter Clark, ed. Goldsboro, NC: Nash Brothers, Book and Job Printers, 1901.

Smith, William A. *The Anson Guards, Company C, Fourteenth Regiment North Carolina Volunteers 1861-1865.* Wendell, NC: Broadfoot Publishing, 1978.

Sorrel, G. Moxley. *Recollection of a Confederate Staff Officer.* New York, NY: The Neale Publishing Company, 1905.

Steiner, Lewis H. *Report of Lewis H. Steiner, Inspector of the Sanitary Commission Containing a Diary Kept During the Rebel Occupation of Frederick, MD, and an Account of the Operations of the U.S. Sanitary Commission During the Campaign in Maryland, September, 1862.* New York, NY: Anson D. F. Randolph, 1862.

Stevens, John W. *War Reminiscences.* Powhatan, VA: Derwent Books, 1982.

Stiles, Robert. *Four Years Under Marse Robert.* New York, NY: The Neale Publishing Company, 1904.

Stocker, Jeffery, ed. *From Huntsville to Appomattox: R. T. Coles's History of the 4th Alabama Infantry, C. S. A., Army of Northern Virginia.* Knoxville, TN: University of Tennessee Press, 1996.

Styple, William B., ed. *Writing and Fighting the Confederate War: The Letters of Peter Wellington Alexander.* Kearny, NJ: Belle Grove Publishing Co., 2002.

Squires, Charles W. "The 'Boy Officer' of the Washington Artillery, Part 1." *Civil War Times Illustrated,* Vol. XIV, No. 2 (May 1975).

Swank, Walbrook D. *Sabres, Saddles, and Spurs: Lieutenant Colonel William R. Carter, CSA.* Philadelphia, PA: Burd Street Press, 1998.

Taylor, Michael W., ed. *To Drive the Enemy from Southern Soil: The Letters of Col. Francis Marion Parker and the History of the 30th Regiment North Carolina Troops.* Dayton, OH: Morningside Press, 1998.

Taylor, Walter H. *Four Years with General Lee.* New York, NY: D. Appleton and Company, 1878.

_____. *General Lee: His Campaigns in Virginia, 1861-1865 with Personal Reminiscences.* Norfolk, VA: Nusbaum Book and News Company, 1906.

Tower, R. Lockwood, ed. *Lee's Adjutant: The Wartime Letters of Colonel Walter Herron Taylor 1862-1865.* Columbia, SC: University of South Carolina Press, 1995.

Trimpi, Helen, ed. "Lafayette McLaws' Aide-de-Camp: The Maryland Campaign Diary of Captain Henry Lord Page King." *Civil War Regiments: A Journal of the American Civil War,* Vol. 6, No. 2 (1998).

Trout, Robert J., ed. *With Pen and Saber: The Letters and Diaries of J. E. B. Stuart's Staff Officer.* Harrisburg, PA: Stackpole Books, 1995.

Turner, Charles W., ed. *Captain Greenlee Davidson, C.S.A. Diary and Letters, 1851-1863,* Verona, VA: McClure Press, 1975.

Turner, V. E. & Wall, H. C. "Twenty-Third Regiment." *Histories of the Several Regiments and Battalions from North Carolina in the Great War, 1861-'65,* Vol. 2. Walter Clark, ed. Goldsboro, NC: Nash Brothers, Book and Job Printers, 1901.

U. S. War Department. *The War of the Rebellion: A Compilation of the Official Records of the Union and Confederate Armies.* 128 vols. Washington, DC: Government Printing Office, 1880-1901.

Venn, Frank H. "That Flag of Truce at Antietam." *Confederate Veteran,* Vol. 4, No. 12 (December 1896).

Von Borcke, Heros. *Memoirs of the Confederate War for Independence.* Gaithersburg, MD: Butternut & Blue, 1985.

Walbrook, D. Swank, ed. *Sabres, Saddles, and Spurs.* Shippensburg, PA: Burd Street Press, 1998.

Walcott, Charles F. *History of the Twenty-First Regiment Massachusetts Volunteers.* Boston, MA: Houghton Mifflin and Co., 1882.

Walker, John G. "Jackson's Capture of Harper's Ferry." *Battles and Leaders of the Civil War,* Vol. 2. Robert Underwood Johnson and Clarence Clough Buel, eds. New York, NY: The Century Company, 1885.

_____. "Sharpsburg." *Battles and Leaders of the Civil War*, Vol. 2. Robert Underwood Johnson and Clarence Clough Buel, eds. New York, NY: The Century Company, 1885.

White, Thomas H. "About The Shelling of Leesburg." *Confederate Veteran*, Vol. 21, No. 1 (January 1913).

Williams, Jonathan Whitehead. *His Life and Times with the 5th Alabama, C.S.A. Company "D" Greensboro Guards*. Greensboro, AL, 1903.

Wilson, Gary, ed. "The Diary of John S. Tucker: Confederate Soldier from Alabama." *The Alabama Historical Quarterly*, Vol. XLII, No. 1 (Spring 1981).

Wise, George. *History of Seventeenth Virginia Infantry*. Baltimore: Kelly, Piet & Co. 1870.

_____. *Campaigns and Battles of the Army of Northern Virginia*. New York, NY: The Neale Publishing Company, 1916.

Wolseley, Garnet J. "General Lee." *MacMillan's Magazine*, Vol. 55 (November 1886 to April 1887).

Wood, James H. *The War: "Stonewall" Jackson: His Campaigns and Battles, the Regiment as I Saw Them*. Cumberland, MD: Eddy Press Corporation, 1910.

Wood, William. *Reminiscences of Big I*. Jackson, TN: McCowen-Mercer Press, 1956.

Worsham, John. *One of Jackson's Foot Cavalry*. New York, NY: The Neale Publishing Company, 1912.

Young, Charles P. "History of Crenshaw Battery." *Southern Historical Society Papers*, Vol. 31 (1903).

Zon, Calvin G. ed. *The Good Fight That Didn't End: Henry P. Goddard's Accounts of Civil War and Peace*. Columbia, SC: University of South Carolina Press, 2008.

Unpublished Manuscripts

Allen, John Owen. "The Strength of the Union and Confederate Forces at Second Manassas." Thesis Submitted for Master of Arts Degree (1993). George Mason University. Fairfax, VA.

Datzmann, Richard C. "Who Found Lee's Lost Dispatch?" Lost Orders File. Antietam National Battlefield Library. Keedysville, MD.

Markell, Catherine Susannah Thomas. "Diary: Frederick, Maryland in Peace and War, 1856-1864." Frederick Historical Society. Frederick, MD.

Neel, James C. "War Reminiscences." Military Collection, Box 71, Folder 36. State Archives of North Carolina. Raleigh, NC.

Schaeffer, Ann R. L. "Records of the Past: Ann R. L. Schaeffer Civil War Diary, September 4–23, 1862." Transcribed by Kira Vaughan. Frederick Historical Society. Frederick, MD.

Venable, Charles S. "Personal Reminiscences of the Confederate War" (Sept. 28, 1889). The McDowell-Miller-Warner Papers, Accession #2969-a, Box 5, Special Collections Department. University of Virginia Library. Charlottesville, VA.

Newspapers and Periodicals

Alexandria Gazette
Baltimore American
Baltimore Sun
Fayetteville [NC] Observer
Frederick Examiner
Frederick News (Post)
Mobile Advertiser and Register

New York Herald
New York Times
New York Tribune
Philadelphia Inquirer
Philadelphia Ledger
Philadelphia Weekly Express
Richmond Examiner
Washington Evening Star

Maps and Atlases

Bond, Isaac. *Map of Frederick County, MD*. Baltimore, MD: E. Sachse & Co., 1858.
Lake, D. J. *Atlas of Frederick County, Maryland*. Philadelphia, PA: C.O. Titus & Co., 1873.
Sachse, Edward. *Bird's Eye View of Frederick, Md*. Baltimore, MD: E. Sachse & Co., 1854.

Secondary Works

Abbott, Eleanor D. *A Sketch of Barbara Fritchie, Whittier's Heroine*. Frederick, MD: Frederick News Post Publishing Co., 1921.
Andrew, Jr., Rod. *Wade Hampton: Confederate Warrior to Southern Redeemer*. Chapel Hill, NC: The University of North Carolina Press, 2008.
Andrews, J. Cutler. *The South Reports the Civil War*. Princeton, NJ: Princeton University Press, 1970.
Armstrong, Jr., Marian V. *Unfurl Those Colors! McClellan, Sumner, and the Second Army Corps in the Antietam Campaign*. Tuscaloosa, AL: The University of Alabama Press, 2008.
Armstrong, Richard L. *19th and 20th Virginia Cavalry*. Lynchburg, VA: H. E. Howard, 1994.
Bartholomees, Jr., J. Boone. *Buff Facings and Gilt Buttons: Staff and Headquarters Operations in the Army of Northern Virginia, 1862-1865*. Columbia, SC: University of South Carolina Press, 1998.
Barringer, Sheridan R. *Fighting for General Lee: General Rufus Barringer and the North Carolina Cavalry Brigade*. El Dorado, CA: Savas Beatie, 2016.
Baxter, Nancy N. *Gallant Fourteenth: The Story of an Indiana Civil War Regiment*. Carmel, IN: Guild Press of Indiana, 1980.
Bridges, David P. *Fighting with JEB Stuart: Major James Breathed and the Confederate Horse Artillery*. Arlington, VA: Breathed Bridges Best, 2006.
Bridges, Hal. *Lee's Maverick General: Daniel Harvey Hill*. Lincoln, NE: University of Nebraska Press, 1961.
Bryan, M. Chris. *Cedar Mountain to Antietam: A Civil War Campaign History of the Union XII Corps, July-September 1862*. El Dorado, CA: Savas Beatie, 2022.
Chambers, Lenoir. *Stonewall Jackson*. 2 Vols. New York, NY: William Morrow, 1959.
Collins, Darrell L. *The Army of Northern Virginia: Organization, Strength, Casualties, 1861-1865*. Jefferson, NC: McFarland, 2016.
Davis, James A. *51st Virginia Infantry*. Lynchburg, VA: H. E. Howard, 1984.
Douglas, David G. *A Boot Full of Memories: Captain Leonard Williams, 2nd South Carolina Cavalry*. Camden, SC: Gray Fox, 2003.
Driver, Jr., Robert J. & Ruffner, Kevin C. *1st Battalion Virginia Infantry, 39th Battalion Virginia Cavalry, and 24th Battalion Virginia Partisan Rangers*. Lynchburg, VA: H. E. Howard, 1996.

Dugdale, Jeffrey. *Confederate Uniforms During the Maryland Campaign, September 1862.* Thatcham, Berks, UK: Banners High, 2021.

Duncan, Richard R. *Beleaguered Winchester: A Virginia Community at War. 1861-1865.* Baton Rouge, LA: Louisiana State University Press, 2007.

Dyer, Frederick H. *A Compendium of the War of the Rebellion.* 3 Vols. New York, NY: T. Yoseloff, 1959.

Ernst, Kathleen A. *Too Afraid to Cry: Maryland Civilians in the Antietam Campaign.* Mechanicsburg, PA: Stackpole Books, 1999.

Evans, Tracy. "Invitation to Battle: Special Orders 191." *Catoctin History* (2014).

Fain, J. Tyree. "Robert E. Lee—Maurice." *Tennessee Historical Magazine*, Vol. 8, No. 3 (October 1924).

Freeman, Douglas Southall. *R. E. Lee: A Biography.* 4 Vols. New York, NY: Charles Scribner's Sons, 1934.

_____. *Lee's Lieutenants.* 3 Vols. New York, NY: Charles Scribner's Sons, 1942.

Freiheit, Laurence H. *Boots and Saddles: Cavalry During the Maryland Campaign of September 1862.* Iowa City, IA: Camp Pope Publishing, 2013.

Gallagher, Gary W., ed. *Lee the Soldier.* Lincoln, NE: University of Nebraska Press, 1996.

_____., ed., *The Antietam Campaign.* Chapel Hill, NC: University of North Carolina Press, 1999.

Gordon, Paul and Rita. *Frederick County, Maryland: Never the Like Again.* Frederick, MD: The Heritage Partnership, 1995.

_____. *Frederick County, Maryland: A Playground of the Civil War.* Frederick, MD: The Heritage Partnership, 1994.

Government Printing Office. *List of Staff Officers of the Confederate States Army, 1861-1865.* Washington, DC: Government Printing Office, 1891.

Harsh, Joseph L. *Taken at the Flood: Robert E. Lee and Confederate Strategy in the Maryland Campaign of 1862.* Kent, OH and London: The Kent State University Press, 1999.

_____. *Sounding the Shallows: A Confederate Companion for the Maryland Campaign of 1862.* Kent, OH and London: The Kent State University Press, 2000.

Hartwig, D. Scott. *To Antietam Creek: The Maryland Campaign of September 1862.* Baltimore, MD: The Johns Hopkins Press, 2012.

Hopkins, Donald A. *The Little Jeff: The Jeff Davis Legion, Cavalry, Army of Northern Virginia.* Shippensburg, PA: White Mane Publishing Co., 1999.

Johnson, Thomas C. *Life and Letters of Robert Lewis Dabney.* Richmond, VA: Whittet & Shepperson, 1903

Jones, Jr., Wilbur D. "Who Lost the Lost Orders? Stonewall Jackson, His Courier, and Special Orders No. 191." *Civil War Regiments: A Journal of the American Civil War.* Vol. 5, No. 3 (1997).

_____. "Ego, Carelessness and Three Cigars: How Lee's Special Orders No. 191 Was Lost." (No Date). Copy at Monocacy National Battlefield Park.

_____. *Giants in the Cornfield: The 27th Indiana Infantry.* Shippensburg, PA: White Mane Publishing Co., 1997.

Keller, S. Roger. *Crossroads of War: Washington County, Maryland, in the Civil War.* Shippensburg, PA: White Mane Publishing Co., 1997.

Kleese, Richard B. *23rd Virginia Cavalry.* Lynchburg, VA: H. E. Howard, 1996.

Knott, Steven W. "Lee at Antietam: Strategic Imperatives, the Tyranny of Arithmetic, and a Trap Not Sprung." *Army History*, No. 95 (Spring 2015).

Koleszar, Marilyn B. *Ashland, Bedford, and Taylor Virginia Light Artillery*. Lynchburg, VA: H. E. Howard, 1994.

Krick, Robert K. "A Stupid Old Useless Fool." *Civil War Times* (June 2008).

_____. "Postwar Dinner Guests Dished and Debated Confederate Heroes." *America's Civil War* Vol. 32, No. 4 (September 2019)

Lewis, David J. *Frederick War Claim: Evidence and Argument in Support of Bill to Refund Ransom Paid by the Town of Frederick, During the Civil War, to Save Said Town and Union Military Supplies from Destruction*. Frederick, MD, No Date.

Longacre, Edward G. *Lee's Cavalrymen: A History of the Mounted Forces of the Army of Northern Virginia, 1861-1865*. Mechanicsburg, PA: Stackpole Books, 2002.

_____. *Gentleman and Soldier: A Biography of Wade Hampton III*. Lincoln, NE: University of Nebraska Press, 2003.

Lowry, Terry D. *26th Battalion Virginia Infantry*. Lynchburg, VA: H. E. Howard, 1991.

McCabe, W. Gordon. "The Real Barbara Frietchie." *Southern Historical Society Papers*, Vol. 27 (1899).

McCall, Kevin E. "Lee's Blind Horse: Confederate Intelligence Operations in the 1862 Maryland Campaign." Keller, Christian B., ed. *Southern Strategies: Why the Confederacy Failed*. Lawrence, KS: University Press of Kansas, 2021.

Menuet, Robert W. "Corporal Barton W. Mitchell and the Lost Orders." *America's Civil War*. Vol. 20, No. 4 (September 2007).

Miller, William J. *Mapping for Stonewall: The Civil War Service of Jed Hotchkiss*. Washington, DC: Elliott & Clark Publishing, 1993.

Murfin, James V. *The Gleam of Bayonets: The Battle of Antietam and the Maryland Campaign of 1862*. New York, NY: Bonanza Books, 1965.

National Park Service. "An Invitation to Battle: Special Orders 191." https://www.nps.gov/mono/learn/historyculture/an-invitation-to-battle.htm.

News Leader, The. "Col. Walter H. Taylor, A. A. G." *Southern Historical Society Papers*, Vol. 41, No. 3 (Sept. 1916).

Palmer, Michael A. *Lee Moves North: Robert E. Lee on the Offensive*. New York, NY: John Wiley & Sons, 1998.

Priest, John Michael. *Before Antietam: The Battle for South Mountain*. Shippensburg, PA: White Mane Publishing Co., 1992.

Reese, Timothy J. *High-Water Mark: The 1862 Maryland Campaign in Strategic Perspective*. Baltimore, MD: Butternut and Blue, 2004.

_____. *Sealed with Their Lives: The Battle of Crampton's Gap, Burkittsville, MD, Sept. 14, 1862*. Baltimore, MD: Butternut and Blue, 1998.

Rich, Russell. "Very Much Diminished: Straggling in the Army of Northern Virginia in the Maryland Campaign." *The Antietam Journal*, Vol. III (Sept. 2022).

Rossino, Alexander B. *Their Maryland: The Army of Northern Virginia from the Potomac Crossings to Sharpsburg in September 1862*. El Dorado, CA: Savas Beatie, 2021.

_____. "Lee's Beaver Creek Plan: The September 1862 Battle He Never Had the Chance to Fight and Why That Matters." *North & South Magazine*, Series II, Vol. 3, No. 1 (June 2022).

_____. "Confederate Defeat at South Mountain: Robert E. Lee's Moment of Hesitation on the Morning of September 14, 1862." *The Antietam Journal*, Vol. IV (March 2023).

Schildt, John W. *The Twelfth Corps at Antietam*. Brunswick, MD: E Graphics, 2012.

Sears, Stephen W. *Landscape Turned Red: The Battle of Antietam*. Boston, MA: Mariner Books, 1983.

_____. "The Twisted Tale of the Lost Order." *North and South Magazine*, Series I, Vol. 5, No. 7 (October 2002).

Sherlock, Scott M. "The Lost Order and the Press." *Civil War Regiments: A Journal of the American Civil War*, Vol. 6, No. 2 (1998).

Sherwood, W. Cullen & Nicholas, Richard L. *Amherst Artillery, Albemarle Artillery, and Sturdivant's Battery*. Lynchburg, VA: H. E. Howard, 1996.

Starr, Louis M. *Bohemian Brigade: Civil War Newsmen in Action*. New York, NY: Alfred A. Knopf, 1954.

Stotelmyer, Steven R. *Too Useful to Sacrifice: Reconsidering George B. McClellan's Generalship in the Maryland Campaign from South Mountain to Antietam*. El Dorado, CA: Savas Beatie, 2019.

Thorp, Gene M. and Rossino, Alexander B. *The Tale Untwisted: George McClellan and the Discovery of Lee's Lost Orders, September 13, 1862*. El Dorado, CA: Savas Beatie, 2019.

_____. "In Defense of McClellan at Antietam: A Contrarian View." *The Washington Post* (September 2012).

Toomey, Daniel C. *The Civil War in Maryland*. Baltimore, MD: Toomey Press, 1983.

Trout, Robert J. *They Followed the Plume: The Story of J. E. B. Stuart and His Staff*. Mechanicsburg, PA: Stackpole Books, 1993.

Wellman, Manly W. *Giant in Gray: A Biography of Wade Hampton of South Carolina*. New York, NY: Charles Scribner's Sons, 1949.

Williams, N. Mahony. *Frederick Directory, City Guide, and Business Mirror*. Vol. 1. Frederick, MD, 1859.

Williams, Thomas J. C. and Folger McKinsey, *History of Frederick County, Maryland*. 2 Vols. Baltimore, MD: Regional Publishing Co., 1997 & 2003.

Index

Allan, William, 115
Anderson, George B., 33; as army rearguard, 33-34
Anderson, Richard H., 24, 32-33, 55; unattached division, 55
Army of Northern Virginia, 13; straggling in, 112-114; weakness of at Sharpsburg/Antietam, 113-114
Army of the Potomac, 100; embedded reporters in, 100
Baltimore and Ohio Railroad, 4, 36; destruction of rail bridge, 36
Baltimore American, 36
Baltimore Sun, 15, 27
Beaver Creek, Maryland, 107-110; as Lee's preferred battleground, 107-108; as better place to fight than Sharpsburg, 109-110
Best's Farm, 4, 9; location of Lee's headquarters, 5
Bloss, John M., 64, 67-68, 70, 72, 76
Boicourt, Enoch G., 71
Burnside, Ambrose, 6, 20, 27-28
Campbell, John, 72
Chilton, Robert H., 22, 54, 91, 120, 124-126, 129, 132; did not sign lost orders, 92, 124-125; did not write lost orders, 120, 126, 129
Cockey, S. G., 5;
Colgrove, Silas, 64, 72-73, 78, 101
Cooper, Samuel, 22
Cox, Jacob D., 20, 27
Dabney, Robert L., 30-31
Datzmann, Richard C., 62
Davis, Angela K., 107
Davis, Jefferson, 2, 15, 20-22
Delashmutt, Elias J., 62
Dinkins, James, 112
Douglas, Henry K., 9, 60, 84, 117, 129
Enslaved persons, 5
Funk, John H.S., 7, 15
Frederick, Maryland, 24
General Orders No. 102, 1
General Orders No. 103, 2, 19
Hagerstown, Maryland, 24
Hampton, Wade, 89
Harpers Ferry, (West) Virginia, 15, 23, 29, 30-31, 44
Hill, Daniel H., 5, 23, 31, 33-35, 57, 60, 63, 78, 91, 114, 124; as army's rear guard, 33; under Jackson's command, 34-35, 35n21; unattached status of command, 35; not told to expect marching orders, 57, 92; did not camp near Frederick, 78-80; on straggling, 114-115
Hotchkiss, Jedediah, 54
Indiana Military Units, 27th Infantry, 63-64, 66, 70, 73, 77
Jackson, Thomas J., 4, 28, 30-31, 33-34, 54, 60, 109; headquarters of, 5, 5n7; proposes defending line of Monocacy River, 30; advocates keeping army together, 30-31; Frederick council of war (Sept. 8), 28-32; placed in command of Harpers Ferry operation, 33, 54; issues D.H. Hill copy of Special Orders No. 191, 34, 54, 91; compels surrender of Harpers Ferry, 109
Johnson, Bradley T., 36
Kershaw, Joseph, 112
Kopp, Peter, 66
Lee, Fitzhugh, 5
Lee, Robert E., 1-2, 4-5, 7-24, 27-45, 54, 81-83, 106-108, 113, 115, 117-118, 121; crosses the Potomac, 1-2; decides to enter Maryland, 1; hopes to encourage Maryland's rebellion, 2, 8-11, 16, 19, 37-38, 106; injuries of, 2, 12; arrives at Best's Farm, 4; believes enemy demoralized and disorganized, 5, 37; plans to shift supply line west, 8, 15, 21-22, 33, 42; and Pennsylvania, 8, 8n13, 22, 37-38, 42, 82, 118; attends dinner in Frederick (Sept. 6), 9; plans to draw enemy west of South Mountain, 10, 27, 30-31, 31n15, 33, 38; writes to Jefferson Davis, 10, 13, 15-16, 20, 38, 42-43, 113; relinquishes initiative, 11, 118-119; changes perspective on fomenting rebellion, 13-14; incomplete understanding of military situation, 14, 20, 37; believes enemy has evacuated Shenandoah Valley/Harpers Ferry, 15, 23, 30; complains about straggling, 15, 113; proclamation of, 16-19; proposes peace negotiations, 21; effort to influence Northern elections, 22; corresponds with D. H. Hill, 23, 82; believes army can operate north of Potomac until winter, 24, 38, 40; believes army has time to reassemble near Hagerstown, 24, 33, 82; hopes to capture Harpers Ferry quickly, 24, 27, 44; understands risk of dispersing army, 27; learns of McClellan's return to command, 27-28; chooses Jackson to lead Harpers Ferry operation, 29; hopes to avoid repeat of Second Manassas, 30; Frederick council of war (Sept. 8), 29-32; on Jackson's command of Hill, 34; and verbal orders, 35; reports enemy

moving toward Frederick, 39, 106; learns Davis is traveling to Maryland, 41; and myth of post-Second Manassas dilemma, 41-42; dictates special orders 45-47; and theory about deliberate loss of special orders, 81; plan after fall of Harpers Ferry, 82, 104-108, 118; late to reinforce Hill at Boonsboro, 108

Long, Armistead L., 12, 128-130, 133, 137; wrote lost orders, 92, 128-130, 137-138

Longstreet, James, 28, 31-32, 41, 60, 97-98 109-110; balks at operation against Harpers Ferry, 28-29; argues for keeping the army together, 31-32; Frederick council of war (Sept. 8), 31-32; claims Davis meeting army in Maryland was planned, 41; reports on spy Henry Harrison, 97-98; does not leave Hagerstown at daybreak (Sept. 14), 108; loses stragglers, 110

Lowe, Enoch L., 4, 42

McClellan, George B., 6, 14, 15n5, 19-20, 23, 27-28, 37-38, 99-100, 116, 118; reappointed as army commander, 6, 27-28; takes command in the field, 19, 38; begins advance toward Frederick, 23, 37-38; operational security and, 99; as victor in Maryland Campaign, 116; advances faster than Lee expects, 118-119, 121

McLaws, Lafayette, 24-25, 31-32, 44, 54, 60, 107, 111; receipt of Special Orders No. 191, 55; straggling in division, 111

Manning, Van, 43

Markell, Catherine, 58, 89

Markell, George, 5;

Marshall, Charles, 10, 16, 17, 24, 46, 92, 115, 129, 132, 135, 138; writes Special Orders No. 190, 46-47, 133, 137

Maryland, 16-17; as Southern border state, 16-18; fears of rebellion in, 17

Mason, Arthur P., 50-51, 131; and Special Orders No. 191, 51, 131

Massachusetts Military Units, 2nd Infantry, 75; 21st Infantry, 79

Miles, Dixon S., 23

Mitchell, Barton W., 62, 72; discovers lost orders 72-73, 76-77, 96, 120

Monocacy River aqueduct, 43, 56, 60

Morrison, Joseph G., 84, 129

New York Daily Tribune, 18

New York Herald, 17; reports on lost orders (Sept. 14), 100

New York Times, 18

New York Military Units, 1st Cavalry, 40

Ninth Corps, 68-69

North Carolina Military Units, 4th Infantry, 33; 27th Infantry, 43

O'Donnell, Columbus, 36-37

O'Leary, Augustine D., 87-89; farm as Stuart's headquarters, 90

Paxton, Elisha F., 129

Pendleton, William N., 35, 85, 107-108, 129; and possession of lost orders, 85

Pennsylvania, 8, 10

Philadelphia Inquirer, 8-9, 19;

Philadelphia Ledger, 18

Pope, John, 20, 28

Poolesville, Maryland, 14

Randolph, George W., 12, 15

Ransom, Robert, 43

Rosser, Thomas L., 83-84

Schaffler, Anna B., 70

Secessionists, 9-11, 14, 9n16, 38

Second Corps, 68

Shinn, James, 33-34

Smith, Gustavus, 12, 15

Smith, Kirby, 2

Snead, Thomas T.L., 36

Special Orders No. 190, 46-47, 50-51, 131-138; difference between special orders and general Orders, 50

Special Orders No. 191, 11, 50-51, 60-61, 103, 120-121, 123-138; meeting leading to creation of, 29-32; two paragraph version of, 50-51; lost copy of, 53; discovery location of, 62-64, 72, 76, 120; importance of loss, 103; handwriting analysis of, 123-130

Stanton, Edwin M., 18

Straggling, 15

Stuart, James E.B., 5-7, 20, 23-24, 40, 57-58, 86-87, 60, 93, 96-97, 101, 117-118, 120, 129; ordered by Lee to divide cavalry, 5; clash with Elijah V. White, 6-7; reports Federal advance from Rockville, 23; urged by Lee to fall back slowly, 24; Roses and Sabers Ball, 40; fails to report advance of enemy on National Road, 40; and Special Orders No. 191, 57-58, 86-90, 93-94, 96, 101, 120; and cigars, 58, 96; headquarters of, 87-90; strange conduct of, 97, 118

Taylor, Richard C., 12, 54, 129, 132

Taylor, Walter H., 12, 17, 17n9, 42, 45, 129; sent to meet Jefferson Davis, 45-46

Twelfth Corps, 64, 67

Urbana, Maryland, 5; Confederate cavalry headquarters at, 5;

Vance, David B., 72

Venable, Charles S., 54, 129
Virginia Military Units, 3rd Cavalry, 14; 5th Cavalry, 14;
Von Borcke, Heros, 5, 40, 58, 88
Walker, John. G., 31, 43-45, 56, 60; Lee orders to destroy Monocacy River aqueduct, 43, 56; problems with postwar writings, 44-45
Washington Evening Star, 100; reports on lost orders (Sept. 15), 100Welch, George W., 71

White, Elijah V., 6-7, 23
White, Julius, 15
White Oak Springs, Maryland, 33
Williamson, Thomas H., 36
Winchester, Virginia, 7, 15, 22, 29; as Confederate army's supply depot, 8
Wolseley, Garnet J., 106
Wool, John E., 37

Acknowledgments

The efforts of a number of people went into the research for this book. After learning from the experience of writing *The Tale Untwisted* with Gene Thorp that there are often problems with printed versions of documents in the *War of the Rebellion* series, popularly known as the *Official Records* (OR), I took it upon myself to collect the copies of as many original documents as I could. These frequently contain details not found in the printed versions in the OR. There are also a large number of documents locked away in state and local archives that do not appear in the OR.

The research for this book benefitted from using those documents, but gathering them required the help of dedicated archive and library professionals. This includes the following people, and my gratitude goes out to each of them. Jody Brumage, an archivist at Heritage Frederick, helped me dig up information on Frederick, Maryland, including an important "bird's eye view" of the area southeast of of town where a corporal with the 27th Indiana Volunteers named Barton Mitchell found the lost copy of Lee's orders.This view by artist Edward Sachse shows that as of 1854, and so presumably as of September 1862, farm fields and pasture ran right to the southern edge of the town. This confirms the veracity of claims made by Hoosier troops that Mitchell discovered the dropped document in a grassy field "adjacent" (i.e., next to) Frederick. Derek Gee and Mary Mannix at the Western Maryland Room of the C. Burr Artz Library in Frederick then helped me narrow down the name of the woman who owned the piece of property where Mitchell probably found the order.

Archivist Kim McKeithan at the National Archives and Records Administration (NA) in Washington helped me secure digital copies of the two-paragraph version of Special Orders No. 191. Seeing this document made me realize there was more to the creation of the order than General Lee simply dictating all ten paragraphs at the same time. He likely did so, but as I discuss in chapter four, Lee seems to have dictated a draft of paragraphs three through ten in a separate document from the first two paragraphs.

Victoria Garnett at the Library of Virginia clarified the subject by sending me scans of a collection of documents held in the Robert E. Lee papers in Richmond. These included a copy of Special Orders No. 190, which contains paragraphs three through ten. After locating the complete ten-paragraph document in the headquarters order book of the Army of Northern Virginia, it became clear that this earlier version of Lee's orders had been created as a draft before Arthur Mason of Lee's staff combined the two paragraph and eight paragraph versions into the final ten paragraph order that appears in the Official Records.

Correspondence written to and from Daniel Harvey Hill during and after the war proved invaluable for gathering the opinions of former Confederate officers and members of Lee's staff. These letters are held by the North Carolina Department of Natural and Cultural Resources (NC DNCR) in Raleigh, and it is thanks to the assistance of Alison Thurman that I was able to secure them. Several archivists and librarians then helped me collect additional writing samples as I needed them. For example, after searching high and low for a sample of the handwriting of Elisha F. Paxton, who served on General Jackson's staff during the Maryland campaign, I finally located a collection at Washington and Lee University in Lexington, Virginia, that Senior Collections Assistant Byron Faidley sent me. Carly Tarne and Matt Guillen of the Virginia Museum of History and Culture in Richmond added the papers of Osmun Latrobe, a staffer with James Longstreet's command, and another rare Paxton document. Taken together, these texts helped me pursue a detailed comparison of the handwriting in the lost copy of Special Orders No. 191 to that of Elisha Paxton, and to eliminate him as a potential writer of the document.

Another subject I researched is the postwar public speaking career of Thomas Rosser. The commander of the 5th Virginia Cavalry during the Maryland campaign, Rosser uttered a comment about Special Orders No. 191 in Raleigh, North Carolina, that made it into *Confederate Veteran* magazine. Rosser claimed the man who lost Lee's orders had been a member of Stonewall Jackson's staff, and that as of the year when he made the statement (1897), the man still lived. I tried hunting down a copy of the text of Rosser's speech to see if he had said anything else about the subject but was unable to find it. I did locate the text of other speeches he made during the same speaking tour and found no comment similar to the one printed in *Confederate Veteran*. This led me to conclude that Rosser probbaly made the comment during a question and answer session with the audience following his talk. Austin Rhea, a Graduate Reference Assistant at the Albert and Shirley Small Special Collections Library of the University of Virginia diligently helped me collect the fragments of Rosser's remarks so that I could evaluate their content.

Helen Anderson of The Huntington Library in San Marino, California, graciously led me through a fascinating virtual reader session that helped me peruse their collection of J. E. B. Stuart's papers. I had hoped to find the copy of Special Orders No. 191 that Stuart claimed to have appended to his campaign report in February 1864, but had no luck. That copy of the orders remains missing, if indeed it ever existed in the first place (see chapters four and six for a discussion of this).

Lastly, no acknowledgements would be complete without recognizing the efforts of the National Park Service's Stephanie Gray of the Antietam National Battlefield Library (ANBL) and Tracy Evans of the Monocacy National Battlefield Park (MNBP). Stephanie dug out rare volumes in the ANBL's collection while letting me peruse the vertical files. Tracy kindly shared all of the research materials she had concerning Special Orders No. 191. These included the only photograph I've seen of Barton Mitchell, and handwritten proof from Mitchell that he could read and write.

This book also benefitted from the keen eyes and sharp comments of several readers. Matt Borders of the MNBP provided me with long, thoughtful observations about the manuscript. Kevin Pawlak, Historic Site Manager for the Prince William County Historic Preservation Division, and a Licensed Battlefield Guide at Antietam, also took a close look at the work. Both readers helped me correct mistakes and hone arguments. Professors James M. McPherson and Allen C. Guelzo of Princeton University did the same, as did my *Tale Untwisted* co-author, Gene M. Thorp. I'm grateful to all of them for the assistance. This book would not be what it is without their help.

Last, but certainly not least, I'd like to thank the staff of my publisher, Savas Beatie. Managing Director, Ted Savas, agreed to publish this book despite the fact that I needed it done within a relatively short time frame, and regardless of the fact that he had a full slate of titles already scheduled to appear. It is a real pleasure working with a publisher willing and nimble enough to get something out quickly and of high quality. To that end, I'd very much like to thank my editor, David Snyder. This book really benefitted from his keen eye for detail. I am humbly grateful as well to Savas Beatie superstars Sarah Closson, Sarah Keeney, Donna Endacott, Veronica Kane, Lisa Murphy, and Lee Merideth. All of you are the best.

About the Author

Alexander B. Rossino, PhD, is an award-winning scholar living in Maryland. He is the author of numerous articles and several books, including *Six Days in September: A novel of Lee's Army in Maryland, 1862* and *Their Maryland: The Army of Northern Virginia from the Potomac Crossing to Sharpsburg in September 1862* (Savas Beatie, 2021).